AN ARCHON BOOK ON POPULAR ENTERTAINMENTS

A.H. Saxon, General Editor

A Seat at the Circus

John Astley, The Equestrian Hero, riding the Gibraltar Charger, presented to his father, Philip, by General Eliott, Governor and Defender of Gibraltar, afterwards Lord Heathfield. (From an engraving by W. Hincks in the author's collection.)

A Seat at the Circus

by

Antony Hippisley Coxe

with
special illustrations by
John Skeaping

Revised Edition

1980

ARCHON BOOKS

Hamden, Connecticut

Library of Congress Cataloging in Publication Data

Hippisley Coxe, Antony.
  A seat at the circus.

  (An Archon book on popular entertainments)
  Bibliography: p.
  Includes index.
  1. Circus—History. I. Title. II. Series:
  Archon Book on popular entertainments.
  GV1801.H5   1980   791.3   79-19155
  ISBN 0-208-01766-6

The Antony Hippisley Coxe Circus Collection is now at the Theatre Museum, Victoria and Albert Museum, London. The author and publisher thank the Theatre Museum for permission to reproduce these illustrations.

Originally published 1951 by
Evans Brothers, London, England

Revised edition published 1980
as an Archon Book, an imprint of
The Shoe String Press, Inc.
Hamden, Connecticut 06514

Printed in the United States of America

for

ARAMINTA

who has so often sat

in the seat next mine at

the circus

Contents

List of Illustrations   *11*

Foreword to the Revised Edition   *15*

Acknowledgments   *19*

I
OVERTURE
21

II
A GRAND PARADE
of the Circus Through the Ages
Ending with a
CHARIVARI
27

III
VOLTIGE
and Other Forms of
TRICK-RIDING
47

IV
THE STRONG MAN
Together with Acts Which Rely on
STRENGTH and BALANCE
61

V

PERFORMING ANIMALS

Mostly of the Domestic Variety

75

VI

LIBERTY HORSES

93

VII

DAREDEVILS

105

VIII

THE INTERVAL

115

IX

THE BIG CAGE

and the Training of

WILD ANIMALS

127

X

AERIAL ACTS

149

XI

LA HAUTE ECOLE

171

XII
JUGGLERS
and Acts Based on
DEXTERITY
183

XIII
GROUND ACROBATS
197

XIV
CLOWNS' ENTRÉE
213

XV
FINALE
225

Glossary   233
Bibliography   241
Index   247

John Astley, The Equestrian Hero, riding the Gibraltar
Charger, presented to his father, Philip, by General Eliott,
Governor and Defender of Gibraltar, afterwards Lord
Heathfield.   frontispiece

Astley's Amphitheatre in 1777, from a drawing by William
Capon.   29

The interior of Astley's Amphitheatre in 1815.   32

The Cirque Olympique, circa 1825.   34

A day-bill of the first American circus to tour England, in
1843.   45

Some of the movements seen in a voltige act.   49

Lucio Cristiani's somersault.   51

Levi J. North, famous American trick-rider who appeared at
Astleys in 1838.   52

The American Riding Machine.   54

The three-men-high of the Fredianis.   55

Hand-to-hand balancing, initial position.   63

Hand-to-hand balancing, final position.   64

Hand-to-hand balancing.   65

The Marinelli Bend, as performed by Ames Adonis.   69

Shirai's combined stilt and perch act.   72

Aubrey, the author's ginger cat, jumping through hoops.   78

Clovis ringing his bell.   80

Clovis taking a bow.   83

The American horse Black Eagle (Howes & Cushing) performing before H.M. Queen Victoria and the Royal Family at the Alhambra Palace.   95

Liberty horses pirouetting in a waltz.   97

Da Capos at the end of Gina Lipkowska's liberty act.   103

The Human Arrow.   109

A "penny-plain-tuppence-coloured" portrait of Henri Martin, the first modern animal trainer.   129

The wild animal den in which lions performed before the invention of the big cage.   132

A "penny-plain-tuppence-coloured" portrait of Isaac Van Amburgh, the famous American trainer.   136

Schreiber's Elephants.   142

The reverse side of a hand-bill for Astley's in 1786 showing the tricks performed by General Jackoo, a monkey.   145

A straight pass.   152

A pirouette pass.   152

A hock pass.   153

12

A plange pass. 153

Passe par dessus. 154

A single somersault pass. 155

A double pass. 156

The grip used by all trapeze artists. 157

Madame Phillipine Tourniaire, one of the first of the great écuyères. 175

Passage. Galopade. 176

Capriole. Piaffe. 177

Volte à droite. Pirouette a gauche. 177

Croupade. Ballotade. 178

Pesade. Courbette. 178

Terre à terre. Mezair. 179

A cascade. 184

A shower. 184

A double shower. 185

A foot-juggler. 191

Signor Colpi's act in 1777, a possible forerunner of the Risley Act. 192

The juggler in the Tarot pack. 195

Professor Risley. 196

A back somersault. 199

A lay-out back. 199

A handspring. 200

A flip-flap. 200

A round-off. 201

A Borani or brandy. 201

A butterfly. 202

A one-hand walk-over. 204

Auriol, the first great French clown. 215

Circus clown. 223

Foreword to the Revised Edition

A Seat at the Circus was first published in 1951. I wrote it because I felt there was a need for a book which tried to explain techniques as well as recount history. Most of the books in my own circus library at that time seemed to use the same source material, such as Thomas Frost's *Circus Life and Circus Celebrities,* "Lord" George Sanger's *Seventy Years a Showman,* and M. Willson Disher's *Greatest Show on Earth.* One found the same stories—and the same mistakes —being repeated so often that there was a danger of their becoming accepted as indisputable fact. However, I wanted to do rather more than correct dates and the names of people and places; my ambition was to try to introduce another dimension. The circus, after all, is essentially a three-dimensional spectacle. History alone, however colorful, seemed a little flat. By describing methods and techniques, as well as when, where and by whom they were used, I hoped to analyze the spectacle as a whole, and to set out my own personal view of what true circus should be. I believed that this approach was particularly necessary at that time because the circus was being denigrated as simply a treat for the children at Christmas.

I do not know how far I succeeded. Looking through my press cuttings I see that the book was reviewed by more than a hundred critics and that most of them were very kind. I got the greatest pleasure from being told that I went to the circus with "the same anxious idealism as others who go in hope and fear to see what the theatre has made of Sophocles and Shakespeare." And the review ended, "Mr Coxe has sawdust in his shoes" (*Times Literary Supplement,* 21 December 1951).

During the last twenty-five years my shoes have collected a lot more sawdust. I would have been quite content to wriggle my toes in it without drawing this to anyone's attention, but for the fact that there has been an upsurge of interest in three major components of the circus: horsemanship, zoology and gymnastics.

There are more young people riding today than every before, and there is a growing interest in high school. The popularity of pony clubs, the inclusion of dressage in many competitions and equestrian events, the appearance of *le Cadre Noir* and the Spanish Riding School in cities far removed from Saumur and Vienna, are proof enough of the growing popularity and heightened understanding of equestrian techniques.

The last quarter century has also seen an increase in zoological gardens, safari parks and nature reserves. Some of the most popular television programmes are about animals. The European, Commonwealth and Olympic Games demonstrate a mounting interest in physical prowess. The gymnastic achievements of Olga Korbut made her an international star overnight. Horses and riders, animals and acrobats are the main ingredients of the circus, supported of course by the clowns. And even here one finds favorable signs. After Fellini's film, a clown song became top of the pops; there are now fifty clown groups performing with street theatre companies, in schools or at private parties in Great Britain alone; the British Arts Council has given a grant of fifteen thousand pounds to Clown Cavalcade, a company which spends four months of the year on tour and the remainder in training, rehearsing and drawing up plans for a Clown Centre.

Whether the circus can take advantage of this great opportunity I cannot say, but when A.H. Saxon and Archon Books invited me to revise my book and bring it up to date, I knew I could not refuse. Apart from my belief that the time is right, every author would like to be given the opportunity to correct at least some of his previous mistakes.

The approach, however, remains the same. This is not an "erudite" work, and it would be stupid to try to turn it into one. I am not an academic, but a journalist and critic. There is one particular difference between a professor and a newspaperman which should be emphasized. The former insists that every source must be recorded, and rightly so. Traditionally, the journalist never reveals his sources, even at the request of government. He would rather go to jail. This is understandable. It is a question of survival; one does not pass one's trump card to an opponent. So, although I have tried to give credit to those I quote in the text, there are few numbered footnotes and no "ibids" or "op cits."

After the book first appeared I was invited to become a member of the *Union des Historiens du Cirque,* an organization which had just been launched by Tristan Rémy and Otto Christl. It demanded no subscription or entrance fee, but every member had to produce a certain number of pages of original research each year, which was distributed to all other members. Some of the work which I undertook is now included in this book. It was Tristan Rémy who taught me never to believe what I heard, and very little of what I read, unless it was a birth, marriage or death certificate. It would be most churlish if I did not acknowledge how much I owe to this meticulous circus historian, how proud I was to count him among my friends and how great a loss his death in 1977 meant to all who love the circus.

The care which must be taken before accepting hearsay as fact was further strengthened after meeting Arthur H. Saxon. His scholarly criticism and advice have been invaluable in revising this book.

It is only when one settles down to bring a book up to date that one realizes how much has happened since it was first published, not only events that have occurred in the interim, but new discoveries about events long past. Revision has not been simply a topping-up exercise; sometimes it has meant a complete reappraisal. In both aspects, *Le Cirque dans l'Univers,* the magazine of the *Club du Cirque,* has proved the greatest help, and I am indebted to its editor, my good friend L.-R. Dauven, for producing such a valuable publication, for answering my many queries and, above all, for reading through the typescript of this revised edition.

For anyone interested in circus research, the greatest event in the last twenty-five years must be the publication of Raymond Toole Stott's world bibliography *Circus and Allied Arts.* It is a magnificent and meticulous work; its present four volumes already list over thirteen thousand sources; furthermore it provides the press marks for most of the titles it lists in the Library of Congress, the British Library and the Bibliothèque Nationale. Raymond Toole Stott has also provided much help.

Then I would also like to acknowledge how much this revision owes to Pierre M. Couderc, who, before he settled in the United States to make films, was a trapeze artiste in France. A mutual friend sent him a copy of *A Seat at the Circus,* and this started a long correspondence, which unfortunately came to a close with his death. The result of his remarkable research into various aspects of the triple somersault were published in *Bandwagon,* the official organ of the Circus Historical Society of America.

When it came to updating costs, I turned to Gerry Cottle, whose good name as a fair dealer is as important to him as his flair for showmanship.

Of the three people whose help was acknowledged in the original edition,* Henry Thétard and Eric Shears have died. The former lives on in his classic *La Merveilleuse Histoire du cirque,* which, as I write, is being reissued in an edition revised and updated by L.-R. Dauven. Although Eric Shears did not write a book, his knowledge of the profession was prodigious and he wrote many articles for circus magazines. Harry Nutkins is still with us and once again I turned to him for help in revising this book, and once again I was astounded by his encyclopedic knowledge.

Finally, there is my wife Araminta, who still sits in the seat next mine at the circus, but who in recent months has been sitting next me at my desk, typing my almost illegible manuscript corrections and saying "Are you sure the so-and-so's are still working?" and "What exactly do you mean when you write such-and-such?"

All these people have made this a better book than it would otherwise have been. All I can say is, "Thank you, very much."

A.D.H.C.
Devon
England

---

* I have let the original acknowledgments stand as written. They follow this foreword.

Acknowledgments

Several thousand books have been written about the circus, and I doubt that one of them is completely accurate. I have no illusions that this book is an exception, though I do know that as it stands it has considerably fewer mistakes than it had in typescript. For this I must thank Henry Thétard, the greatest chronicler of the circus to date; E.M. Shears, a retired performer who, having spent a lifetime in show business, has given me invaluable technical details as well as the benefit of his keenly critical eye; and Harry Nutkins, the finest amateur critic we have in this country, whose love of the circus is as deep as his knowledge of famous acts. To these three, the historian, the professional and the true *aficionado*, I am especially indebted for reading my typescript and offering corrections, criticism and advice.

At the end of this volume you will find a bibliography listing the books which I treasure most in my own collection. All these have stimulated my interest and given me much enjoyment. Some have provided me with an incentive to do my own research; others have offered me confirmation of half-formed theories. Where they have provided me with material, I have tried to make acknowledgment in the text; but I welcome this opportunity of tendering to all these authors my most grateful thanks, especially to Henry Thétard for his *La Merveilleuse Histoire du cirque*, the most comprehensive reference book so far published.

Finally I would like to say how much I appreciate the time which circus directors, performers and amateur enthusiasts have so readily made available, and the knowledge and experience which they have generously imparted. I started listing them by name: Mills, Schumann, Medrano, Butson, Carré, Rancy, Houcke, Paulo, Fossett . . . but the list became unwieldy, and I hope that these nine will represent all the others and accept my thanks on their behalf. As for the circophiles, I must express my gratitude to my fellow members of the Circus Fans Association, both in this country and in America, the Club du Cirque of France, and the Club van Circusvrienden of Holland.*

A.D.H.C.
London
1951

---

* I have left these acknowledgments as they were originally listed in the first edition. Others have given great help in this version. My thanks to them are expressed in the foreword to the revised edition.

I

OVERTURE

A seat at the circus—as near to the sawdust as we can get—a seat called in England a "starback," because of the design on its cover, at one time described by Americans as a "red" because of its color, and occasionally referred to in France as a "Pullman." But the seat which I offer you is not necessarily at an English or an American circus, nor is it particularly associated with any country in Europe. It is to be found at The Circus—which may be the first you ever saw or the one you hope some day to see.

This book has one purpose: to help you to enjoy the circus. In watching any spectacle one's pleasure depends to a large extent upon the depths of one's knowledge. To enjoy a cup final one must know what the teams are trying to do and the rules which govern their play. In the Olympic Games breaking the record for throwing the javelin or running a race is only fully appreciated by those who realize what is entailed in javelin throwing, or know how long it usually takes to run a certain distance. True appreciation, then, requires some knowlege of both history and technique.

The theatre, the ballet, the cinema and music all have their own critics who, armed with such knowledge and experience, keep the public informed of what is good or bad—and, if they are good critics, why it is good or bad. But in England and America the press employs no circus critic. The tickets for the first night of a circus go to the dramatic critic, or perhaps to the man who reviews the books. They don't know much about it, because it's not their job. The circus is nobody's business, or, as I prefer to think, it's everybody's business. It is up to the audience to fill the gap.

Just as any professional critic must have knowledge and experience, so must the ordinary circus-goer have a yardstick with which he can measure achievement. That is what this book sets out to provide—something by which you can gauge the difficulty of the feats you witness in the ring, and compare the great performers of today with the famous artistes of the past. But no such book can ever replace experience. This volume is a primer which, I hope, will help you in the early stages to form your own standards and remain of some use while experience is still being gathered. All this may take some time; for not only does the circus stretch round the world, but it will lead you back over two centuries in history, and its subjects range from the build of a horse to the anatomy of laughter.

The pattern of this book is based on a circus programme. I have tried to put it together so that a fast act follows a slow one, and so that animals may break the monotony of a long sequence of human performers. This is not a perfect plan because acts today cannot always be put into pigeonholes: juggling is now sometimes combined with the slack wire, a sense of balance is needed for wire-walking as well as in the perch act. But the various turns which are grouped together in each chapter are united by certain dominant characteristics, and this should help one to analyze the circus as a whole.

What I have written is neither simply a history nor a technological treatise, though it contains a bit of both. It deals with the technical "how" and "why" as well as the historical "when" and "where"; I have even tried to deduce from these a "wherefore."

The circus has one great advantage for the amateur critic. It is always direct in its appeal. If a trick is extremely hard to accomplish, it is usually fairly easy to see what makes it difficult. One should always trust one's own opinion as a spectator before believing such phrases as "never before achieved," "unparalleled feat" or "the only artiste in the world." Such qualifications roll glibly off the circus proprietor's tongue; and so they should, for he would not be much of a showman if he did not indulge in some form of exaggeration. These descriptions merely provide a baroque frame for the spectacle itself; and, providing the act is good, you will feel no more disappointed than you do when you realise that the lions are a little less ferocious than you thought, and the aerialists are not quite so suicidally inclined as you supposed when looking at the advertisements.

The exaggerations of circus publicity are more irksome to the historian than anyone else. There are so few ways in which statements made a hundred years or so ago can be checked. When the circus moves on, what does it leave behind apart from its own rain-washed posters and a few crumpled throw-aways? Newspaper reports, perhaps, but of doubtful accuracy; and impressions left in the minds of the spectators, impressions which have become faded by forgetfulness or distorted by much retelling.

There you have one of the reasons for my choice of a ringside seat. It gives us the best chance of seeing what really happens, and appreciating the subtleties as well as the principles of that kaleidoscopic entertainment which the circus bills of the last century so rightly described as "an evening dream of wonder." We are here to enjoy what goes on in the ring, both at the performance and during rehearsal. In the interval we may catch a glimpse of some of the proprietors and performers when they are off duty in the "back-yard." But it is their work that I want most to describe. So let us take our ringside seats.

We are early. The band is still playing out in front to the queues at the box office, spurring them on with the blare of its brass. For those inside, the music weaves a subtler but more insistent spell. The snatches of those simple tunes, muted by distance and the hum of conversation, remind the hearer of all the circuses he has ever seen, and infuse the audience with a feeling of nostalgic expectation.

There is nothing quite like a circus band. Apart from the music it plays—the traditional airs such as Fucik's "Entry of the Gladiators," Teike's "Old Comrades," Sousa's "Bullfighters," and all the "oompah" tunes we know so well—it seems to have a special knack of taking anything from classical music to the latest "pop" tune and making it its own. I never listen to Marquina's "Spanish Gipsy Dance" or Bratton's "Teddy Bear's Picnic" without thinking of wire-walkers or performing bears; and when my son was four years old, on hearing "Der Walkürenritt" played on the radio, he never failed to say "Geraldo's trapeze music!" He was not quite right, because trapeze acts are usually accompanied by a slow waltz. The Geraldos, however, their blue silk cloaks covering their white tights and leotards, did make their entrance to Wagner all the same. But our band has not yet climbed up the narrow ladder to its place above the plush ring curtains. The auditorium is still no more than half full. And the programme sellers and ushers have some minutes left before they are called away to put on their spangles as performers. So we have time to look around.

Immediately in front of us is the ring—a circle of sawdust forty-two feet in diameter, surrounded by a ring fence. From this, tier upon tier of seats rise steeply in concentric circles. The rake of the seating is important, for if it rises back gradually to a low horizon one's eye will wander up and over that gentle slope of faces. But here the rows of seats fall steeply to the ring, and one is forced to concentrate on the spectacle.

More important to the circus-lover than the rake of the seating is the necessity for each tier, except the first few rows which are broken by two entrances, to surround the ring completely. The audience should hold the spectacle in its midst. One finds almost the same thing, on a larger scale, in a football stadium or a bullring, and in each case the audience reacts in the same way. By providing the setting themselves, the spectators become a foil to what goes on in the ring, and in so doing they become a part of the spectacle.

The almost hermetic feeling produced by an unbroken ring of spectators initiates a reaction, not only between the public and the performer, but also within the audience itself. Emotion is intensified and runs round the arena like an electric current. Break the circuit and the power goes out of the reaction. Think of a cup-tie played in a stadium which is bounded on one side by an empty wall, or imagine a bullfight staged in an amphitheatre of which a segment remains open, and you will realize how great a loss such a break must cause.

For years many British circus proprietors, imbued with their national love of compromise, tried to combine the circus and the theatre in one building. By cutting into the auditorium with a proscenium and stage, they disrupted the unity between the public and the performer and confused the basic principles of two completely different forms of entertainment.

Any performance presented on a stage, framed by a proscenium, is a spectacle based on illusion. We have always known that Hamlet was really Lord Olivier or Sir John Gielgud, and that the massive walls of the castle were really no thicker than a lick of paint. In the theatre scenes must be played *against* a background, and they can only be watched from the *front* of the house. Go backstage and the illusion is lost. You will find yourself in exactly the same position if you look at the back of a painting—in a world of canvas, struts, and the plain, ungilded back of the frame.

Just as the theatre has a parallel in painting, so does the circus have an analogy in sculpture. You can walk round it. It can be seen from all sides. There can be no illusion, for there are eyes all round to prove that there is no deception. The performers actually do exactly what they appear to do. Their feats of dexterity and balance and strength must never be confused with the make-believe world of the actor. "Props" should not simulate anything or provide a background; they are machines on which, or with which, actual manifestations take place. Even the everyday phrases of the performers outside the ring reflect this characteristic; for while an actor says he will "play his part," the circus artiste tells you he will "work his act."

The circus, then, is the spectacle of actuality. But what is a spectacle? Although the dictionary hints at the part played by the audience, it is not very helpful; it simply says "a public show." A fuller explanation is given by Pierre Bost in *Le Cirque et le music hall* (Paris: Au Sans Pareil, 1931): "A man alone with his thoughts is not a spectacle. . . . A spectacle demands that Man, brought face to face with either events or other men, should react to them. . . . An unhappy man is not a spectacle until he weeps or shouts. Therefore there must be something physical about a spectacle; boxing is a spectacle, chess is not."

There are, of course, many kinds of spectacle; those produced by the pugilist, the football player or the matador are very different from those of the trick-rider, the acrobat or the animal trainer. In the boxing ring, in the *plaza de toros,* or on the football field, the course of the spectacle is never predetermined. In the circus ring it is. Everything is calculated and timed to a fraction of an inch and a split second. Just as every wire in the apparatus of a flying trapeze must have its stress and strain, so every gesture of the performer must have its meaning. On the stage over-production may mask under-rehearsal. In the circus over-production just looks silly, and under-rehearsal is unforgivable.

By now the auditorium is nearly full. From all round there comes the rustle and quick chatter of expectancy. Since the audience is part of the spectacle, it is worth studying. The first thing one notices is that it does not appear to be confined to any particular category of people. Here you may recognize a poet. In the royal box sits a princess. Over there is a cabinet minister, and next to him a

25

plumber's mate. There is no special circus-going public. The wise are there no less than the foolish, and the young no more than the old. It is, as Joyce Kilmer wrote in *The Circus and Other Essays* (New York: Laurence J. Gomme, 1916), "vulgar. Its enemies say so; and its friends, with grateful hearts, assent. It is *vulgar*, of the crowd. To no play upon the stage can this lofty praise be given. For the circus, as it is today, would thrill and amuse and delight not only the crowd that today see it, but the crowd that might have come from the days before the Flood, or from the days of our great-grand-children's children."

Too many people have said that the secret of the circus is to be found in its appeal to the childlike simplicity which lies in every one of us. What self-effacing nonsense! What a pitiful underestimation of the wisdom of the young! And what a pathetic misinterpretation of the circus! Children appreciate—in an intuitive and half-formed way, perhaps—the same fundamental qualities which appealed to Toulouse-Lautrec, Degas and other great painters; not merely the "atmosphere," the color and the movement, but the realization that here in the ring men and women find expression by actually doing something which calls for such prowess that we are filled with wonder. We can hardly believe it, yet we know it's true.

Everything is now ready for the parade. Outside the ring doors the performers are lined up. And, although the patterned sawdust has not yet been disturbed, somehow the audience senses that all is set. Spectators settle back in their seats. The chatter and rustle die down with the houselights, and the silent pleasure of anticipation increases as the lighting on the ring grows brighter.

II

A GRAND PARADE
of the Circus Through the Ages
Ending with a
CHARIVARI

The parade is on. Spanish wire-walkers, Rumanian bar acts, Chinese contortionists, Czech animal trainers, Swedish acrobats, American Indians, French clowns, Italian jugglers, English riders . . . horses . . . dogs . . . elephants . . . monkeys . . . bears. . . . It seems as if the whole world is represented in the procession which marches so magnificently across the ring. That is just as it should be, for the circus is international. It is the only truly international entertainment that exists, provided by every nation on earth for every country in the world.

The parade does more than stress this cosmopolitan aspect. It gives us a brief summary of what we are going to see. These artistes and animals who pass before us across the arena are rather like the actors who assemble on the stage to take a curtain call; though here they introduce themselves, while in the theatre they say farewell. The parade shows us the scope and scale of the entertainment as a whole. If one looks upon the circus as a feast, one must not think of the parade as one of the courses, but rather as a menu—a visual programme of events which gives no idea of how well the dishes will be cooked or served.

A parade is anonymous; one can do no more than pick out the acts by their generic terms: acrobats, trainers, horses, elephants and clowns. As yet we have seen no particular style or personality, and so we begin to wonder how this rider or that juggler will compare with other great riders or jugglers of the past. When each performer returns to the ring to work his particular act, then we can see what he does and how he does it, but for the moment let us see how he came to be here at all. Let us look at the evolution of the circus; for the history of the circus is a parade in itself—a parade which stretches back in time as well as across the world in distance.

The velvet curtains below the orchestra are pulled aside, and through the ring doors, heading the procession, comes the equestrian director. When he reaches the center of the ring he turns aside and, lifting his silk hat, salutes first the audience and then the whole company which passes before him. The title "equestrian director" reminds us that the circus was started by an eighteenth-century horseman; while the strong man, wearing those faintly ridiculous gladiatorial boots, recalls the fallacy of trying to trace the history of the circus back to ancient Rome.

The elongated circuses of Maxentius, Domitian, Hadrian and Nero, which were three times as long as they were wide, and even the elliptical amphitheatres such as the Colosseum, were all designed for spectacles, the principles of which were exactly the opposite of those that underlie the circus of today. Races between horses, either ridden or driven, and encounters between man and beast, which had to end fatally for one or the other, were the chief attractions of the Roman programme. In the Circus Maximus, 3,500 beasts were killed during the reign of Augustus alone. Human beings, horses and wild animals still appear in the arena, but now the ring is specifically designed so that one horse shall not compete with another but maintain its relative position, and should a trainer or an animal get killed it is a most unfortunate accident.

Credit for inventing the modern circus must be given to an irascible ex-sergeant major turned trick-rider, called Philip Astley: the place, Lambeth; the date, 1768. He had discovered that by galloping in a circle while standing upright on his horse's back he could use centrifugal force to help him keep his balance. So the first ring was formed. The ring is the quintessence of the circus, and when the acrobats, rope-dancers and clowns appeared in Astley's arena, the circus was born. Yet it had been conceived some years previously. In his memoirs, Henry Angelo describes how, while Astley was still in the army, he astounded Lord Pembroke and his neighbors at Wilton, near Salisbury, when he made his horse gallop in a circle while giving a demonstration of trick-riding.

Astley's Amphitheatre in 1777, from a drawing by William Capon. (From a print in the author's collection.)

During the second half of the eighteenth century trick-riding developed into popular entertainment. M. Willson Disher in his book *Fairs, Circuses and Music Halls* (London: Collins, 1942) explains how horsemanship was "no longer an urgent necessity but an accomplishment. . . . Only wealthy and enthusiastic noblemen maintained their own manège. . . . Riding-masters found themselves without employment . . . [which explains] the growing numbers of riding-masters, English or Irish, who gave displays of trick-riding at home and abroad."

The reason a cavalry rough-rider and not a riding-master invented the ring may well lie in the fact that riding-masters were steeped in the tradition of the manège, and the manège has always been rectangular. Although prints of Astley's rivals such as Bates, Johnson and Chiarini do exist, I have yet to find one that shows them riding in the ring. On the other hand, some posters specifically billing circuses—those of Dietrich Gautier and Johann Lenz are examples—show performances taking place in a rectangular manège as late as 1825.

The pleasure gardens which surrounded medicinal springs, or lay at the back of taverns and teahouses, were a favorite setting for these exhibitions. But it soon became apparent that trick-riding, although the mainstay of the programme, was not quite enough.

From the fairgrounds came the tumblers, acrobats, rope-dancers and all those whose acts were based simply on their own physical skills—they realized that a ring was the ideal place in which to perform. A little later they were joined by the animal trainers.

Why did the supporting programme—the acrobats, rope-dancers, jugglers and others—forsake the fairground for the ring?

The chief attraction of the big London fairs during the first half of the eighteenth century was the actors. The leading ladies and men came from the principal theatres of the metropolis; and during the two or three weeks' duration of St. Bartholomew's Fair, the playhouses of central London were closed down. But the jealousy of the theatre licensees and the increasing rowdyism of the pleasure seekers on the fairgrounds brought petitions and legislation against the showmen. In 1750 St. Bartholomew's Fair was limited to three days, while puppet shows and theatrical booths were banned altogether. Although, either by permission or connivance, these theatrical booths were back by 1757, the leading actors were absent. The three-day limit still held, and the stars of those days were not tempted to leave the greenrooms of the patent theatres for the rowdy discomfort of a fairground fit-up. So the fairs went into decline. In 1760 Southwark Fair was abolished, and the only reason St. Bartholomew's lingered on was because of the revenue it brought Lord Kensington.

The same situation had arisen in Paris. Rivalry between the patent theatres and the fairground booths had brought in orders of restraint. Way back in 1719 the Comédie Française had obtained the suppression of all exhibitions except those devoted to rope-dancers and marionettes. An uneasy political régime, growing increasingly aware of the disquiet of the people, enforced new bans and restrictions. As in London, the fairgrounds became haunts of the underworld. Perhaps the showmen foresaw that when the Revolution came—and showmen have a keen nose for coming change—measures would be taken to suppress their means of livelihood. At any rate, that is what happened, although the two great fairs of St. Laurent and St. Germain actually died out a few years before this law came into force.

So when Astley went to France to present his "daring feats of horsemanship" before the king and the French court, he found that in Paris, too, showmen were ready to leave the fairgrounds. In 1782 he returned to lay the foundation for the French circus. His son John became a favorite performer of Marie Antoinette, who called him the English Rose. Later, under the Franconis, the circus became the most popular as well as the most elegant entertainment in the French capital.

Astley's journeys into Europe did not stop at Paris; he went as far afield as Belgrade. During his lifetime he was responsible for building nineteen permanent circuses. Yet it was his one-time leading horseman, Charles Hughes, who took the circus beyond the Balkans. Hughes had quarreled with Astley and set up his Royal Circus in opposition to Astley's Amphitheatre in Lambeth. He then quarreled with his partners and went off to buy thoroughbreds for Catherine the Great. He took some of his company over to Russia as well as the stud, and there, after delivering the horses, he gave an exhibition of trick-riding. He was rewarded with a circus, specially designed for him, in the royal palace of St. Petersburg, and the promise of another in Moscow. Some authorities hint at more intimate favors. Anyhow, by 1793 trick-riding—the principal attraction of the circus—had reached Russia.

By this time the circus had also spread westward to America. In that same year, John Bill Ricketts, a pupil of Hughes, built a circus at Philadelphia. While Ricketts was soliciting the patronage of George Washington, Benito Guerre was presenting his feats of horsemanship in Spain. Spain had also produced a number of trick-riders, and amongst them was Juan Porte, who founded a circus in Vienna in 1780.

Each country has produced its circus dynasties, but since these families have always spent much of their time in travel, they have intermarried and achieved an internationalism within themselves. Today there are Cookes in the United States with Cooke cousins in England. In England there are Pinders with Pinder connections in France. Over there are Gautiers related to Gautiers in Sweden . . . and so it goes on.

The story of the circus is like the conjuror's set of Chinese rings. The rings are separate. Suddenly they are linked in a chain. You look again, and they form an overlapping complex pattern. Yet, in a second, once more they are all separate, each one a single entity.

The parade continues, and the sight of the grooms each leading two plumed and caparisoned horses across the ring gives one the clue to the character of the circus in its early days. For, in looking at the history of this entertainment as a whole, one can distinguish three main trends, three dominating influences which, without fundamentally changing its pattern, have each in succession emphasized a particular aspect of its design. During the first ninety years or so, the prevailing feature was the horse.

Even in England, where one proprietor after another insisted on mixing up the circus with the theatre, the plays produced were equestrian dramas, the plots of which were written with an eye to the horses that came down off the stage into the ring. Hughes started this misalliance between the theatre and the circus; Astley, unfortunately, copied him and gave the idea to the Franconis. But the French, who have always shown a subtler appreciation of the circus than the British, soon dropped the idea and applauded horsemanship without histrionics, relegating the lavish equestrian dramas and zoological pantomines to the hippodrome, which provided more room for such spectacles. In Germany, too, the cult of the equestrian drama soon died out, though it lasted longer there than in France.

Meanwhile, the English persevered, even to the point of producing *Il Trovatore* and *Richard III* with actors on horseback. *Mazeppa*

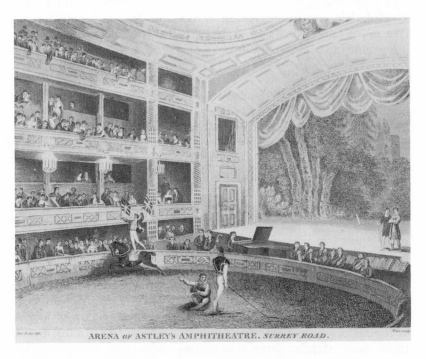

ARENA *of* ASTLEY'S AMPHITHEATRE, *SURREY ROAD*.

The interior of Astley's Amphitheatre in 1815. (An engraving from a drawing by George Jones, in the author's collection.)

was probably the most famous piece, chiefly because in one production Adah Isaacs Menken showed more of her fleshings than was necessary; but it was run a good second by *The Battle of Waterloo*. Military subjects naturally formed many of the plots. But the circus was not quite dead. Tucked away in the middle of the bills one finds "Scenes in the Circle." And in the provinces a less sophisticated audience applauded a purer form of horsemanship simply because the tenting shows were unable to carry all the props which the more theatrical productions demanded.

Long before "Lord" George Sanger put on his pantomine with a cast of seven hundred human actors, thirteen elephants, nine camels, fifty-two horses and twelve other species of animals in 1876 at Astley's, the French had made high school riders the stars of the circus.

In the middle of the last century Jules Janin, the French dramatic critic, asked a Parisian clubman if he had seen Caroline Loyo ride the new bay she had trained. "Alas, I did not. You see I went to Florence to see the Pitti Palace," was the reply. This brought forth the rebuke, "Sir, when Caroline rides a new horse one does not go gallivanting off to look at Pitti Palaces. One stays at the Circus."

At that time the Cirque d'Eté in the Champs Elysées was a social rendezvous which almost rivaled the Opéra in splendor. But the circus was primarily a man's entertainment. There the Jockey Club had its own private box, while behind the ring doors other members of the aristocracy paid constant tribute to the performers. As a center of fashion it maintained its position for nearly sixty years, and it has been described by Arnold Mortier as "the place where all the world mingles, where all languages are spoken, and where for an hour the most blasé public on earth swoons over the antics of a clown or holds its breath in suspense over a horse's hoofs." Although nothing remains of the original building, except some subterranean passages where the street cleaners keep their brooms, a less sophisticated audience still holds its breath over a horse's hoof, for above ground the site is marked by a children's merry-go-round. The Cirque d'Hiver, the sister establishment on the other side of Paris, however, is still run as a circus.

Soon a new influence was to be felt, which, although it never supplanted the horse, did alter the balance of the programme. In 1859 the success which followed Léotard's invention of the flying trapeze and Blondin's achievements in crossing Niagara on a tightrope drew the attention of the world to that first group of showmen who left the fairground to join the equestrians of the circus: the acrobats, rope-dancers and jugglers. Subtle distinctions were made between acrobats and gymnasts, and the latter were categorized as either aerial or parterre. Later the feats of the Hanlon-Voltas, Sandow, the Craggs, the Scheffers, Cinquevalli, Caicedo and others all accentuated the purely human element. The appreciation of gymnastics became a cult, and people in every walk of life became amateur acrobats. This was particularly noticeable on the Continent, where there were few facilities for organized games and sports, which in England provided an outlet for this athleticism.

The Cirque Olympique, circa 1825. (From a lithograph by G. Engelmann, in the author's collection.)

The acrobats and gymnasts of the circus reached their greatest success at the beginning of this century, particularly in Germany. While in London the greatest stars appeared on the music hall stage, in Berlin they still remained faithful to the sawdust. But, no matter where they appeared, World War I caused their decline. Many were killed or injured and others deprived of time and place for practice; furthermore, the depression that followed made directors look for ways of saving money. This they achieved by relying on more house numbers, which left little room for outside acts. These numbers were found amongst the wild animals and their trainers, which had formed the second group of performers to leave the fairgrounds for the circus.

So we come to the third phase, the rise of animal acts, which, while not achieving the total eclipse of either man or horse, put both further into the shadow.

The German animal dealer Hagenbeck started it as far back as 1887; but at that time he diluted the strong animal flavor of his programme with Sudanese, Esquimaux, Somalis, Kalmucks, Patagonians and Hottentots. The other German proprietors followed his lead. At the same time the Americans, with their inherent desire to possess the biggest of everything, were showing an almost idolatrous respect for the elephant. They even went so far as to judge the importance of a circus by the number of these animals instead of the number of horses in the show.

With the deterioration of economic conditions the preponderance of animal acts grew. In the menagerie tent elephants, lions, tigers and bears brought in extra gate money—which contributed substantially to their upkeep—and in the ring they performed. No acrobat or juggler served this dual purpose. So today one finds many circuses possessing their own wild animals as well as their own horses. Sometimes even the dogs and monkeys belong to the proprietor. In these circuses more than half a programme of twenty acts may consist of house numbers; the rest is likely to include several acts which double, that is, a troupe which works, say, a riding act under one name and perhaps a clown entrée under another. In such a company the animals greatly exceed the human performers. Yet of the jugglers and acrobats that remain the best are as good as they ever were, though there are fewer of them. If a performer has pride in his calling—and all the great ones have—more work and less pay won't keep him from appearing in the ring. He may grumble a bit, but he knows that those who drop out are never the best.

The horses with their tossing plumes, the acrobats in tights and leotards, the elephants and bears have all, for one brief moment, held the ring as the parade passed by. The changes that they symbolize have been brought about by time. Place has also altered the emphasis, not of the main international pattern of the circus, but of its scale and character.

Were we to select an American performer from the company, he would tell us how in the United States the circus grew up as the country developed. The continuous opening up of the West put the accent on traveling shows, most of them making their journeys first by road and then by railway, while some used canals and one or two steamed up and down the broad rivers in floating palaces.

Just as the settlers had to fight for existence, so did the circuses. They fought not only the prejudice of the country-folk, many of whom thought that even a parade was an "iniquitous spectacle," they fought the country-folk themselves. The circus battle cry of "Hey Rube!" has led to many overturned wagons, ripped canvas, fired tents and quite a few deaths on both sides. They fought storms, floods, blow-downs and other acts of God. They eventually fought the confidence tricksters and card-sharpers who trailed along in their wake, and even the short-change men in their own payboxes. And they won through. Little shows—such as Quick and Mead's, which in 1826 had no more than four wagons, nine horses, a fifty-foot big top and an orchestra which consisted of one hurdy-gurdy—eventually became gigantic combines in which a thousand people produced simultaneous spectacles in three rings and four stages for an audience of sixteen thousand.

This growth came about through a complicated series of partner-ships and mergers. When in the 1840s the vermilion wagons of Welch's National Circus joined the ultramarine wagons of Lent's New York Circus, the combines were comparatively small. But soon the bewildering interchange of partners began in earnest. The end of each season became the signal for a sort of general post amongst proprietors. This formation and reformation of aggrega-tions and combines could only lead to one thing. It happened in 1929 when the Ringlings, who, apart from their own show, had already acquired half a dozen others, including Barnum & Bailey, bought out the rival Circus Corporation of America which owned five more. In this way all the big circuses came under a monopoly.

In the early days the amalgamation of two or more shows meant the development of the individual spectacle. This, together with the fact that one season's partner might become next year's rival, led to more and more extravagant publicity. Andrew Haight, who lost seventy-five thousand dollars in one circus venture, found that it paid to take a whole page of advertising in the local newspapers; and that if there were no hoardings or walls large enough for his posters, it paid him to build them. He discovered that in a street parade three brass bands made three times as much noise as one, and that noise meant ballyhoo and ballyhoo meant business.

Soon street parades in America reached the height of baroque splendor, rivaling even those put on in England by "Lord" George Sanger. A procession of twenty or more richly carved and gilded wagons, carrying tableaux, bandsmen or wild animals, cunningly interspersed with horses, riders, elephants and clowns, with a blaring steam organ, called a calliope, bringing up the rear, would lure the townsfolk to the circus field in much the same way as the Pied Piper led the children of Hamelin into the mountains.

The showman's love of the baroque was not confined to the carving on the bandwagon. On the posters flamboyant pseudonyms were used in place of the simple word "circus." Shows went out under names such as "Equescurriculum," "Hippolymiad," and "Cirqzooladon"; they were called "Egyptian Caravans" and "Paris Pavilions," and described as "Nickel-Plated." But behind all this fantasy serious work was going on. Spencer Q. Stokes built the first American riding machine, for training trick-riders. "Doctor" Gilbert Spalding, who had started his career in a chemist's shop, invented quarter-poles, those posts which support the canvas roof of a big top between the king poles at the center and the side poles at the perimeter. The famous clown Dan Rice* was another who contributed to the technical side of the circus. While running his own show in 1852 he experimented with lighting the ring by electricity. Although he decided to give up this form of illumination because of "the injurious effect it had upon those suffering from pulmonary complaints and the tender brains of young children," at least he blazed the trail.†

Electric light, quarter-poles and the riding machine are now used in circuses all over the world. But the circus has not wholly accepted three rings, nor the "bigger-and-therefore-better" policy,

---

* In *The Ways of the Circus*, George Conklin, the lion trainer, tells how Dan Rice was particularly fond of drink, and afterwards toured America giving temperance lectures. At these lectures he took frequent sips from the water carafe in front of him—which contained pure gin. After his audience had gone home Dan would chuckle and say, "What fools people are, anyway."

† One cannot help thinking that the real reason was more likely to have been the unreliability of the dynamos. Times change: in 1886 Powell and Clarke, tenting in Ireland, billed their show as being "illuminated by the recently invented American Circus Electric Light," and the performers included the Electric Family, who "by a freak of nature . . . possess the marvellous power of conveying electricity to anyone approaching them." The medical profession at that time not only accepted but approved. "Doctors," the handbill says, "advocate electricity as a cure for nervousness, rheumatism, weakness, giddiness, indigestion, sluggish liver, want of energy, overworked brain, tic, toothache and several other afflictions."

which under a monopoly has led to taking producers and designers from the theatre instead of letting the circus develop along its traditional lines. Americans themselves may feel that in the fantastic but bewildering, exciting but overpowering circuses of today something is lost. As long ago as 1941, Woolcott Gibbs wrote in the *New Yorker:*

> We went to the circus on the opening night, and we're damned if we know just what to make of it. The tan-bark has turned a lovely blue; the roustabouts have been dressed like Dutch boys . . . the big parade, that used to blare and prance around the ring glides by . . . cushioned on air and whimsy; the Black Jaguar and Berber Lion snarl from a chromium jungle, bathed in a cold, artistic light. . . . We don't know exactly what seemed wrong. . . . All we do know is that the symbol, the essence of the whole performance isn't a beautiful yellow-haired girl on a high-stepping horse, as it was when we were young. It's a handful of blue sawdust sifting gently through the fingers of an air-conditioned ape.

Once more we are back at the parade, and if we have to ask the English jockey-rider how the circus fared in Great Britain, we should find that here the story ran in exactly the opposite direction: instead of fewer and bigger circuses, they grew in numbers but became much smaller. Tradition is stronger than in America, but it is rather too hidebound. Tradition should flow on, not stagnate behind a dam labelled "Good-enough-for-father"; it was in father's day that grandfather's standards were left behind.

During the last century the circuses belonging to the Sangers, Pinders, Ginnetts and Cookes competed on their home grounds with shows brought over by Van Amburgh, Barnum and Bailey, French, Franconi, and many others. They did more than hold their own against this foreign competition. The Sangers, "Lord" George and "Lord" John, put on the richest, gaudiest, grandest shows that England has ever seen. They were at the top of their class, but others followed close behind. What is more, Sanger, Ginnett, Cottrelly and Pinder made frequent and successful tours on the Continent, and the last two stayed there. The Cookes invaded America. In South Africa, the Bells and Frank Fillis were followed by the Boswells, and the Harmstons made the Far East their tenting ground.

I have a letter in front of me from Adele Wirth, written in 1947. It reads "My Dad's show—Willison's Great World Circus—toured India, Burma, the Malay States, Java, Siam, China and Japan in 1896–1897; then went from Yokohama on to Honolulu, Vancouver and the USA. Among the artistes we had the Hartley Family of trick-cyclists, riding old penny-farthings, the Fredericks Family— my grandparents and aunties. One of these girls, a strikingly pretty blonde, married Frank Eldred, Willie Harmston's half-brother. . . ."

Frank Brown, whose father had appeared at Astley's, developed the circus in Latin America and became a naturalized Argentinian. English names topped circus posters all over the world, but in Britain the circus turned inwards and dissipated what talent remained by breaking up into smaller units. Charlie Keith, clown and circus proprietor, saw the danger as early as 1879. "I am compelled to confess, and I believe it will be owned," he wrote, "that cheapness at home is often thought more of than talent, and that travelling circuses have of late years degenerated in England. . . . To see the circus in all its glory one must visit the Continent." Soon the growing emphasis on wild animals was to make the public realize that one season's show was very much like the next. The circus went into a decline.

It was saved by Bertram Mills, who, first at Olympia and then with a tenting show, proved that a first-class programme, as good as anything to be seen on the Continent, could be made to pay. Like Sarrasani in Germany, who was at heart a businessman, he showed what could be achieved by organization. No circus in the world was run so cleanly, so smartly, so efficiently or effectively as that of Mills in its heyday. It is a great pity that between the wars no one followed his example.

I once asked the director of an English family circus why he did not put on something bigger, or at least better. He shrugged. "I thought money would be tight this year," he said, "so I put on pretty well the cheapest programme I could. Look at it! Packed out every night. It must have something that pleases them. Why should I take a gamble on anything better when I know it would only cost more? And why should I make it bigger, when I know that all it would mean is more worry?"

At the end of World War II there was a boom. The smaller family shows had struggled on through wartime restrictions, petrol-rationing and the blackout. To meet the demand, these split still further and catchpenny proprietors also invaded the field. In the early days of peace there were eighty circuses in England, some of them "rogue" shows, presenting a programme which bore no relation to that which was announced on the bills. As money got tighter these dropped out. Apart from Cyril and Bernard Mills, who tried to maintain the high standard set by their father, and the Blackpool Tower company, very few proprietors could say that their circus was as good as ever, and families rarely joined forces to produce a better programme.

Then Clem Butson (who had been responsible for the excellent programmes at the Blackpool Tower) produced a circus for Tom Arnold at Harringay which, act for act, often surpassed Olympia. The Harringay arena, built as an ice-skating rink, demanded a different type of production. The empty space between the forty-two foot ring and the steeply raked seating had to be turned into a hippodrome track and filled with color and movement. This called for parades, show-girls and chariot races. Some may have found this rather reminiscent of an American three-ring circus; but where else could one then see the Schumanns, Gilbert Houcke, the Geraldos or the Ibarras?

Two exceptions to the usual run were the summer circuses of Smart and Chipperfield, which grew to rival that of Bertram Mills. But in 1964, Cyril and Bernard Mills decided that they should stop tenting and Dick Chipperfield took his circus to South Africa for a spell. Then Harringay was sold and the Mills found that Olympia was no longer a viable circus venture, so that London was without a Christmas circus. Some people felt that television was to blame. Yet since then a newcomer to the circus has seized on this medium and exploited it to his own ends. Gerry Cottle started with a small show in 1971, when he was twenty-five years old. Within four years he had arranged for his tent, equipment and part of his programme to be used in a series of television spectaculars, and provided the setting and artistes for a children's circus thriller serial.

In 1978, members of the Chipperfield family were back on the road with two circuses, and both they and the Smarts provide programmes for television at Christmas and Easter. Gerry Cottle has taken his show as far afield as the Persian Gulf, where he performed before the Shah of Persia and the sultan of Muscat and Oman. He was also the only British circus proprietor to run his own traveling school, with a fully qualified teacher. The children were educated free. Then, in 1979, he ran into financial difficulties. The Persian general who had sponsored his circus's season in Iran failed to meet a seventy-thousand-pound bill, and subsequent events in that country make it improbable that the debt will ever be paid. Bad weather and high taxation contributed to his troubles. His creditors decided to form a committee to help him retrieve his and their losses. This meant cutting out items like the circus school.

Gerry Cottle does not come from showman stock; the Chipperfields and Smarts do. The Chipperfields gained a great deal of experience in fairground menageries, which has stood them in good stead when organizing and stocking safari parks. Billy Smart, founder of the circus which bears his name, was an amusement caterer who made his name running fairs. This influx among circus proprietors of showmen from the fairgrounds also took place in France.

In France "parade" has a rather different significance from the English word. It is still most often used to describe the free performance which is given on the show-front of a fairground booth to draw the crowd. This is, indeed, the origin of the circus parade, and the name "parader" is still used to describe those who perform in front of fairground booths in England. It did not take the showmen long to realize that if the sight of a few performers lined up outside a tent would make people flock to the entrance, then many more could be gathered in if the performers were to parade through the streets. Such a procession usually ended with a final display—or *postiche,* as the French showmen say—in front of the booth. From there it was but a step to continue their march across the ring so that those who had already taken their places were also able to see the parade.

The parade soon became an integral part of the show even in the permanent amphitheatres of Paris. When at the end of each summer season the company from the Cirque d'Eté in Paris left for the Cirque d'Hiver, they formed a procession which marched through crowd-lined streets from the Champs Elysées to the boulevard du Temple. When the Cirque d'Eté was demolished this procession could no longer be held, but one can still see the parade in its original form on the show-fronts of a number of little circuses in the fairgrounds of France. Sometimes the performance which is given free outside is better than that for which one pays inside; the stronger the rival attractions, the better the bait must be.

Most of the proprietors of the big circuses traveling over the Continent today were reared in the competitive atmosphere of the fairground. The Bougliones who, unlike any English circus family, have a strong dose of Gypsy blood in their veins, started with a few lions in a menagerie and did not turn to the circus till 1925. Since then they have achieved a remarkable success, which dates back to the day they bought a job lot of posters which had been ordered and forgotten by the original Buffalo Bill. Although the famous frontiersman had been dead for many years, the public were completely taken in. They flocked to see Colonel Cody, who looked more like a redskin than a scout; and the Paris audiences which, during the twenties, rushed to see his "rough-riders of the world" in the suburbs did not realize that the "cowboys" were Gypsy horse-copers, or that the elephants in the programme were to be seen much nearer home at the Cirque de Paris in the avenue de la Motte-Piquet, whence they came every night in a pantechnicon directly their act was over. The Bougliones did so well that in 1934 they were able to take over that doyen of the French circus, the Cirque d'Hiver.

Before World War II the great rivals of the Bougliones were the Amars, who originally came over from Algiers with a troupe of hootchi-kootchi dancers. They then became owners of a fairground menagerie and finally circus directors. When the family split, their importance declined, and Pinder's Circus became the Bougliones' greatest rival. Although the wagons were still painted yellow, as they were in Arthur Pinder's day, this circus was then run by the Spiesserts. They, too, were menagerie proprietors on the fairgrounds before they came to the circus. Charles Spiessert—or Spessardy, as he sometimes called himself—honored tradition and reestablished the street parade. He built a number of floats carrying sea monsters and royal barges; a lion couchant in gilded plaster headed the line of beast wagons. A chariot bearing the *carillon Pinder* and a magnificent bandwagon provided the music. Interspersed with clowns, elephants, horsemen and with an airplane circling overhead, this parade showed how, by building on the foundations of the past, one could make tradition live today.

Charles Spiessert died in 1970, and soon after Pinder's Circus was bought by Jean Richard, who in 1978 was running four circuses in France. Unfortunately for a man who has done so much to keep the circus alive, this season was not a success and Jean Richard was forced drastically to reorganize his affairs.

The same story of menagerie proprietors becoming circus owners can be told of the Krones, who ran one of the largest circuses in Germany. Traditionally, the great family circuses were directed by horse-trainers and riders, such as the Schumanns, Renzes, Carrés and Strassburgers. But today most are descended from *banquistes,* the name by which showfolk are known amongst themselves, and which has the same derivation as *banquier*—for the bankers and the mountebanks were those who set up their *bancs* or trestles on the fairgrounds of the Middle Ages.

The finest traveling show in Europe today is undoubtedly that belonging to the Knies, which celebrated its 175th anniversary in 1978, although it was not until 1919 that it became the Swiss National Circus. The first member of the family to take to the road was born in 1784, the son of the doctor who attended the Empress Maria Theresa of Austria. Since then seven generations have appeared before the public. Today their circus is distinguished not only by the brilliance of the acts, particularly those performed by members of the family, but also by the inimitable sense of style in every aspect of production, right down to the publicity material. Their posters are works of art of an extremely high quality.

What, you may ask, about Eastern Europe? Well, the circus parade, which has led us through England, France and America, which has touched at points in the Far East, South Africa and other places nearer home, can also take us behind the Iron Curtain. At the State Circus in Moscow you may watch a parade which, while it remains completely in the grand tradition, makes excellent use of new production techniques. One programme opened with a fanfare of trombones played by clowns in the orchestra balcony. Then across a brilliantly lit ring marched the artistes in a dazzling procession; as the last performer passed through the ring curtains, the lights went out and back through the darkness came the whole parade in fluorescent costumes of many colors, gleaming luminously in the ultraviolet rays of black light.

After World War II, the Russian circus seemed, for a time, to be used as a hoarding. The sawdust ring, for instance, might be patterned as a poster in praise of the Red Army; a pyramid of acrobats was said to represent the bourgeois social structure, the bearers being the peasants, who on their shoulders supported successive tiers representing clerks, soldiers, priests, aristocrats and finally as top-mounter the Czar. Today that kind of thing seems to have disappeared. After all, the circus pure and simple can so easily and forcefully show both the inhabitants of the remotest parts of the USSR and capitalists abroad what superb athletes, what brilliant horsemen, what magnificent animals and what remarkable trainers the Soviets can produce.

Sixty permanent amphitheatres, thirty tenting shows and ten stage circus companies employ 8,000 people. The new circus in

Moscow seats 3,400 and has four interchangeable rings, for ice and water spectacles as well as for illusionists and circus acts proper. The famous circus school started in 1927 has trained some 2,000 performers, though not all have stayed in the sawdust ring.

The Soviet circuses that I have seen both in and out of Russia have shown great imagination. The apparatus, particularly for aerial acts, has been most originally designed to demonstrate human achievement. Costumes and lighting have imbued the spectacle with richness and color, and the whole programme has been produced with a sense of occasion.

I have only seen one circus from the German Democratic Republic, and it struck me that the undoubted originality of the performers had been let down by the banality of the production, particularly in costume and lighting. However, the other two tenting circuses in that country may make amends, and the circus school in East Berlin has indeed turned out some original acts.

There are also state circus schools in Poland and Bulgaria, producing performers for nine Polish tenting shows and a permanent circus in Warsaw, and for five Bulgarian tenting shows and a permanent building in Sofia.

In the 1930s I remember visiting two permanent circuses in Budapest. Fenyes, in the Angol Park, seems to have disappeared, but Beketow's old building, which became Fövárosi Nagy, has recently been reconstructed. Three circus companies tour Hungary under canvas. Rumania has one permanent and one tenting circus. In Czechoslovakia you will find three circuses and in Yugoslavia two more, all five working under canvas.

That is the overall picture, the background of the circus as I see it. The parade is over, and the time has come to study the individual acts in more detail; but first there is still the charivari.

Close on the heels of the parade come the clowns, tumbling and bumbling about the ring. What they do and how they do it will be described later, but their place in the circus as a whole should come here.

A spectacle which, although it causes a mental reaction in the audience, is so essentially physical in its presentation, should contain contrast. The riders, the trainers, the acrobats and the rest are too much concerned with action to try to impart ideas. That is the job of the clown, and in doing so he reverses the process of the other artistes. Instead of physical action producing mental reaction, the clown gives expression to an idea and obtains a physical reaction from the audience.

Besides their entrée, or special number, clowns run into the ring between the acts. They should provide the grotesque after the beautiful, the comic after the serious, the laughter after the thrill, as well as keep the audience entertained while the ring boys are changing the "props."

But the ring has already been raked, and it is now clear for the first act on the bill.

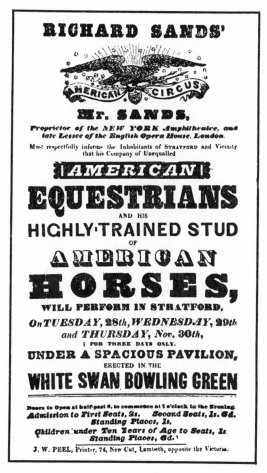

A day-bill of the first American circus to tour England, in 1843. (From the author's collection.)

III

VOLTIGE
and Other Forms
of
TRICK-RIDING

The orchestra shatters the hush with Strauss's "Thunder and Lightning" polka, and a horse and rider hurtle into the ring. They circle the sawdust like a whirlwind, and as they pass one sees that the rider has neither stirrups nor saddle. There is just a surcingle or "roller" in front of him, with a handgrip on either side of the withers and a loop, low on the off-side. The horse has its head, yet from the constant urging one would think that it could not move fast enough. Then suddenly the rider flings himself from the horse's back, turns cartwheels and somersaults alongside and, seizing the handgrips, vaults on again. While mounted he goes through movements such as the scissors, so that at one moment he faces the tail and the next moment the horse's head. But he does not remain on the horse's back for long. He seems to spend as much time leaping on and off as he does astride his mount. This is the voltige act.

There are several variations. In *voltige à la Richard,* for instance, the horse is neither bridled nor saddled, it does not even carry a halter or surcingle, and when it clears an obstacle the rider also jumps over it alongside his mount, often complicating his leap with a somersault. This act is said to have got its name from Davis Richard, an American who killed himself in 1860 while with the

Renz circus in St. Petersburg. However, as A.H. Saxon points out in his *The Life and Art of Andrew Ducrow,* the same act was performed long before by the mulatto rider Joseph Hillier, one of Ducrow's protégés. This act led to a type of performance known as the *voltige infernale,* in which Johnny Woodson excelled at the end of the last century. It consisted of some ten circuits of the ring, both horse and rider going hell for leather, and ended with a particularly high jump at the ring doors. Both *voltige à la Richard* and *voltige infernale* lost much of their former glory when coco-matting replaced the sawdust in the rings of permanent circuses.

One can also see *voltige à la cowboy,* in which lariats are brought into play, while *voltige Tcherkesse* has a Cossack flavor. Here the routine includes lying across the horse's back with one foot in the loop attached to the surcingle, and, leaning back and downwards into the ring, the rider picks up a handkerchief from the sawdust as the horse gallops by. A favorite position for a Cossack rider is the shoulder stand: that is, upside down with one shoulder on the base of the horse's neck and the feet straight up in the air. The *djigit* riders of Russia perform even more startling tricks, passing not only under the belly but between the back legs of a galloping horse.

The basic movements of the voltige act are not difficult, but they must be presented with a sure sense of style and timing. In vaulting to the back of the horse, both legs should come down well to the front, and as the horse draws abreast the legs and body are thrown up and back, pivoting on the hands which hold the grips. For a moment trunk and legs lie straight out, high above the horse, then the legs part and the body falls into the ordinary riding position. It is by looking out for neatness in movements such as these that one learns to appreciate style. The difficulty of timing comes in varying the tempo of the human movements while the animal maintains a fast, even pace. Against the steady rhythm of the horse the rider must provide the acrobatic melody.

A good voltige act requires a sound knowledge of both riding and acrobatics. It makes an excellent opening number if it is taken at great speed and is performed by one person, for then it whets the appetite for what is to follow. But like all good *apéritifs* it should be dry, brisk and taken in small quantities.

Bareback numbers, now usually known as jockey acts, are rather similar to voltige acts, but in *Le Jockey d'Epsom,* as it was once called, more time is spent actually on the horse's back: in standing on one leg, in jumping from the knees to an upright position, in leaping over a whip or in dancing. There are less wild acrobatics

Some of the movements seen in a voltige act top, the take-off; centre, the elevation which results from a good take-off; and below, the single-knee balance and the scissors. (Drawings by John Skeaping.)

and more feats of balance, so the horse has broader quarters and is slower. It is the type known in the American circus as a rosinback because of the rosin which is rubbed on its coat to keep the rider from slipping. When the rider jumps onto the horse's back, he usually takes a preliminary run across the ring, and sometimes he makes use of a springboard called a "cushion."

An Englishman called Billy Bell is always given the credit for inventing this type of act in the 1870s. But Tourniaire was billed as "the English jockey" on the posters of Astley's Amphitheatre in 1843; and twenty-three years before that Andrew Ducrow enacted the rôle of the jockey. After a while it became a special routine, the distinguishing characteristic of which was a series of leaps from the ring to an upright position on the back of the horse without any help. Later performers, many of whom were British, also took it up. Dressed as for the turf, Bradbury at Salamonsky's circus in Riga, Hubert Cooke, who was killed in the ring of the Circus Strepetow at Odessa in 1917, and a number of others all became famous jockey riders.

About a hundred years ago, at Renz's Circus in Berlin, three English jockey riders, Wilkes Lloyd, Adolph Wells and Hubert Cooke, together with three foreign performers, Sasha Gérard, Alfredo Rossi and Hermann Althoff, all competed against each other. On that occasion Wilkes Lloyd made six running ground mounts during one circuit of the ring; that means running across the ring and jumping onto the horse in a standing position six times while the horse canters once around the ring.

The great English circus family of Clarke produced several outstanding jockey riders, the finest of whom was John Frederick. Even other riders admitted that he had no rival; and to prove it he issued a challenge of £1,000 to anyone who could even copy his act, let alone surpass it. This consisted of four complicated routines of flip-flaps, round-offs, pirouettes, handstands and somersaults on the back of a cantering horse.* He is one of only two people who have ever achieved a double somersault from the back of a horse to the ground. In the early days of this century he and one of his brothers could command a salary of 3,500 francs a month. Not only his two brothers but his niece and nephew all worked as jockey riders.

While a voltige number looks better performed by one person, a jockey act appears at its best with two or three. Both men and

---

* These and other acrobatic movements are described on pp. 199-203.

women can work it together, though women are rarely seen and somehow seem slightly out of place. After the Clarkes came the brothers Houcke, and the three Reinsches, all of whom made their names in this type of riding. Nowadays "to do the jockey" has come to mean more a method of presentation than a definite act with its own set of tricks.

The highlight of the Reinsch Brothers' act was when one of them somersaulted from the back of one horse to the back of another which followed behind. Chotachen-Courtauld, the Franco-Chinese rider, performed a lay-out back somersault from one horse to another in the mid 1930s at the Cirque Medrano. Lucio Cristiani went one better; he threw a somersualt—but not a layout back— which took him right over the second horse to land on the back of a third as they cantered round the ring.

Lucio Cristiani's somersault. (Drawing by John Skeaping.)

If one turns a somersault from a moving platform, the platform does not move from under you, as most people seem to think. The movement of the horse is imparted to the rider and Lucio had to throw himself backwards in making his somersault—not just wait in the air for the horse to come under him. The horses, however, moved neck to flank, and this meant a shorter jump than he would have had to throw if the horses moved in strict Indian file. Lucio, Belmonte and Mogador Cristiani also made simultaneous back

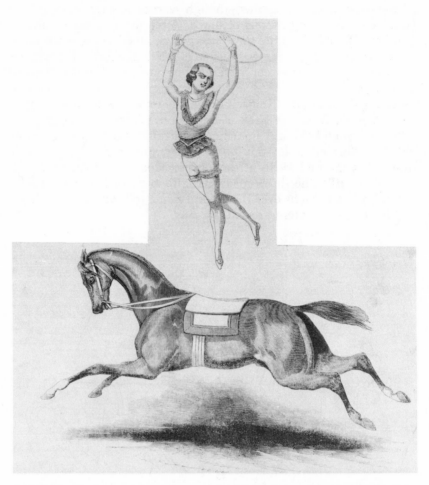

LeviJ. North, famous American trick-rider who appeared at Astley's in 1838. (From a newspaper cutting in the author's collection.)

somersaults from three horses, two of them to the horses behind and the third to the ground, while passing hoops over their bodies. In the 1950s, the Alexander Serges Troupe in Russia included a performer who turned a double somersault from a two-men-high column standing on one horse, to land on a following horse. To turn a somersault on one bareback horse is no mean feat. It was first accomplished by an American, and the credit is usually given to John H. Glenroy, through some say Levi North preceded him by seven years. There are very few accurate records of the tricks which were performed in the first fifty years of the nineteenth century, but I believe that North used a pad, a flat platform strapped to the horse's back, which makes the trick much easier, while Glenroy was the first to turn a somersault bareback. I have not been able to find out whether another American, billed as "Mr. Aymar," used a pad when he threw "his back somersault feet to feet with the animal at full speed" at Astley's in 1843. This reminds one that, apart from such a feat being simplified by a pad, there is the question of how a somersault is turned. It should be made as Aymar made it, feet to feet, but in the early days if a pad was not used it was more often accomplished feet to fork—in other words the rider did not land standing up, but astride—which again is much less difficult. Only one thing seems clear, and that is that the first somersault on horseback was turned by an American. America has produced a number of excellent riders, and among them was Billy Sholes. In a conversation he once had with his friend Bob Sherwood the clown, he tells of another interesting point of technique. Some time after Sholes had retired Sherwood asked him why he had not stayed with the circus in some other capacity. "Bob," he replied, "I just couldn't do it—I couldn't hang around with the crop of riders they have doing principals today. Look at them! Not a single one who can make a running ground jump without grabbing hair."

That disparaging remark "grabbing hair" explains how a leap from the ground to the horse's back should *not* be made. A good rider should land as delicately as a snowflake on the horse's quarters, never near the withers where he can seize the horse's mane until he gets his balance. He must therefore be light, supple and full of grace. Nothing looks so clumsy as a stiff, heavy jump, followed by a tottering struggle to keep upright.

Trick-riders start their training young, particularly if they are born into a family of specialists in this type of work, for there is always a demand for experienced top-mounters who weigh little, which often means that they must be as young as the law allows. After the child has learned to ride astride, a "mechanic" is rigged up in the practice ring. This apparatus is the same as the American riding machine which, as I mentioned in the last chapter, was invented about 125 years ago by Spencer Q. Stokes. It consists of a central post which supports an arm rather like the jib of a crane; the base of the arm pivots round the post. At the top, a rope is reeved through a pulley. One end of the rope is fastened to the rider's belt; the other leads down to the hand of the attendant, who

The American Riding Machine. (Drawing by John Skeaping.)

pushes the arm round the ring so that the pulley is always above the horse's quarters, and who can take the weight of the rider when he slips. This simple gadget is now used for training bareback riders all over the world. Once the rider has learned to keep his balance

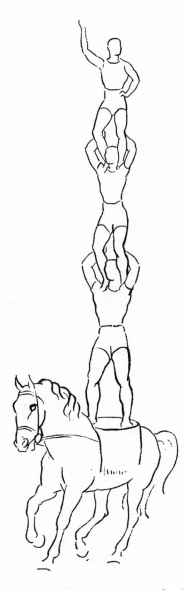

The three-men-high of the Fredianis. (Drawing by John Skeaping.)

while standing, more exciting movements can be introduced, culminating in the somersault. Then all that is needed is constant practice.

In the family riding act one sees not only more riders, but more horses as well. But while the horses are always kept outside the ring until they are needed, the human performers are there in front of us all the time. When they are not actually riding, they walk round and round in the center of the ring exhorting those on horseback with cries which may once have been "Allez," but which now sound more like screams of delight. And directly the trick is achieved they stand with one arm half-raised and the other pointing towards the performer, directing the attention of the audience to his praiseworthy feat with a final cry of "Hup!" I enjoy the work of this supporting chorus almost as much as that of the person who does the trick. The ecstatic whoops and yells give the act a refreshing spontaneity besides adding quite a lot to the excitement. But the tricks must be good. No amount of screaming will replace fine workmanship—though it can enhance it.

The routine of the family troupe consists, for the most part, of building various human pyramids on two, three or four horses. In the 1950s the Loyal Respinskis, the Sobolewskis and the Carolis achieved much the same act as had the Five Olympians a hundred years before. Three horses cantered round the ring in line abreast. Two men stood on their backs, each straddling two horses. On their shoulders stood a third. No one, however, has surpassed the three-men-high column which the Fredianis accomplished at the beginning of the century. They used a single horse which, it is true, carried a pad; but on this stood one man who bore a second man standing on his shoulders, and on the shoulders of the second man stood a third. The middleman, Aristodemo Frediani, worked in the ring long after his riding days were over. He became the famous auguste Beby.*

The different balances which are held on horseback are usually interspersed with various forms of acrobatics such as the running ground mount. If one studies this movement it seems to have an almost algebraic quality. The rider walks up to his horse, pats its rump as it canters by, then turns smartly around and runs, with a quick change of step, across the ring to make his leap. By the time he lands, his horse will have completed its course round half the ring. Remembering that the ring should always be forty-two feet in diameter, one could express this trick by a formula something like this:

---

* An auguste is the stooge to a clown. Whereas the clown has a white face and usually wears a sequined costume, the partner, the auguste, can paint his face any way he chooses and wear the most eccentric clothes.

$$\frac{42}{x} + T = \pi\frac{21}{y}$$

where T = the time the rider spends in the air,
       x = the speed of the rider,
       y = the speed of the horse.

The traditional finale for a family riding act is for all the performers to be carried out of the ring on one horse. Even the member who has been acting as ringmaster finally throws down his whip, runs across the ring and lands astride the horse's neck, in front of the others, where he is forced to grab hair to keep his balance; while the comedian at the tail end also has to grab hair to stay on at all.

Speed should be the keynote of a successful troupe of riders, but this is not always achieved. One of the reasons is that a rosin-back must have a smooth gait above all else. Many a rider has been injured in falling from a horse because it suddenly changed its speed or step. Then, like the horse in the jockey act, it must have broad quarters and be capable of carrying a heavy load. It is not easy to find one which is fast as well.

The Baker Boys, who frequently appeared at Olympia as the Cumberlands or the Corinthians, were one of the fastest family riding acts that I have seen. Although they did not turn any somersaults from one horse to another, Billy, Dicky and Pat Baker, urged on by the shrill screams of Sylvia Doksansky (herself an excellent top-mounter), worked with high spirits and a dashing verve. The story of how Bertram Mills first found their elder brother, Tommy, in the small tent that his father had pitched on Willesden Common, of his outstanding success at Olympia, of the great loss suffered by the British circus when he died of peritonitis at the age of twenty-two, all this has often been told. But its repetition serves to remind us that it is the small family show which often produces the biggest names. The Fredianis first presented their three-men-high on horseback in the little thirty-foot ring of their own circus. It took them a long time and many falls before they could work in the full-sized ring at the Nouveau Cirque.

In order to keep one's balance while standing on the back of a horse one must lean inwards to overcome centrifugal force. The angle at which the body must be inclined depends on the diameter of the ring. That is why circus rings are usually made the same size. C.B. Cochran, I believe, once built a circus ring slightly larger than normal. The Corty-Althoffs, who were to appear in it, took one look and refused to perform unless it was rebuilt to the regulation size. Given time, of course, any act can be adapted to suit a bigger or smaller ring. Thétard told me that Sarrasani's ring measured fifty feet across, and that it took the Reinsches eight days' rehearsal to get used to it.

Although a standard ring makes all riding acts at home anywhere in the world, the size is particularly important to those acts which rely to a great extent on balance, such as bareback acts, and particularly the *pas de deux*, for this routine needs little more than a highly developed sense of equilibrium. It was a popular act in Victorian days, when a gentleman in evening dress straddled two horses and supported a lady in ballet skirts while she took up various poses; or when two men appeared in classic costumes for the variation known as *jeux romains*. Today it has become more athletic and the costumes are less formal. Acts such as that of the Medrano Sisters* are directly descended from the *pas de deux*, but seem more akin to the work of the family riding troupe. In the *pas de deux* grace and style are more important than dash and excitement, and for these qualities the Pissiuttis have never been surpassed.

At the end of the last century the jockey act and the *pas de deux* were given a more prominent place on the bill than the other riding acts because they were performed without a pad. All pad-acts were then divided into two kinds: those in which the artistes turned somersaults and pirouettes, which were known to the profession as trick-riding, and those where they merely leapt over obstacles, which, according to Monsieur Farini of the Westminster Aquarium, "were not so honoured." They would bring the performer a mere seven pounds a week, against the one hundred pounds a week paid to the trick-rider. Today the pad is only used for bears, lions or tigers which are occasionally persuaded to ride on horseback.

The lady bareback rider† still flourishes. Somehow the sight of a principal lady rider, dressed in a short dancer's skirt, close-fitting bodice, tights and cross-gartered ballet shoes, leaping through a paper hoop, or sitting, with ankles crossed and toes pointed, on the

---

* Their real name is Swoboda, but this Austrian family adopted the name Medrano—much to Jérôme Medrano's understandable annoyance.

† She is now sometimes called a ballerina, and she is said to work a ballerina act, but this should be applied only to a high school act in which a ballerina dances on the ground alongside the horse.

broad quarters of a skewbald rosinback, sums up the whole spirit of the circus. The horse, standing with arched neck, and the rider, toying with her cutting whip while the clown kneels with one leg in the sawdust to mime his undying devotion . . . the ludicrous repartee, which somehow never seems to grow stale, that he then exchanges with the ringmaster . . . the crack of the whip which sends the horse ambling on and the clown out of the ring rubbing his behind . . . the blowing of kisses . . . all this is so bound up with tradition that it seems happily inevitable. Even the obstacles which are cleared by a principal lady rider are traditional: balloons,* the paper-covered hoops *through* which she jumps, and the banners and garters, which are either broad flags or narrow ribbons, *over* which she leaps. With the emancipation of women, their acts became more spectacular, rivaling some of the acrobatic movements of the jockey rider. Between the wars the Australian rider, May Wirth, used to turn a forward somersault with a half-twist on horseback.

Two other types of riding acts which were once popular have been rightly dropped from the programme of today. They are the *manoeuvre* and the *quadrille,* and they were very much alike. In spite of such variations as the *Manoeuvre des Bandeaux* (in which a maypole was used), the *Manoeuvre des Hussards,* and the *Quadrilles sous Louis XIV,* the movements were always based on the steps of some formal dance. Any number of riders from six to twenty took part, but although they may have been a pretty spectacle, a glorified form of Sir Roger de Coverly on horseback is hardly suitable for a circus.

Finally there is the courier act. It is still to be seen and well deserves its place on the programme. Throughout a long history the same routine has been known by many different names: The Courier of St. Petersburg, *Le Postillon de Longjumeau,* Chico's Post, *La Poste,* and now Rolf Knie presents it as Ben Hur, but the act is the same. The rider stands upright astride two horses and, forcing his mounts apart, allows other horses to pass under his legs, snatching up their long reins as they go, until he drives six, seven, eight or nine tandem-fashion while he straddles three more.

Andrew Ducrow invented this act in 1827. The scene is supposed to portray the journey of a courier on his way to Russia, the horses which pass beneath him representing the countries over which he

---

* I have heard it said that the word balloon originally referred to a short cylinder through which the rider jumped. A paper-covered hoop is still called a *ballon* in France, and the cylinder is called a *tonneau.* It seems likely that just as there are broad banners and narrow garters, there were also the broad *tonneaux* and the narrow *ballons* which eventually became hoops.

must travel. Though one can forget this symbolism when watching the act today, it is as well to count the horses. Ducrow used nine in this act, but a few years later the French rider, Paul Cuzent, was working with twenty-four. The name by which the act is generally known—The Courier of St. Petersburg—serves as a memorial to Cuzent, for he died as the result of a hard and bitterly cold ride from Pavlovsk to St. Petersburg in 1856. He came of a famous circus family, all of whom were excellent horsemen. He was also a composer, but even his music shows equestrian influence. His best-known work is called "The Infernal Gallop of the Last Judgement."

If Paul Cuzent is a great name, Andrew Ducrow is a glorious one. In his day he was the subject of more prints and engravings than nearly any other stage or ring performer. Many of these portraits show him in some of the equestrian roles he created: The Vicissitudes of a Tar, The God of Fame, The Yorkshire Foxhunter, The Roman Gladiator, Mercury, or Paul Pry.

Although he was a brilliant rider, the emphasis in most of his acts was on characterization, and so the only one of his many roles which has come down to us today is the one that demanded the least acting ability but provided the best example of horsemanship —The Courier of St. Petersburg.

This flamboyant character, who enjoyed such a success in France that he was crowned with laurels, and into whose bedroom women broke to strew it with flowers, was born and bred in the circus. His training included most branches of the profession, and he appeared as a rope-dancer and equilibrist before he turned to riding. He became the proprietor of Astley's Amphitheatre and married Louisa Woolford, the idol of Dickens and Thackeray. When he died he was buried in Kensal Green Cemetery, and he is still considered a sufficient celebrity for his name to appear on the list of famous people who lie there. He left behind him a phrase which, although changed in wording from the original, has maintained its meaning: "Cut the cackle and get to the horses."

IV

THE STRONG MAN
Together with Acts Which Rely on
STRENGTH *and* BALANCE

After the whirlwind speed of the voltige number, and the ecstatic shouts of the riding troupe, one needs an act which is quiet and in comparison a little slow. The routine must not be limp or loose because, at this early stage of the programme, a feeling of tension must be maintained. One wants to see some form of effort, but it must always be under control. The strong man can best provide this.

The wreath of laurels round his head, the cloak of imperial purple and, of course, those gladiatorial boots, make him half imposing, half ridiculous. But somehow the Roman costume in which he makes his entrance suits him. It is a *fin-de-siècle* appearance which is in keeping with his "phenomenal feats of strength." Strong men were more popular in Victorian times than they are today; and the props they use, the anvils which are laid across their diaphragms, the horseshoes they twist in their hands and the iron bars they bend across their biceps all seem to belong to a less mechanized age than ours. So when occasionally one still comes across them, or their still more amazing female counterparts, it is difficult to be critical; one is inclined to view their act with nostalgic tolerance—so long as it is kept short.

Strong men left the fairgrounds for the ring early in circus history

—Andrew Ducrow's father was billed as the Flemish Hercules—but it was not until the end of the nineteenth century that they held an important place in the programme, and even then they never became completely absorbed. They have always been an independent lot. Today the street performer most commonly seen in Paris is the strong man, working his act in front of a length of tattered carpet on which are displayed the barbells, weights, chains, hammers and cannonballs of his profession; his counterpart in London is his cousin the escapologist.

A hundred years ago these performers used to specialize in holding a cannon on their shoulders while it was fired. Henry Thétard tells us how Toch supported a cannon weighing 365 kilos in this way, and that through an oversight a double charge amounting to 400 grammes was fired. There were also cannonball kings, who actually caught the projectile in midair. Holtum was probably the most famous, but the act was invented by Alexandrini. In *La Merveilleuse Histoire du cirque* (Paris: Prisma, 1947), Henry Thétard tells us how this unfortunate man died. One may imagine him taking part in a street parade, sitting astride his cannon, nonchalantly smoking a cigar and waving acknowledgment to the crowd. The cigar slips from his fingers and falls down the barrel which is charged with explosive, and he is blown sky-high. Thétard says this happened when Hengler's company was parading through the streets of Manchester in about 1875; but this is one of the few occasions when that admirable historian is wrong. Alexandrini was blown up in Borrisoleigh, Co. Tipperary, on Friday, 3 July 1885, while with Powell and Clarke's Circus. He died at Thurles three days later, and there lies buried.

Gradually this type of trick died out and its place was taken by weight-lifting. In Sandow's day those who joined the circus lifted elephants. I saw this accomplished at a small tenting circus in the 1920s. An elephant, with a sling fastened round its body, was led beneath a bridge on which, between two handrails, stood a strong man in a body harness. On lowering his torso the harness could be hooked to the sling. Then by thrusting downward on the handrail and straightening his legs, he lifted the elephant clear of the ground. Fifty years later I was delighted to find Khalil Oghaby lifting an elephant at Gerry Cottle's Circus.

Of all the acts of strength I have seen, Katie Sandwina's performance was the most remarkable. She was billed as "Catherine the Great," and when I saw her in Carmo's Circus in Dublin, this magnificent flaxen Juno made her entrance in a Roman chariot. Motorcars were driven across her prostrate body; merry-go-rounds holding four men were supported on her diaphragm; blocks of granite, set on her torso, were shattered by road gangs wielding sledgehammers as she lay across a bed of nails; and she caught a cannonball on the back of her neck. In most lifts the weight can be increased gradually, but in catching a cannonball in this way the same size, weight and shape must be used from the beginning. Only the height from which it falls can be increased.

Today, however, most circus audiences want a different type of *tour de force;* and with good reason. After all, there is always a possibility that the weights are not quite as heavy as they seem. One can never be quite sure that the man picked from the audience isn't an accomplice—unless it happens to be oneself. No element of doubt must enter the circus, and so, with the rise of the acrobat, a new and better type of act was evolved which could not be faked. In place of barbells, cannonballs and chains, another man was used. Feats of strength and muscular control are now mostly performed by the hand-to-hand balancers. Their wholly human achievements seem better suited to the circus, and in form such acts seem nearer to the Greeks than to the Romans.

George Stanglemeir, who founded the Trio Rasso, was one of the first to see the advantage of this kind of act. But these early

Hand-to-hand balancing, initial position. (Drawing by John Skeaping.)

performers were a little heavy. Although their "props" had disappeared, the physical bulk of the strong men had not yet given way to more classical proportions. Gradually a more athletic type appeared; and today, when tights and léotards* have been replaced by no more than a pair of trunks for men and a *cache-sexe* and brassière for women, the muscular control shown by such acts can be appreciated to the full. Two movements in the hand-to-hand balancer's routine give me particular pleasure. In one the bearer first lies face upward in the ring and supports his partner hand-to-hand so that he stands vertically but upside down above him. Then, while keeping his partner in the same position, he slowly twists his body so that he lies face downward. The second feat follows this, for having twisted his body back so that he lies face upward again, it is the top-mounter's turn to show what he can do. Slowly lowering his legs, he brings them between the bearer's arms. His body leans back until he lies horizontally in the air above his partner. In the final movement which follows this slow and careful change of position, the legs are shot out with a quick jerk, bringing the trick to completion with the crisp finality of a whip-crack.

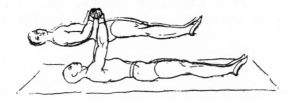

Hand-to-hand balancing, final position. (Drawing by John Skeaping.)

In all hand-to-hand balancing one should first be struck by the beauty of both the attitudes themselves and the movements by which they are achieved. But one should also be conscious of the immense effort and rigorous control which these poses and movements demand. It is for this reason that the torso and legs are best left uncovered. If the general effect is one of easy grace, then it is the detail—the play of muscle—which should reveal the strength and skill which is required. I once read of an act in which the performers appeared in evening dress. Suddenly the tailcoat of the bearer split, and the audience was surprised to see the muscles of

---

* Léotard is the name given to the tight-fitting singlet often worn by acrobats in the last century. For an account of its origin, see p. 151.

his back standing out like knotted cord. Presumably on normal occasions this act went for nothing.

Sometimes hand-to-hand balancing is combined with contortionism and the performers work on a low pedestal. Occasionally artistes cover their bodies with diamanté. In this way the Colbergs and the Spurgats, who both billed themselves as "The Crystal Wonders," increased the spectacular appeal of their acts, but it does not help one to appreciate technique, and it seems more suited to the revue or music hall stage. The same applies to those artistes who cover themselves with glycerine and gold-dust and bill themselves as "Golden Statuary." These performers do no more than take up what they consider to be classical poses, such as "The Slave" or "The Cymbal Player," on and around a black drum. The drum slowly revolves, but apart from this there is no movement; and the only effort needed is to keep still. I find it difficult to think of a more boring act for the circus ring.

Hand-to-hand balancing. (Drawing by John Skeaping.)

In the middle of this century there was a revival of the finger balance. Unus, Tay-Ru, Jolly, Spike Adams and others appeared to balance upside down on one index finger. Cyril Mills assured me that so long as the first joint is covered with some form of splint, there is no need for any further artificial aid, but usually some form of grip is also included. Even so, the muscles of Jolly's hand and wrist were proof of the extraordinary strength that this act requires. Occasionally a pointed iron splint, which is strapped to the wrist and which runs down past the palm to the tip of the finger, is used. But whatever device is employed, the performer should first show it to the audience; the smaller it is the greater the feat becomes. If he shows one nothing, one suspects that his whole arm may be artificially stiffened, for it is impossible to stand on one finger without some outside assistance.

Closely allied to hand-to-hand balancing is head-to-head balancing. Here less variety is possible, and so the performers often make use of "props" to maintain interest. They may play musical instruments or juggle, the bearer working the right way up and the top-mounter upside down. Although such an act can rarely be compared with that of the hand-to-hand balancer, the Uessems, by accentuating the need of a meticulous sense of balance, presented an act which has never been surpassed. The bearer stood on a rolling globe. He balanced a partner head-to-head, so that his feet were in the air. On this middleman's feet stood a third man. They thus built up a column—three men high, center man reversed—on an extremely insecure platform.

A globe rolled by one person is one of the oldest acts in the business, and it is still frequently seen in the smaller circuses. The routine is made slightly more complicated by setting obstacles in the ring between which the sphere must pass. I never thought it possible to produce a first-class act with rolling globes until I saw Vera, Dora and Gerda Rogge at Tom Arnold's Circus at Harringay in 1950. The three girls remained on top of their globes while juggling, dancing on their points, standing on each other's shoulders and performing many other tricks. But the really original touch came when all three rolled their globes up a steep, narrow and rickety incline, maneuvered two right-angled corners before reaching the top which was twelve feet from the ground, and then rolled their globes down again. Their father, who belonged to the fourth generation of circus performers, started training them when they were five years old. When I first saw them they were eighteen, seventeen and fifteen, and their work was beautifully confident and mature. After a while the act split up—although many have copied it. Gerda is now Miss Atlas, the Strong Woman. Vera died after a fire in her caravan in Czechoslovakia. Dora married Frank Foster and is now billed as Rogana, who after a short routine on the globe works the familiar dagger and sword balance with great style.

More difficult than plain globe-rolling is the roller balancing act. In this the performer stands on a short board lying across a cylinder which moves backwards and forwards along the narrow top of a high pedestal. He is usually accompanied by a partner for a balancing routine, or else juggling is introduced; both help to build up the act. But roller-balancing has the disadvantage of looking at its best from the front. It cannot be fully appreciated in the round. Yet the young Spaniard Abilio performs an astounding routine. He balances on seven cylinders. Working from the pedestal up, these are arranged as follows; two vertical, one horizontal, two more vertical, one more horizontal (lying at right angles to the first horizontal) and one more vertical which supports the board on which Abilio stands.

A variation of the rolling globe was *La Balo Misteriosa* (*sic*) which was seen at Tom Arnold's Circus in 1949. Here a ball of about two feet six inches in diameter appeared to roll up a spiral by itself. When it reached the top it broke open and out stepped a young woman. Although this was billed as "The First in the World," a similar act had been presented as long ago as 1880 by Leon La Roche, who rolled the globe both up and down before breaking it open to take his bow.* He appeared at Olympia when Barnum and Bailey's Circus visited London. The strange story of the man who invented this act is told by A.H. Kober in *Star Turns*, where he is called "Ludwig R.," since he was actually a one-time circus rider called Ludwig Rauch. According to Kober he was a man who seemed plagued by occult forces. Every five or ten years he fell into a kind of trance, and each time on regaining consciousness he felt some strange power urging him to make a complete change in his life. In 1908 he is reported to have said, "I am only afraid of 1918 and 1923." He lost all his money in 1918, and Sarrasani, the German circus director, had great difficulty in persuading him to roll his globe again. Then, in 1923, he committed suicide while crossing the equator.

What his performance was like I do not know, but the act presented at Harringay would have been better had it been simpler and faster. The production, in which the ball was first brought in by Father Christmas on a sleigh, and then wound its way up a spiral disguised as a Christmas tree, seemed very theatrical and detracted from the extraordinary effort that this act must require. Leon La Roche and his successors were all, of course, contortionists, and that brings us to another type of act based on muscular control.

The training of circus children includes "bending," and in the small fairground circuses of France one often sees the young

---

* In his book *Attractions sensationnelles*, Adrian suggests that Lepère may have been the first to develop this act and that La Roche did not appear until later.

daughter of the proprietor performing these excercises in the ring. She does the stride splits* on a tabletop, then leaning well back she touches the crown of her head with her toes. Or with her head held on the carpet in a fixed position she may describe circles with a curious crablike walk, her body changing from being stomach uppermost, when her feet are behind her head, to being back uppermost as her feet come to the front. Such tricks are an elementary form of contortionism.

The contortionist should not be looked on as a freak. Midgets, dwarfs, giants and fat ladies are not in the same category, for their characteristics arise from glandular deficiency. Midgets, who are perfectly proportioned but less than four feet six inches when fully grown, and giants, who must be more than six feet six inches tall, usually owe their abnormality to an underactive or overactive pituitary gland. Dwarfs, whose arms and legs are out of proportion to their heads and bodies, are generally found to possess an under-functioning thyroid gland. These people have no control over their strange appearance. The talent of the contortionist, however, is very much under his control; in fact it is usually the result of long and arduous training. Posture-masters, as they used to be called, had appeared on the fairgrounds long before Astley invented the circus, and they soon invaded the ring. Then in 1813 a man was born in London who gave his name to this type of act, and the pleasant title of posture-master was replaced by the clumsy name of Klischnigg, a word which is still used in the profession. Later H. B. Marinelli added his name to the contortionist's vocabulary by inventing the posture known as the Marinelli Bend. This performer's impersonation of a snake was so successful that when he was rehearsing at a circus in Frankfurt, the horses and elephants stampeded in terror and did a lot of damage. When he retired he became an artiste's agent of international repute, with offices in most of the great capitals of the world.

In *Acrobats and Mountebanks*, by H. Leroux and J. Garnier, there is a story which reads like a press agent's handout. It describes how a certain contortionist was so fond of gambling that, in order to raise money for a bet, he sold his own skeleton for a thousand guineas; and forever after traveled with his coffin, addressed to the surgeon who had bought him, together with full instructions for his embalming.

---

* There are two ways of doing the splits: the legs can either be stretched out in front of and behind the body, which is called the stride splits and is the easier, or the legs can be worked out to either side of the body in the center splits.

The Marinelli Bend, as performed by Ames Adonis. (Drawing by John Skeaping.)

Walter Wentworth was another contortionist who achieved some success at the end of the last century. He specialized in what he called Packanatomicalisation. He is reputed to have got into a box measuring twenty-three inches by nineteen inches by sixteen inches, and then to have had six dozen bottles, each about the size of a baby soda, stowed all round him. More recently, Albert Powell combined some amazing dislocations with work on a fixed trapeze, which to my mind is certainly better than wriggling around as a snake, or even crating oneself with empty bottles. Contortionists are either front benders (more often called posturers) or back benders. Both types have certain movements in common, such as shoulder dislocation. In this the wrists, bound together behind the body, are brought over the head to the front of the body—a movement which is sometimes extremely painful to beginners. Posturers can bend forward until the body is brought back through the legs. They can also tuck one foot behind their head. Back benders specialize in more serpentine movements. Marinelli was a back bender, and Walter Wentworth a posturer. Chester Kingston, who worked dressed as a Chinese, is the only person I have seen who was equally good as a posturer and a back bender. A good contortionist should never give one a feeling of disgust; he should amaze one with the suppleness attained by the human body. Most people today seem to find it easier to accept this point of view when one uses the Chinese contortionist as an illustration. It was the same a hundred years ago when posture-masters were often called Chinese nondescripts. Few people experience any sense of revulsion when watching a Chinese no matter what strange position he may adopt. Yet I doubt if anyone can prove that an Oriental has any more physical aptitude than a European for this work. The Chinese make excellent contortionists, but to show why they should excel is just about as difficult as to explain why at one time the greatest trapeze artistes were so often French, or the best tent-masters have always been Czechs. The reason the public is more willing to appreciate the Chinese may be partly due to the fact that they so often combine their contortions with other tricks. Perhaps the plate-spinning, which frequently accompanies a difficult dis-articulation, is the sugar which makes the pill more palatable.

Contortionists, no matter what country they come from, must start young and practice constantly. Unless they have a tendency to put on weight, which with so much rehearsing is very unlikely, there is no reason why they should diet; though a posturer should not eat for four or five hours before his work. One thing contortionists never do is anoint themselves with "Snake Oil," "Angle-Worm Oil" or "Lizard Oil," which used to be sold on circuses as the contortionist's secret.

The disadvantage of the straight contortionist act is that one cannot immediately appreciate the skill which is required. In balancing this is obvious. The necessity of coordinating muscular control with the inherent sense of equilibrium is apparent to all. In hand-to-hand balancing it is the bearer, or under-stander, who does most of the work, but when a top-mounter is supported by an inanimate object such as a globe, he must take the active part. It is the same with stilt-walking, an accomplishment which can be learned at a very early age. There are records of a girl who apparently enjoyed her training at the age of three and a half. Her mother was a stilt-walker who accomplished a trick which I have never seen done by any other performer. She took off one stilt and, flinging it across her shoulder, went through the arms drill of a soldier. Nowadays stilts are usually associated with clowning, but before the circus was born they were regarded more seriously. An early professional stilt-walker was engaged to follow the court of Charles V of France, and a popular sport in the Midi was stilt-racing.

In the modern circus it is occasionally used in other acts besides clowning. Blondin crossed Niagara on stilts; these were short iron rods forked at the end to straddle the rope and fixed to the soles of his boots. Shirai, the Soviet performer, worked a perch act on stilts, in which he supported three men on a giant trident strapped to his arm.

The ordinary perch act originated in the Far East. During the last century the circus lured a number of oriental tumblers, jugglers and equilibrists to Europe, and among them were the perchists. One man would support a tall bamboo pole either in a socket in his belt or simply on his shoulder. Up this a second man would swarm and go through various balances on top, usually with one foot held in a loop attached to the pole. Steel gradually replaced bamboo, but the act remains fundamentally the same—a beautiful combination of balance, acrobatics and strength. There have been many excellent perch acts in recent years, such as the Polis, in which the under-stander, like Shirai, supported three partners; the Four Palms, who worked with a fine sense of technique; and the Georgys, whose perch-on-perch act has never been bettered. In this the top-mounter becomes a middleman who supports a second perch up which a third performer climbs. Some time after appearing at Olympia this act split up, but the members were brought together again at Harringay, where the girl who climbed to the top fell, breaking a collarbone and receiving several other injuries.

Perches are not always supported by a performer; sometimes they are fixed at the base. In this case they are usually extremely high and what is lost in artistry is gained in thrills. They sway over at alarming angles, with the performer standing sometimes on his hands, sometimes on his feet at the top. In America they are known as sway-pole acts. Alberty worked this routine on a sixty-foot pole, and the two Ortons appeared at a height of ninety feet at Olympia, their two perches being slung in midair. They worked at an even greater height out in the open. So do the Nocks from Switzerland. In all these acts the bending poles and the curve of the human figure as he checks the outward swing by leaning inwards add grace to thrills.

Captain Bunte, whom I once saw in Budapest, produced another variation by supporting a partner astride a motor-bicycle on top of his perch. The Zavattas and the Rockleys went even further; in their acts the top-mounter looped the loop on a motor-bicycle inside a small circular track. Less sophisticated, but of more interest to the circus historian, was an act I saw some forty years ago, in which the bearer had a cylinder strapped to his back in

Shirai's combined stilt and perch act. (Drawing by John Skeaping.)

which a cyclist looped the loop. I seem to remember this cyclist and his brother, both sons of the bearer, appearing on the same bill in a roller-balancing act. Their name was Bale—the American superstar Elvin Bale's father, uncle and grandfather. I find such acts show little grace, and the introduction of machines, particularly ones as noisy as a motor-bicycle, destroys the feeling of physical prowess.

Ladder-balancing acts are very similar to perch acts, especially when they are supported by a bearer, though the strain never comes on his shoulder, for ladders are always balanced on the soles of his feet as he lies on his back in a cradle, known as a *trinka*. Sometimes a breakaway ladder is used, in which one side and all the rungs collapse, leaving the top-mounter on what is virtually a perch balanced by the bearer on one foot. These numbers are really part of the repertoire of the foot-juggler or antipodist. The art of balancing objects is closely linked to the work of the juggler, and he will be dealt with later in this book. Unsupported ladders, on the other hand, are almost a form of stilt-walking; the performers rock the ladders from side to side to maintain their balance in much the same way as the man on stilts has to mark time when he is not actually walking. The Raspinis, who were brought to England by Mills and appeared with his circus both in London and the provinces, excelled at this work, combining it with head-to-head balancing and juggling.

All balancing depends to a large extent on the eye, and that brings us to another type of act, which, although again akin to juggling, might well be included in this chapter. It consists of rope-spinning, whip-cracking and knife-throwing; it occasionally includes sharpshooting, and is often billed, with a rather charming naiveté, as Western Pastimes. The chief drawback to this kind of act is that while the rope-spinning, whip-cracking and so on are admirably suited to the ring, the *pièces de résistance* more often than not consist of knife-throwing and sharpshooting, which are much better seen on the stage. They look awkward in the ring because they are worked in one direction. Someone must always be seated behind the board with its human target. And no amount of elaboration can overcome this—not even a thrilling and complicated act which I first saw performed by Collins and Elizabeth, in which a wire-walker hurled knives at his partner as she spun round on a circular target. A similar act is being performed today by the Two Tornados. If sharpshooting looks dangerous to the audience one suspects that it is a fraud. Many tricks are indeed faked. The clay

73

pigeons brought down by Buffalo Bill were not hit by bullets but by buckshot.

One of the finest sharpshooters was a woman who, seventy-five years ago, appeared as Mademoiselle Diana in a William Tell act. She shot an apple off her own head by firing her rifle at the trigger of another, set in a stand some yards away and pointing straight in her direction. This could not be worked in a circus. The William Tell act has a place in the ring, but it is performed by clowns.

Before leaving those who work with weapons, one should perhaps mention the sword-swallower. Although nowadays he is generally relegated to the sideshow, you may still find him in the ring of the small fairground circuses, following in the footsteps of the famous Chevalier Cliquot. This man could swallow the twenty-two inch blade of a cavalry sword, or a bunch of fourteen bayonet swords fourteen inches long. The sensation of the act came when the Chevalier bent his torso in all directions while the swords remained in their unnatural scabbard. On one occasion his contortions bent the sword so much that he wounded himself on withdrawing it. Sometimes instead of lowering the blade down his oesophagus he allowed it to be shot down by the recoil of a rifle.

Sword-swallowers are not to be found in the big circuses of today, and their passing need not be mourned. In such acts there is little beauty, little dexterity, and whatever muscular control may really be required remains invisible. I believe that so long as the swords are well oiled they slip down easily enough after a little practice. Even the human target is a better circus act than this. And once they were not merely outlined with bullets or knives. As we have already seen, cannonballs were shot straight at them and caught in their hands. But these were strong men, which brings us full circle and ready for the next act.

V

PERFORMING ANIMALS
Mostly of the Domestic Variety

After the human performers have run into the ring several times and acknowledged their call, the men with a bow, the girls with a kiss blown left and right—a gesture which has been described as "like they were drawing a hair out of their mouth"—the ring-boys bring on the props for an animal act.

Before the dogs or geese appear someone in the audience is bound to look at the programme and say, "I do hope they're not cruelly treated." So let me deal with the question of cruelty first.

Only the craziest lunatic would say that no trainer has ever been cruel to his animals, or that somewhere in the world someone may not be cruel today. Perhaps in some remote valley of the Welsh mountains a shepherd is beating hell out of his sheepdog. Who can say?

Even in what we complacently call civilized society there are criminally negligent people in every walk of life, among nurses and schoolmasters and clergymen no less than among animal trainers. There are worse. Hardly a week passes without a newspaper carrying a story of some sadist cruelly treating his own child. But although few people would stigmatize all parents as perverts, some persist in believing that all animal trainers in the circus are cruel.

Animal trainers outside the business, of course, don't count. Shepherds, sportsmen, horsebreakers are never suspect. Yet while it is extremely improbable that this type of owner will be visited by an RSPCA inspector unless evidence of cruelty or suspected cruelty is given, the circus trainer is always open to inspection. And he welcomes an unbiased observer. It is nonsense to say that training and rehearsals always go on behind locked doors. I have dropped into training quarters unannounced and watched rehearsals unobserved. I have never seen any cruelty. London County Council inspectors were always given passes to Olympia for the whole season, so that they could come and go as they liked. A president of the RSPCA spent several months at the winter quarters of a circus, watching the lions being trained. Neither his report nor that which followed the visits of any LCC inspector has ever been made public, but the findings—if anything so completely unfounded can be called by that name—of the "antis" have been published.

The "antis" are a group of people, too hysterical to be rational and too bigoted to learn, who state categorically that no animal can be trained to work under professional conditions by kindness. Their comments would hardly be worth a mention were it not for the fact that it was through them that I gained personal experience in animal training, which may interest some of those who read this book.

No sooner does a journalist write the truth about circus animals than in come letters and brochures informing him that he is completely misguided because circus animals *must* be cruelly treated. When I first received these I was not prepared to believe or disbelieve them, any more than I was prepared to believe or disbelieve the protestations I knew I should receive from the trainers if I asked them what truth these allegations held. It seemed silly to expect that animals could be turned into such consummate actors that they would appear to the public twice, or three times a day, as if they thoroughly enjoyed doing their tricks while all the time their hearts were breaking; but I decided to settle the question once and for all by carrying out an impartial test myself.

How I trained a troupe of animals to perform in a circus ring, on the music hall stage, in a fairground booth and in cabaret, as well as to be heard the radio and to appear on film, all without cruelty, will be described presently. But first I should like to point out that when I mentioned this in a Sunday newspaper, I immediately got a letter from one of the "antis" informing me that unless I denied I had done any such thing, legal proceedings would be started against me. Although I asked my solicitors to tell the writer to go ahead, I heard no more. Did this person threaten me with such a rash and foolhardy action without first finding out the facts? It is possible, for the literature of the "antis" shows little forethought or careful study of the subject. Or did the writer back out because he realized that I knew the fallacy of his belief?

In order to see if animals could be trained to professional standards entirely by kindness, I chose the most recalcitrant kind I could think of which could be kept in a house without much extra expense or nuisance. They were ordinary domestic cats. As far as I could find, less than a dozen people had succeeded in persuading these aloof, enigmatic tigers-on-the-hearth to work in public. They are not imbued with the herd instinct. They acknowledge no master, and by human standards they are essentially lazy. But I must admit that cats are the animals I like most.

Since my method of training was not in the least original, but merely typical of the way all animals are trained, this would seem an appropriate place to give a full description of the act I produced, and the method by which it was achieved.

The ring or stage was set with six pedestals each carrying the name of the cat, two belfries, a tight-rope, five hoops, a circle numbered from 0-9, twenty-four champagne bottles, a small box slung twelve feet in the air, a ladder and a seesaw. Into the ring came Aubrey, a ginger, Clovis, a tabby, Fitzpatrick, black with touches of white, Nicolas, white with touches of black, Caroline, all white, and Marianna, a tortoiseshell. Sexes and colors were all as mixed as I could manage. Each jumped onto its own pedestal and bowed an introduction to the audience. Clovis, purring all the time, mounted the ladder and walked the length of the tight-rope, went back to the middle, turned round, made his way to the far end and sat up and bowed. Aubrey jumped from one pedestal to another through first one hoop, then a second, a third and a fourth, each decreasing in diameter until he was making a standing leap of over nine feet through hoops ranging from two feet six inches to one foot three inches in diameter. Clovis next walked along the tops of the twenty-four champagne bottles, sat up and bowed. After that, Nicolas made a seven-foot jump through a blazing hoop. Aubrey and Clovis each rang a bell by standing on their hind legs in the belfry and pulling at the ropes. These two cats then jumped onto the seesaw, while Fitzpatrick, walking up and down the center, brought each into the air in turn. Aubrey and Clovis returned to their pedestals and Fitzpatrick walked round the figured board, stopping at any number called out by the audience, and adding or subtracting any two numbers whose answer came to less than nine. Caroline then came off her pedestal, swarmed up the rope and, on reaching the box, released the flags of all nations in a grand finale. A "chariot" pulled by a poodle then made its appearance and each in turn jumped in, Caroline on the boot, Fitzpatrick on the box and the rest inside and so made their exit.

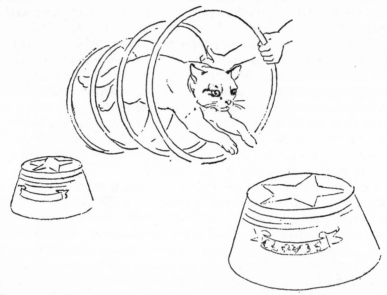

Aubrey, the author's ginger cat, jumping through hoops. (Drawing by John Skeaping.)

You will notice that Marianna did nothing but sit on her pedestal. She was pretty but dumb and I only used her for dressing the act. You will often find that in any act one or more animals appear in the ring merely to swell the numbers. Yet the one thing Marianna did—sitting still without getting off her pedestal—was the most difficult thing to teach any of the cats.

This is how it all was done.

I started with Aubrey and Clovis. They came from a feline nursing home, where they had been born a few months before. I place great importance on this for they were my best performers, and I am sure that these kittens, which had been regularly fed and kept under scrupulously clean conditions, had never been frightened—even accidentally.

Each cat received its food on its own pedestal and nowhere else. If one got down without being given its cue, it was gently but firmly replaced and told that that was not what was wanted. When they stayed on their tubs for a few minutes they were rewarded with a piece of meat. These few minutes gradually grew until, after some months, they would stay on their pedestals for twenty minutes or more.

They were rehearsed for less than an hour every day. For the rest of the time they had the run of a London house and garden. I watched them climb about the branches of a fig tree and I soon noticed the difference in their characters. Clovis would walk along the narrowest bough, balancing delicately and stopping to sniff at a leaf. Aubrey would leap from branch to branch, crouch, hugging the bark, and nearly fall out of the tree in a sudden wild attempt to catch his tail. So Clovis was taught to walk first along a narrow board and then a tight-rope. When he reached the end he got a little bit of raw minced beef. In the same way Aubrey was persuaded to jump through a hoop from one pedestal to another. These tubs were placed quite close together at first, but as soon as he learned what was required the distance was gradually increased.

Neither cat was ever *forced* to do anything. When Aubrey jumped, he immediately got his reward. When he got off his pedestal and walked over to the other, he was not rewarded; but since the reward came from the ration of meat he was allowed every day, and which he got whether he did his tricks or not, there was never any question of starving him to make him work. He soon learned that the *quickest* way to get his meat was to do his trick, but he never found it was the *only* way.

Training became absorbingly interesting, and I found out many things about animals which, had I not started to train them, I would never have suspected. I searched for records of other performing cats, and I found that in 1832 Signor Capelli's cats "beat a drum, turned a spit, ground knives, struck an anvil and rang bells." I realized that four of these tricks were probably based on two movements, *striking* an anvil or drum, and *turning* a grindstone or spit, but at that time I could not see how they could be taught. However, I did think of a way in which cats could be persuaded to ring bells. Only that morning Clovis had tugged at the breakfast tablecloth to get at some fish. So I made them little belfries, with ropes attached to the springs of old-fashioned house bells. Between the strands of the ropes, just out of reach of a cat standing on its hind legs, I tucked a piece of meat. They clawed the

Clovis ringing his bell. (Drawing by John Skeaping.)

rope to reach the meat and found that they could pull it down to their mouths. The sound of the bell didn't worry them.

Then the second phase of training started. By decreasing the size of the meat in the rope while increasing the amount given from my hand, I eventually got the cats to forget that the rope had once held meat, and they pulled the ropes while looking towards me. It was this simple trick which led Tom Driberg, then "William Hickey" of the *Daily Express*, to describe Aubrey and Clovis as "Cat Campanologists."

They were rehearsed every day at lunch time and fed immediately afterwards. Sometimes I only gave them a little food in the middle of the day and the bulk in the evening. So it went on.

One night after a circus party I was driven back home by Coco, the clown. He came in for a nightcap, saw the "props" and asked what they were for. When I told him, he wanted to know what the cats did, so then and there I put them through their paces. They worked perfectly at 2:30 a.m. At the end of the performance Coco said, "Listen—you must get another cat and teach it to count." It took me six weeks, working for about twenty minutes a day, to teach Fitzpatrick to add and subtract—or rather to appear to do so, for all he had really been trained to do was to stop and sit up on his haunches whenever I gave him a special cue.

Nico joined the troupe, and being a good jumper with no sign of fear, he became a fire-leaper. When he got used to jumping through a hoop bound with asbestos, I put a drop of methylated spirits on either side and lit it. This didn't worry him, so very gradually the area of flame was increased until he jumped through a complete circle of flames.

Then I was given one of Norman Hartnell's white cats which I called Caroline. I wanted to teach her to climb a rope, but this trick caused me more trouble than almost any other. Caroline loved climbing trees, but when she was given a rope she would make a start, yet directly her hind legs left the ground she would drop off. I was afraid that I would have to give up this trick. The only thing that made me go on was the thought that since it was natural for a cat to climb, failure would disprove a conviction which was growing in my mind. I was beginning to realize that any trick which developed an animal's natural attributes could be taught with considerably less severity than that experienced by a child in a kindergarten.

Then, luckily, Bob Beasy, who was also a circus clown and another good friend of mine, came to the rescue. He had toured the world with his own famous troupe of performing cats and he told me what was wrong. Hemp or sisal rope is so hard that a cat finds it uncomfortable when the full weight of its body is taken by its claws. The rope had to be cotton. I bought a cotton rope, but with little better results; the claws seemed to get entangled in the fine yarn. It was only when Bob generously gave me the rope which he had used that Caroline would climb without a moment's hesitation. That rope was not laid up in the ordinary three strands; it was plaited in the form of a square sennet.

Every day the routine was meticulously followed through to the accompaniment of gramophone records. In the cats' minds these tunes became so identified with their tricks that on one occasion when Bertram Mills gave a talk on the radio and they played him in to "The Entry of the Gladiators," all the cats rushed to their "props" and started their act by themselves. I was out at the time but came back in the middle of the broadcast, and when Mills was played out to the same music and once again the cats rushed to their pedestals, I had not the heart to prevent them doing their tricks.

Whenever I could I took them to other houses, to children's parties and to church halls. Each time they went to a fresh place I let them roam about for two or three hours, so that they could thoroughly satisfy their curiosity before they were asked to perform. Before they appeared in cabaret at the Café Anglais, I let them have the run of the restaurant for three afternoons before rehearsing them on the dance floor, so they would become accustomed to the atmosphere and not be lured off their pedestals by the smell of *sole bonne femme* or *poulet en casserole*.

On 6 March 1937 they went on the air, purring, miaowing and ringing their bells. How could they be taught to purr to order? They weren't; they had always purred while doing their tricks and they miaowed because they always asked for their supper. But a number of people must have suspected that I alternately stroked them and pulled their tails. A day or two later, in response, I believe, to some listener's request, round came the RSPCA inspector. He took one look at the cats and begged my pardon for bothering me. I invited him to come and see the cats being trained any time he liked.

Private parties, cabaret and radio were not enough. I wanted to see if animals trained on these lines would work anywhere. I accepted a film offer and I also worked them on a fairground. I rehearsed them for television, but the strong lights which were then used seemed to worry them. In a film studio they were able to rest between shots and the film was afterwards cut to give a continuous performance, but at Alexandra Palace this was not possible and I decided not to let them appear on television. Then they had a chance of appearing in music hall. I had no wish to become a professional variety artiste, so I got someone else to present them. After a bad start they soon settled down, though I don't think they were ever quite so quick or sure of themselves as they were with me.

Finally I myself worked them in Ginnett's Circus. Aubrey, Clovis, Fitzpatrick, Nico, Caroline, Marianna and I appeared in the ring nine times a week, and the only amateur was me. Under professional conditions the cats behaved like troupers, except on one occasion at rehearsal when they heard a sea lion bark for the first time and they all fled. But once they were shown where the noise came from they took no more notice of it than of a horse's whinny.

Clovis taking a bow. (Drawing by John Skeaping.)

Then came the war and the act broke up. Aubrey and Clovis, who were always my star performers, spent the rest of their days a few doors away from my house, and when I was in London would visit me on Sunday mornings.

Once, and once only, did I punish one of my cats. One day at

rehearsal twenty-five minutes of cajolery would not persuade
Aubrey to jump through his hoop. I gave him one slap with the
palm of my hand. The result was that he refused to work for four
days and I learned my lesson. That was the only time that any of
my cats refused to work and the only time I hit one.

While checking through the original typescript of these para-
graphs I learned that Aubrey, the last of the troupe, had died. He
was sixteen years old. The friend who looked after him said that she
"could never have another cat. None could compare with Aubrey;
he was almost human." He was certainly a willing and eager pupil
except on that one occasion, and like his brother Clovis, he was a
great performer and a charming and lovable companion.

There is nothing original in any of the tricks or the method I have
described. Trainers had been using a similar method long before
I.P. Pavlov called it "conditioning reflexes." This great Russian
psychologist found that he could make dogs salivate at the sight of
a light and the sound of a bell or metronome. He even discovered
that if a bell was habitually rung half an hour before a dog was fed,
eventually saliva would rush to its mouth exactly half an hour after
it heard the bell, whether it was fed or not.

Pavlov was born over one hundred and twenty-five years ago. He
began his investigations into the salivary gland in the 1890s. At this
time the circus in Russia was in its heyday and enjoyed the
patronage of society and the intelligentsia. It may well be that the
trained animals which appeared at Ciniselli's circus in St. Petersburg gave Pavlov the idea of investigating their psychological
behavior. In fact, I suspect that there is a strong connection
between Pavlov and Vladimir and Anatol Durov, whose families
have now been appearing in the ring for three generations.
Vladimir founded an animal training school, which after the
Revolution became a state-sponsored scientific laboratory. As a
young man he had attended Professor I.M. Sechenov's lectures on
"Higher Nervous Activity" at Moscow University. Perhaps he met
Pavlov there. Pavlov's findings were seized upon by the Behaviorists, who, I am told, as psychologists now run the followers of
Freud a good second in American popularity. It is interesting to
find that the scientists have not spurned the animal trainer's system
of patience and reward, and it is amusing to think that a school of
psychology may owe some of its success to a dog that was given a
lump of sugar when it jumped through a hoop in a circus.

In the circus different types of animals naturally require slightly
different handling, but the principle is the same. Cats will usually

smell their food before they eat, pigs are less fastidious, dogs have become so domesticated that they sometimes copy human beings without any persuasion at all, and I have often seen ducks in a farmyard run to their feeding pen directly they hear the clatter of a tin pail. Clermont, a clown who trained pigs, birds, cats and dogs, once said, "Imagine sometimes it is you who are the performer and the animals who are the trainer. . . . If such a thing happened to me I like to think that my act would go on exactly as it does now."

Once or twice I have been asked why I and other trainers have never accepted the five hundred pounds offered by the "antis" to anyone who can train animals to work to a timetable by kindness. The answer is that in a number of lawsuits brought by the "antis," damages and costs have been granted to circus producers and trainers, but the "antis" have not yet paid up. Few can afford to spend valuable time and then have to wait for their money.

Since Coco, the performing stag, brought all Paris to the Cirque Franconi in the days of the First Empire, there is hardly a domestic animal that has not appeared in the circus. Horses, bulls, pigs, donkeys, mules, hares, goats and geese have all made their bow. Peacocks, beetles, fleas and—though hardly domestic—even ant-eaters have all been trained, if not for exhibition, then in the course of studying animal psychology. For this purpose even a fish has been trained to enter a cylinder at a signal from an electric light.

Highland cattle and bulls are occasionally presented in the ring, which may demonstrate remarkable training, but hardly makes a satisfying spectacle. I can think of no characteristic in these animals which could be developed through training to make an interesting act. I would always prefer to see performing goats, for they at least have an inherent sense of balance. I remember some years ago in Paris stopping to watch a street performance near the Champs Elysées. A man was beating a drum and a very small child was persuading a goat to climb a high pedestal. It needed little inducement, and there, high above our heads, on a platform no bigger than a coffee saucer, stood the goat—vaguely reminding one of Uncle Sam. I threw a few francs into the hat and walked on, glancing up at the name of the street as I passed. It was the rue du Cirque.

In my opinion monkeys, which will be dealt with later in the book, are the only animals which may be dressed up. They are sufficiently like human beings for clothes to look natural. An act in which dogs appear in trousers and skirts always appears to me to be a little vulgar, and it usually lacks the crispness of an act where the dogs appear simply as dogs. In the finest animal acts the performers show off their mental attributes no less than their physical characteristics. The stubbornness of the mule is best seen in its antics to prevent a rider from mounting it.

Small animals are rarely shown in a circus because their performances generally lack spectacle. Rabbits have been trained, but their cousin the hare is more frequently seen. Hares are quicker, and the sight of one walking on its hind legs and beating a drum has amused the public since the Middle Ages, although they are too small to be shown in the large circuses of today.

A flock of pigeons, on the other hand, can produce a fine spectacle. The act in which a dozen wheeling birds are brought fluttering down at the crack of a gun to sit on the barrel still has a rather touching charm, though in recent years this trick has been done a little too often, and familiarity has bred boredom.

Although performing cockatoos and parakeets are rarely seen in flight, their brilliant plumage contributed to the spectacle in acts like that of Fanny Nomano. There is a tendency for such turns to be played in one direction, which is reminiscent of the music hall. Sometimes they contain good tricks which demand real training, but too often a cheap effect is gained from the birds whirling round on a mechanical contrivance, like a roundabout, which they have only to grip tightly with their claws. Fanny Nomano would never have been content with anything so simple. She taught one of her birds to hoist the flag of any nation selected by the audience,* and another turned a rollover somersault. One way of training a bird to turn head over heels is to scratch it at the back of the cranium, which causes it to lower its head. When it can see between its legs it is shown a piece of sugar. In an effort to get the sugar the bird will fall over on its back and immediately right itself by jumping up sideways. In fact the bird does not turn a somersault at all, but the movements are made so quickly that it has every appearance of doing so.

Often animals of different species are taught to live and work together. This act is usually known as "The Happy Family" and, I believe, was first introduced by a stocking-weaver from Coventry in the 1830s, who learned about animals from an Indian snake-

---

* This is only one degree removed from the scientist, experimenting in brain research, who has trained a white rat to pull a certain chain to get at its food.

charmer. Birds, rats and mice have been trained to work with their natural enemy the cat. This is achieved by preventing the cat from fulfilling its immediate inclination to kill. Felines do not always kill for food; the hunting instinct remains long after the primary cause has been forgotten. That is why they play with dead mice, and often make no attempt to eat the rats and birds they have caught. But, as with humans, the instinctive desire to kill diminishes with the growth of understanding. If you hold a cat in one hand and a rat in the other, their first reaction is one of hate. But soon their coats will stop standing on end and they will begin to show an interest in each other. Very gradually you can bring them together until their noses are practically touching. Interest replaces hatred and then familiarity makes even interest wane. After a cat has become thoroughly acquainted with rats, mice and birds, they can be placed at intervals along a tight-rope and the cat will step delicately over them, taking no more notice of them than an inquiring sniff.

Rats alone have appeared in several acts trained by Vladimir Durov. In one of these he played the part of the Pied Piper, and lured hundreds of rats to the call of his pipe. They swarmed all over him. On one occasion they found a scratch on his neck and, thinking it was their supper, started to nibble at his flesh. In another act a troupe of rats loaded and manned a model ship. The company was headed by a captain who steered the vessel from the bridge. This commanding officer's name was Captain Serko, and his story, as told by Durov in his book, *My Circus Animals* (London: George Routledge & Sons Ltd., 1937), seems to epitomize all the tragedies of Russian literature.

Serko had been married to a little grey rat who bore him nine children, and he had proved himself to be a tender and solicitous father. Then, because of his "strong imposing figure and deep hoarse voice, which was very impressive in giving brisk important orders," he was made captain of Durov's ship and did not see his wife for two years. One day a fight broke out between two of the rat stevedores over a crate of raisins; the captain went to settle the dispute and found that one of the combatants was his long-lost wife. Duty and love fought in Captain Serko's breast, but love won and he had to be shut in his cabin.

"Then," writes Durov,

> the mechanic, sitting up on his hind legs, pulled the string and pressed the lever. The regulator began to revolve, the machin-

ery to throb. Clouds of steam rose above the boat. The sailors pulled up the anchor. At this moment the doors of the captain's cabin flew open with a loud bang, and the captain rushed towards his dear grey rat.

As luck would have it, the hatchway was open. Serko did not notice this in the clouds of steam, and, running towards his friend, he fell into the engine room.

I heard a low, weak squeak. When I looked down through the open hatch I saw Serko, all broken, lying on the cog-wheels with closed eyes, and his paws were twitching.

I called him. He answered me twice, then ceased to twitch and lay silent.

Tears rose in my eyes while the public clapped and laughed, little suspecting that this brave captain was dead.

Like rabbits, rats are really too small to appear in a modern circus.

The story that pleases me most is how Durov trained Chuska, the Parachute Pig. On the balcony of his villa on Krestovsky Island in St. Petersburg, he arranged a pulley through which a rope led to a well-padded harness. Into the harness he put the pig and hoisted her into the air. When she struggled he gave her a bowl of her favorite food, and soon she realized she was so safe that she actually went to sleep in the sling. In this way she became accustomed to being raised and lowered in the air. Then he built a small platform and on it put an alarm clock. Gradually he coaxed her to jump off the platform to get her food when the alarm sounded. After weeks of training, a small Montgolfier balloon was filled with hot air, and on the suspended platform stood Chuska and the alarm clock. The pig's harness was attached to a parachute which hung by a thin thread from the envelope. Up went the balloon. At so many thousand feet, "d-r-i-n-g" went the alarm clock. "My God! My food," thought the pig, and jumping off the platform came sailing gently down to the ground.

The most recent pig act I have seen is that of Uwe Schwichtenberg, whose animals were caparisoned—and behaved—like liberty horses. This East German trainer also presents donkeys and an exotic group of zebras, camels, buffalos, guanacas, a llama, a yak and an emu.

Dogs, as one might imagine, are comparatively easy to train. Yet it is this animal that the over-sentimental always suspect of being most cruelly treated. A hundred years or more ago they might have found justification for their fears. An old circus rhyme used to run:

> Risley Kids and slanging buffers
> Lord only knows what they suffers.

Of Risley Kids more will be told in the chapter on acrobats, while slanging buffer is the term which used to be given to performing dogs. In an age when children were driven down the mines to drag trucks full of coal, animals did not escape their share of suffering. But the phrase today is as meaningless and archaic as the whipping boy.

The relationship of man and dog is particularly interesting because no other animal has become so domesticated. In *Circus Parade* (London: T. Batsford Ltd., 1936) John S. Clarke devotes an excellent chapter to the relationship of man and beast, and this is what he says of the dog:

> In the conquest of the natural environment man necessarily divorced himself from the rest of his fellow-animals. They remained in a state of nature; he became artificial. He brought one animal along with him—the wolf, which he transformed into a dog. As man lost touch with nature, so did the dog. That is why the man is not merely the dog's master, he is his very god. Of no other domestic animal, not even the horse, can this be said. Man is lonely, and he has made this one animal as lonely as himself. It is dependent upon him, not for food alone, but for *sympathy*. There is an *affection* between man and dog, and the wonder of it is that the dog seeks it always, the man only at times.

That is why dogs are easier to train than other animals, and so can be persuaded to do more complicated tricks. It also explains the fervency of some people to stop dogs from performing them. I have already pointed out that the best tricks are based on a natural movement or attitude, though it is carefully developed to produce an interesting spectacle. It is often so hidden as to be far from obvious, especially to the uninitiated, whose minds are so clouded with sentimentality that they have lost the power to reason.

"Don't tell me," people have said, "that it is natural for a dog to walk on two legs." Yet dogs have been known to walk on their hind legs without being taught at all. I knew a poodle, with no circus connections whatsoever, who preferred to walk this way when he was with human beings, but not when he was alone with other dogs. He had never been taught a single trick, yet, after he misbehaved, he would stand himself on his hind legs in a corner *before his misdemeanor had been discovered.* He was copying the actions of a little girl in the house who was sometimes sent to stand in the corner for being naughty.

It is quite natural for some breeds of dog, such as pointers and setters, to freeze in one position. Develop this characteristic and you will soon have a dog which will appear to do a one-paw balance on your hand. I use the word appear because in this case it is not the dog which does the balancing, but the trainer; the dog merely remains rigid.

A dog walking on its forepaws is not natural in itself, yet the training required for this trick is merely the development of a natural action in which one position is prolonged. When a dog jumps off a stool its forelegs touch the ground while its hind-quarters remain for a second almost vertically above them. By supporting the hind legs for a gradually increasing length of time the dog will soon become accustomed to this position. There is only one secret—you must know what kind of dog to choose.

Training, on humane and scientific lines, can teach us to understand all those other animals whom we forsook so many million years ago. And we have a lot to learn. To imbue them with human feelings and failings is not fair either to them or ourselves.

A.J. Cummings once told me that during World War I two horses from a gun-carriage team were eating their corn side by side. Suddenly one kicked the other so violently that its leg was shattered, and the animal had to be destroyed. Yet at the time it was kicked it did not even look up from its food. One might deduce that in this case the horse felt less pain than any human would expect. But one cannot generalize; some animals may be more sensitive to physical suffering than humans, some may be less.

Fear and pain are unknown quantities which need never be used in training domestic animals. There is another unknown quantity which is somehow connected with the natural dignity of an animal. I heard once that a man taught some cats to play the piano, or at any rate to strike the notes with their paws. The sight of this so amused a friend that he burst into guffaws of laughter; the cats stopped playing and would never go near the piano again.

I have saved till last a story which shows how tampering with an animal's natural dignity may even be dangerous. I very much doubt that it is based on fact, but it will serve as a fable for those who think that an animal can be made to submit to any form of degradation.

M. Edouard Garnier in *Les Nains et les géants* quotes the following report which appeared in a Lille newspaper in July 1882:

> A mountebank, who gave his address as an hotel in the rue St. Pierre, was recently arrested in connection with a most horrible tragedy, entirely caused by his crassly stupid and cruel behaviour. Six months ago he hired a youth who, although eighteen years old, was only 62 cm. high. . . . His idea was to turn this remarkable dwarf into a trainer of miniature tigers, which were in reality to be nothing more than cats with coats dyed in yellow and black stripes. On the 12th of July last, at the fair of Beaupré-sur-Saone, one of the cats sprang at the neck of the little trainer and knocked him off his feet. Within a second all the other "tigers" were upon him, and before anyone could come to his rescue, the dwarf, his eyes torn out and his face ripped away, was dead.

VI

LIBERTY HORSES

"Training secrets?" Bertram Mills once said. "There are none. Patience, understanding and carrots are the eternal triumvirate. There is no other way with a horse, and never was." I don't entirely agree with the last three words, but then Mills was probably thinking of the liberty number as it is performed today, the magnificent display of sixteen well-matched horses wheeling round together in perfect formation. In the old days the act—and sometimes, perhaps, the method—were different.

All through history the performing horse has provided the omen which foretold the birth of the circus. In the illuminated manuscripts of the Middle Ages riderless horses are to be seen dancing on their hind legs and beating tabors. In the golden age of Queen Elizabeth I, Banks and his horse Morocco achieved European renown. This is the "dancing horse" which Shakespeare tells us could do calculations in *Love's Labour's Lost* (I, ii). Before and since then there have been many other horses and trainers whose tricks have so mystified their audiences that both man and animal have been accused of witchcraft.

On the eve of the birth of the circus the number of these acts increased, and one which was popular in London at that time belonged to a man called Zucker. Even eighteenth-century showmen used rather ambiguous billing. From a quick glance at this trainer's handbill one is led to suppose that "all lovers of curious performances" were invited to see "MR. ZUCKER and his learned little horse from Courland." It is only after a more careful scrutiny that one finds above the boldy italicized surname a minute line which reads "The Brother of the Famous."

Most of the tricks which this animal performed can still be seen in the small family circuses whose owners cannot afford a troupe of liberties. Adding and subtracting by pawing the ground, nodding or shaking the head, and pretending to be lame are tricks whose history is much older than the sawdust ring. But the circus increased the popularity of these acts, and this led trainers, both professional and amateur, to attempt more difficult tasks. Simple arithmetic was left far behind, and by the beginning of this century London audiences had seen the horse Alpha write his name on a blackboard with the chalk held between his teeth; while in Paris, Germinal had amazed amateur trainers by writing the name of his master, Dr. Rouhet, in the same fashion.

Two of the three "R's" had been taught. The third came when M. de Kroutikoff's horse Antar showed he could read a word on a blackboard by spelling out the same word with lettered blocks. Perhaps it would be better to say that these horses appeared to have mastered reading, writing and arithmetic, because they really had not the slightest idea what they were doing.

When a circus horse stamps out the number of players in a football team, distinguishes the letters of the alphabet, or shakes or nods its head in answer to a question, it is merely reacting to a sign. If you watch the trainer more closely than the horse you will see that the direction in which he points his whip, or the position of his arm or leg, changes according to the right answer. In other words he is giving the animal its cue. Sometimes the sign is nothing you can see and only those who have extemely good ears can hear it. Once or twice an animal has been trained to react to a sign which the audience would never guess, and which could be given, without a confederate, in the trainer's absence.

Just before World War I, "strange Morocco's dumb arithmetic" was far surpassed by the remarkable achievements of "the equine calculators of Eberfeldt." Their trainer was a rich diamond merchant called Karl Krall. His ambition was to "establish a proof of the inherent intelligence of animals, and to show that horses, above all other animals, should be freed of their base servitude because they had a soul just like human beings." To demonstrate his belief he chose, rather oddly perhaps, to make his horses give the cube root of 7,890,481 and solve equally complicated sums. He got an enormous amount of publicity, for nine times out of ten Muhamed and his stable companions, Zarif, Hanschen and Berto, gave the correct answer. Maurice Maeterlinck tells how he asked Muhamed the cube root of a certain number without thinking, and was surprised to find the horse did not answer: "But Muhamed was right because the number had no cube root." Krall's horses solved the most complicated sums even when he was not present. The only reasonable explanation of a horse being able to answer a problem known only to the audience is that the spectators themselves gave the animal its cue without knowing it. This theory is backed up by the fact that when the sum was chosen by someone who left the audience before the horse could answer, and which was unknown to those who remained, the horse failed. Perhaps a feeling of unconscious tension, a sense of expectancy or an almost imperceptible leaning forward as the horse approached the correct solution gave the animal its cue. There are other ways, less subtle but just as mystifying, of telling a horse when to stop pawing the sawdust of a circus ring. There is no reason, for instance, why a

The American horse Black Eagle (Howes & Cushing) performing before H.M. Queen Victoria and the Royal Family at the Alhambra Palace. (From the author's collection.)

signal should not be transmitted by radio, causing oscillations in a minute piece of electronic equipment hidden in the animal's mane. According to P. Hachet-Souplet, one-time director of the Insitut de Psychologie Zoologique, this method was used before World War II.

However, once it is realized that the results of all such tricks can only be achieved by deception, the interest lies less in *what* is done than in *how* it is done. And again one comes up against the old question of pretense. In the circus one should feel that animals at least know what they are doing, even if they don't always understand why they are doing it.

Yet the training for all tricks, faked or natural, is based on patience and reward. Years ago impatience and punishment also came into a horse's training, but those days are over.

Here is an example of how the same trick can be taught in two very different ways. The repertoire of most educated horses has for many years included the removal of a handkerchief bound round its foreleg. The old method of getting a horse to do this was to put a pointed piece of wood or a sharp stone inside the bandage. The horse, finding this irksome, naturally tried to remove it. But there is no need to cause the horse any discomfort at all. A lump of sugar placed inside the handkerchief provides a different incentive. If, each time the horse loosens the handkerchief, the size of the lump of sugar is decreased, while the reward from the hand is increased, the horse will soon forget the handkerchief ever held sugar and remove it simply for the lump given afterwards.

In these two cases, which will look better, the animal which with every sign of distress tugs off the bandage to obtain relief, or the horse which removes the handkerchief and, with every sign of pleasure at having achieved what was intended, trots up to its trainer for its reward?

Another trick often performed by a horse is finding a national flag hidden in one of a series of boxes. Here again patience, understanding and reward are the secrets of training. Oats are first wrapped in the flag and it is placed in an open box which is small enough to force the horse to remove the flag to get at the oats. Then by degrees the oats are replaced by a reward given after the trick, and the lid of the box is gradually closed until the horse has to nose it open. That is all there is to it. But acts like these have not got enough spectacle for the big tenting shows of Knie, Althoff or Togni, let alone the vast audiences at Madison Square Garden. Here a group of horses is needed.

Linking the act of the educated horse, where one horse does a series of tricks, to the modern liberty act, in which a series of horses work in unison, is the Equine Kindergarten, for here the members of the troupe all do something different. Horses or ponies imitate rocking horses, play on a seesaw, strike at a strength-testing machine and work merry-go-rounds.

Liberty horses pirouetting in a waltz. (Drawing by John Skeaping.)

The amount of patience and understanding required to produce an act like this is enormous. To get just two horses to work a seesaw is no mean feat. Before the horses step onto the plank it must be secured so that no movement is felt when they are persuaded to take first a step forward and then backward. Only when they have complete confidence can the blocks which wedge the ends be gradually decreased in size. At first the movement of the board is barely perceptible, but as the wedges become smaller each end goes alternately higher and lower as the horses move to and fro. The same long process of building up confidence is necessary in training an animal to rotate a cylinder while balancing on top of it. Yet although a horse will move backwards and forwards on a seesaw, I have never heard of any horse being trained to move a cylinder forward, which means, of course, that once the cylinder is moving forward the animal has to take a series of short steps backward.

I find that any act which requires a lot of "props" is usually boring. Too much time is spent in setting the ring; and once the performance does start, there rarely seems any reason why it should end. Because the routine is formless, it lacks that sense of inevitability which is so important in the circus. Furthermore, the seesaws, the roundabouts and the rest of the apparatus detract from the horses themselves. So of all the routines which can be presented at liberty, the straightforward act in which horses simply change their positions and show their movements as a team is really the best, as long as the routine is well-designed. Two horses which are perfectly matched are always better than a badly selected troupe of sixteen. But eight, twelve, sixteen or twenty-four animals —either all of the same shape, size and color, or else contrasting in groups of four—wheeling round, turning and changing formation, can be a magnificent sight. There is an almost machinelike perfection in the movements of a group of well-trained liberties, yet their precision can never be compared to the monotonous regularity of the horses on a merry-go-round. However faultless their performance may be, their tossing manes, nodding plumes and swishing tails give this act a feeling of quivering energy, suppressed excitement and fiery individualism, which is often evidence of their large proportion of Arab blood.

They are not all Arabs by any means; Trakehners, Frieslands, Norwegian Fjord horses, even Percherons and Zeelanders have all appeared in the ring. Lipizzaners, although better known as high school horses, can be seen in Freddy Knie's splendid liberty act. All Lipizzaners are descended from one of six stallions born between 1765 and 1819, although the foundation of the stud at Lipizza goes back to 1580, when Archduke Charles of Austria introduced six Andalusian stallions. The last lot of Lipizzaners belonging to Knie that I saw bore brand marks showing that they were descended from Pluto, Favory and Maestoso.

There are also liberty horses which are described as "tiger spots," which sounds very misleading until one realizes that originally the word was French, *tigré*, which means spotted, but somehow the accent got lost. The smaller circuses have for years shown a marked preference for colored horses, which is the phrase used to describe piebalds and skewbalds. But the most showy of them all are those with Arab blood. According to Bernard Mills they are also the ideal height, ranging from 14.1 to 15.1 hands.

Sometimes the trainer of a liberty act works from the back of a horse. This is rarely successful because the contrast between one horseless man and a group of riderless horses is lost; and when he is mounted the movements of a trainer are apt to become exaggerated. The sense of speed and the atmosphere of excitement—both of which come from the animals—are greatly intensified if the trainer stands quietly alone in the center of the ring. Lulu Gautier provided an excellent example of this. Dressed in a top hat and grey morning coat, he calmly watched his four blacks, four bays and four chestnuts going through their paces while he smoked a cigar. Such showmanship makes a most effective number.

Ponies are more difficult to train than horses, and Shetland ponies are particularly stubborn. However, once they have been trained, they bring another kind of contrast to the act. The sight of eight fine grey Arabs is enhanced by eight small black Shetland ponies trotting by their sides, and the contrast is given point by the ponies running under the horses' bellies. But once this has been appreciated, the ponies should make their exit. They tend to make a routine fussy if they are in the ring all the time, for their scampering confuses the rhythmic cantering of the horses.

Zebras are even more difficult to train. They are stubborn and vicious. The tricks that they can be taught are limited, yet when they appear together with horses their strong markings tend to dominate the scene. So long as they can be taught an interesting routine they are better seen on their own.

Like all things in the circus which give the appearance of suavity and ease, the simplest liberty acts need many months of training.

Take one horse, make it canter round in a circle and you will find that after two or three turns it will work its way towards the center. So the first thing to do is to train the horses to move round the maximum circumference of the ring. The animal must be able to accomplish this in both directions, clockwise and widdershins. For this you will need a lunging rein and a long whip.

Most people who have had anything to do with horses know

what a lunging rein is like, but very few of them realize the peculiarities of a ring whip. The stock of the type favored by most trainers, including Albert Schumann, is made of wood from the nettle-tree which grows around Perpignan in France.* This is extremely light, pliable and hard. The lash is made of hide, ending in a short length of cord. As with all whips it is this cord that makes the crack. And in a ring whip the crack is most important.

A whip is not used to punish the animals, or even to sting them into motion; it merely gives them their cues. Every position and every sound has its meaning. In *Les Animaux savants* (Paris: A. Lemerre, n.d.), P. Hachet-Souplet devotes no less than four pages to the management of the whip. He describes *le coup droit*, which sends the horses to the ring fence, *le coup lancé vertical*, which brings them to the center; then there is *le coup roulé déroulé*, which is the sign for increasing speed, besides *le coup droit coupé*, *le coup droit coupé brisé*, *le coup lancé*, *l'ellipse*, *le balancier*, etc. The whip, in fact, can best be compared with a conductor's baton.

With the whip in the right hand and the lunge in the left, the horse is taught to canter counter-clockwise round the ring. Then it is made to change direction by tracing the letter "S" across the center of the ring. It takes more time to teach a horse to travel in a clockwise direction because, I have heard it said, horses prefer to move counter-clockwise. But I think there is a different reason. Man is right-handed and holds a horse from its nearside. On leading it into the ring he naturally turns right so he is not squashed between the horse and the ring fence. And what is more important is that the trainer holds his whip in his right hand and so finds it easier to direct the horse from the right to left.

After this elementary training the horse is taught to pirouette and, without a rider, do some of the complicated steps of *la haute école*, which will be described later. Other lessons include kneeling, lying and sitting down. Sitting up would be a more correct phrase than sitting down, because this position is really the movement of getting up stopped and held while the forelegs are stretched out and the hind legs and rump are still on the ground.

So far we have been dealing with only one horse. When the troupe come together there are other things to be taught; but first think what it must be like to make just two horses canter round the

---

*There is, however, a difference between what the French call a *chambrière* and what they refer to as a *perpignan*. The *perpignan* is a whip used by wild animal trainers. A *chambrière* is less supple, and often the stock is made of cane.

ring in opposite directions.

In a troupe of horses each member must be so well rehearsed that he automatically finds his right position, whether they are moving round the ring in single file, two abreast, four abreast or eight abreast. After the basic movements have been taught, the trainer will want to work out a routine of his own; and it may be necessary to ride the horses through their paces or keep them on a lunge until they realize exactly what is wanted of them.

Finally there are the little touches of showmanship to be introduced. The trainer may want to emulate Edouard Wulff and Adolph Althoff, who both claimed to have been the first to teach each horse of their troupe to stand in a line and put its head over the neck of its neighbor. Or he may wish to train them to walk around the ring with hind legs and forelegs alternately on the ring fence. Or again he may decide to make them waltz round in pairs. Such finishing touches bring out the personality of the trainer.

Wulff was a great showman. He always shaved his face to copy the moustache, beard or whiskers of the reigning king of the country in which he was performing. He was also an excellent trainer, and well over two thousand horses passed through his hands in the course of his career. The Carré family have always been less ostentatious, but they have met with just as great success, and the Emperor Franz Josef had a tobacco pipe specially carved for Oscar Carré, showing the trainer with eight of his liberties rearing up on their hind legs around him. Two of his grandsons came to work in England: Harry, who for some years trained the horses at Chessington Zoo Circus, and Freddy, who as Pepino II ran a miniature circus of his own. There were two other brothers, Albert, more often called Tully, who worked as a horse trainer and rider all over the Continent, and Ernest, who trained horses for the Circus Schreiber in Sweden. They were the fifth generation of circus trainers. Today, Ernest, Harry and Freddy are dead, and Tully now has a riding school in France. But their name lives on in the permanent circus in Amsterdam, which is still called Carré.

One cannot mention liberty horses without referring to the name of Loyal. Though this family enjoyed its greatest success in the last century, they have achieved lasting fame by giving their name to the one circus character who is constant to all programmes. In France any blue-coated equestrian director is called "Monsieur Loyal," and in the scripts of a clown's duologue you will find that it is the name which appears where we would write the word "ringmaster." Yet most of the present generation of Loyals seem to specialize in training pigeons. In 1948 the programmes at Olympia and Harringay both contained almost identical acts worked by Loyal cousins.

The greatest horse trainers in the world, however, are still the Schumanns. There is a saying on the Continent that when a Schumann cracks his whip even a wooden horse will dance. This family can trace its history back to the Master of the Horse to the Grand Duke Karl of Weimar. His son Gotthold, who was born in 1825, was apprenticed to a German circus proprietor called Wollschläger. In his company were three other apprentices. When they left, each went his own way; one branched northward, one to the south, one eastwards and the other to the west. In the countries in which they made their homes each ran its most famous circus: Carré in Holland, Renz in Germany, Salamonsky in the Baltic States and Schumann in Scandinavia. And the success of each circus was derived from its horses.

The circus dynasty founded by Gotthold Schumann has never been equalled. His great-grandson Albert appeared at Olympia and with Tom Arnold's circus at Harringay; and I doubt whether anyone who saw the brilliant liberty and high school acts which he presented has ever seen anything better. Never miss an opportunity of seeing a Schumann in the ring. They may turn up anywhere. I first met Albert's younger brother Max in the Coleseu de Recreios in Lisbon, a hideous building designed by Eiffel which changes from opera to circus according to the season. Their headquarters for many years was the permanent circus in Copenhagen; though Albert and Max's sister Cecily, after her marriage to Johnny Kayes, could be found on Kayes Brothers' Circus in England. Unfortunately, Cecily died, and her brothers had to give up the Circus Schumann in Copenhagen. I heard that the landlords wanted to use it for other purposes, but the citizens insisted that it should remain a circus. They got their way, but too late for the Schumanns to retain the direction. Now you must look for them in other parts of Europe. If you ever hear that Katja Schumann is appearing in a circus, then it is worth making a journey of a hundred miles to see her perform. She is a high school rider of exquisite talent.

Some people find liberty numbers boring. I myself have occasionally been tempted to slip away, but only when the tempo is not sufficiently varied or the routine lacks imagination. In the finale to one of Albert Schumann's acts the horses cantered round in Indian file, while Albert, with his back to the exit, appeared to take no notice. At each circuit the last horse, on reaching the ring doors, pirouetted and disappeared through the curtains. At first the audience failed to appreciate exactly what was happening, but as the number of horses grew less, still with no sign from their trainer, the applause swelled to a roar.

Da Capos at the end of Gina Lipkowska's liberty act. (Drawing by John Skeaping.)

This was a quiet and subtle end to the act. The finale of Mills's horses, when they were presented by Czeslaw Mroczkowski, was an excellent example of a sustained climax. After the troupe had left the ring, one horse after another would hurtle back to make an even more spectacular exit—even walking backwards on their hind legs —in the routine known as *da capos*. When Gina Lipkowska, Czeslaw's wife, presented this group, the beautiful stallion that danced upright out of the ring was preceded by a small Shetland pony also on its hind legs. Here the spectacle gained much of its effect by the contrast in size. All liberty routines should also include a contrast in speed. A very popular trick is that in which the horses, bearing numbered shields, are first shuffled and then sort themselves out into the right sequence. I remember once seeing a troupe beautifully presented, by, I think, Karl Strassburger, going through this routine at a walk. Since it followed a very fast sequence its effect was doubled. It appeared much more deliberate than when carried out at speed. Strassburger had a flair for giving his liberty acts a new twist and introduced some original effects by using fluorescent trappings. Today tradition is well maintained by Alexis

Gruss, whose liberty act with Portuguese horses, Frieslands and Palominos is by far the best in France today.

In watching any liberty act first look for the matching of the animals. If the harness distracts the eye, either it is badly designed or it is hiding the imperfections of the horses. Like a hat on a woman, harness and plumes should enhance the look of the wearer and add a touch of color. Chessboard combing, which is sometimes seen on the quarters of an animal, accentuates the glossiness of its coat. See if the horses appear to be in top condition and have that dash and fire which give an act sparkle. Compare this with the control and repose of the trainer; he should give *you*, as well as the horses, a feeling of quiet confidence. Next take note of the routine itself, the element of contrast, the balance of interest and the sense of surprise, all of which contribute to the spectacle. A good routine never flags and has no dull moments. Remember that a few well-matched and competently trained horses in a short brisk routine are worth twenty-four badly chosen old crocks going through their act any which way. In 1950, Albert Schumann presented a liberty act at Harringay in which there were never more than four horses in the ring at the same time. He first showed four beautifully matched greys whose routine opened with two maintaining a steady walk, abreast of each other, round the ring, while the other two cantered round and round them in a variety of patterns. All four then circled the ring at equal distances, jumping in and out of four low wicker cylinders about six feet in diameter, suddenly stopping or pirouetting together at a sign from Albert's whip. The ring seemed full of precision and movement. Mere numbers are not enough. For all its spectacle, a carousel of fifty or more horses is never so fine a sight as a well-trained troupe of sixteen.

Counting forty Shetland ponies on the ring-fence, Edouard Wulff managed to pack one hundred and twenty animals into the ring. For this he built up a series of circular platforms, from the highest of which he could survey the concentric rings of horses circling alternately in opposite directions beneath him. Remarkable as this may be, it does not show the subtleties of horse training, any more than writing the Lord's Prayer on a postage stamp demonstrates the art of calligraphy.

VII

DAREDEVILS

There are some acts in the circus which simply set out to thrill, without taking much account of the skill of the performer. Though the preparation may take time, the routine itself is usually confined to one swift, death-defying action. Such a performance is easy to describe, but hard to classify. In England we have no word which accurately sums up the performer. The French call him a *casse-cou* —a break-neck—and I suppose that the most suitable English word is daredevil. But even this term is a little too general. It could be applied equally well to a racing motorist or the driver of a car which somersaults above the sawdust. Yet while the former must possess great skill, the latter needs no more than calm nerves.

In making a car loop the loop the real work is done on the drawing board by the engineer who designs the ramp down which the car is to hurtle, and who calculates the upward curve at the bottom which will throw the machine into a somersault. Yet the man who has spent many hours working out problems of speed and momentum, centers of gravity, stresses and strains, receives little credit. It is the driver, trusting his life to these calculations, who gets the applause. Sometimes, of course, the inventor is the same person as the performer, and I would not begrudge Marcel and André Desprez a single handclap. They were the creators of a

thrilling act in which their car plunged down a long ramp built up
above the seating, leapt into the air and turned a double somersault
before landing. And as if that was not sensational enough, the
Raluys turned a triple in their automobile.

Some daredevils, however, have to do more than pray to God and
sit still. Raoul Monbar, for instance, tobogganed down a steep
incline, shot off the upward curve at the end at a hundred miles an
hour, and at the top of his flight grasped the bar of a trapeze eleven
meters above the ring. An act similar to the plunging car or sled is
achieved on a bicycle. One feels that here again more skill is
needed; the rider has to keep his balance, he may have to alter
speed and even steer a course. The Ancillottis were a troupe of
highly skilled trick-cyclists long before one of them rode down a
track which looped the loop at the bottom. This trick amazed
circus-goers at the turn of the century, but a few years later Ugo
Ancillotti found he could leave out a section of track at the top of
the loop, and so leap a ten-foot gap upside down on his bicycle. He
appeared as Act No. 17 with Barnum & Bailey in 1904, and the
programme reads: "Here Diabolic Audacity Sits Upon His Throne
While Trembling Amazement Whispers 'Nothing Remains'."

But the author of the programme was wrong. The next year saw
two Ancillottis

> undertake a fearful frolic and frightful flight with Fate. Bid-
> ding a bold defiance to Death while safely accomplishing the
> most fearful and frenzied feats ever performed. Not a reckless
> risk of life, but a hazardous dual achievement, so full and
> fraught with peril as to fascinate, enthrall, astound and please
> all spectators. Approaching each other from widely separate
> starting points, the artistes meet and are seen flying in space in
> the same direction, one upside down, when striking opposite
> sections of the apparatus they ride safely away in opposite
> directions, thus presenting a double paradox.

Although the act had undoubtedly become more thrilling, the
press agent's description, fulsome as it was, seems to have lost the
feeling of awe which was apparent in the previous year's programme. The reason is not far to find. The motor car had made its
appearance, and no human achievement could stand up to that
novelty. In heavy black type we read

The Absolute Limit to which Mortals May Tempt Death with Impunity and Where a Final Period is Placed to Further Effort. L'AUTO-BOLIDE, THE DIP OF DEATH. . . . An astounding and audaciously awful abysmal act with a fascinating, furious, fugacious, flitting flight doubly discounting all devilish deeds ever done. . . . A peerless, perilous, pre-eminent, puzzling, prodigious plunge, perfectly and prettily performed.

The press was almost as ecstatic. One paper quoting the programme said, "It was all that and more so." The actual routine which caused spectators to leave the performance "with white faces and haunted eyes" would be a sensation even to the sophisticated audiences of today. The ramp ran straight down at a steep angle, then, instead of curving up at the end, *curled down under itself and then up*. There followed a forty-five foot gap which the car traversed upside down before striking another curved ramp which led it down to the ground. Draw the letter "S" and trace the curve from the top, outside the first loop and inside the second, imagining a break in the center, and you will get some idea of what Mademoiselle de Thiers accomplished in her little red car (which, incidentally, "had in its interior no sparking devices") nearly eighty years ago.

Sensational acts of this sort usually came at the end of a performance, in order, as Bost wrote in *Le Cirque et le music hall,* to produce the most brutal effect and leave the audience stunned. But though it may be good psychology to send the public away dazed and with its heart still in its mouth, I like to leave the circus with a more substantial and lasting impression. A few years ago I saw a programme which ended with a man being shot from a cannon. The gun was gradually edged into the ring. The barrel was meticulously elevated to the correct angle. The white-coated figure gave a leisurely salute before he slid slowly down inside the barrel. Then came a tense moment of waiting. All this built up an almost unbearable feeling of tension. I experienced the same empty drag at the bottom of my stomach, the same constriction of the throat, which I had always felt before going back to school, and which came back during the war after the wail of the sirens or the order "Action Stations." And yet, unlike the air raids, the flash, bang and rapid flight of the projectile in the circus seemed over all too quickly. I left my seat with a slight feeling that the lengthy and laborious preparation was worth something more than one swift flight through the air. Some may have shared this vague sense of dissatisfaction, but most of the audience probably felt quite content. Human cannonballs have thrilled the public ever since 2 April 1877, when a young girl called Zazel made the first flight from muzzle to net at the Westminster Aquarium. The act was such a success that the "beautiful lady fired from a monstrous cannon" was kept in the bill for two years at a salary of £120 a week. Others soon followed Zazel's trajectory. To many the flight proved fatal. Out of some fifty human projectiles more than thirty have lost their lives, mostly by falling outside the net.

In America such work became the speciality of an Italian family called Zacchini. According to an article in *Life*, at one time nearly three dozen Zacchinis lived at Tampa, Florida, all connected in some way or other with being shot from a cannon. More often than not human projectiles black out at the moment of impulsion and only regain consciousness at the top of their five-second flight, leaving very little time to twist into a safe position for landing. Where Zazel employed elastic springs, performers today use compressed air. A pressure of two hundred pounds a square foot in a barrel elevated to forty-eight degrees will shoot a man one hundred feet up in the air to a net two hundred feet from the gun. But the Zacchinis' usual flight was a quarter of this distance and for this they were paid no more than $150 in the 1950s.

Zazel travelled about thirty feet from a cannon slung in midair, which, judging from a photograph, could not have been more than ten feet long. The Zacchini cannon was mounted on a truck; the barrel was twenty-three feet long and the whole thing was reported to have cost about twenty thousand dollars.

A variation of Zazel's Human Cannon Ball was an act known as the Human Arrow. In this a girl was fired from a giant cross-bow at a target thirty feet away. As she hit the bull's eye, the target swayed back and the girl fell into a net which was stretched beneath. Here again the human element seems to be more in evidence. It is an act which might well be worth reviving, but I should like to see the stock of the bow made of some transparent material so that looking up one could see the "arrow" lying in position and the bowstring actually shooting her into the air. The girl should pierce the target before falling into the net, and she might even be dressed in an asbestos suit and set ablaze so that she traces a fiery course high above the ring. Such an act would have certain advantages over the most modern cannon. One would see exactly how it is done. There would be no need to fake the loud

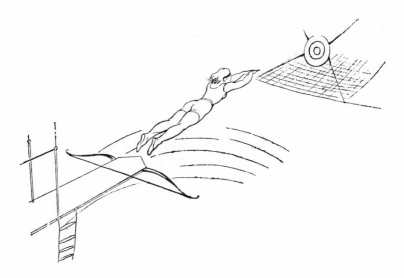

The Human arrow. (Drawing by John Skeaping.)

report, the flash and the cloud of smoke which, however picturesque they may look, have nothing to do with the firing of the projectile. Then another advantage would be that one could see a definite objective; the arrow has not merely to fall into the net but to hit the bull's eye first.

The trouble with most daredevil acts is that no sooner does one person accomplish something original, than he is copied by dozens of others. Few can imitate a really good trapeze artiste because few have his skill, and the complexity of his movements allows room for variety. But the short and simple number of the daredevil, thrilling as it may be, allows little chance of introducing any distinguishing characteristics.

Some daredevils specialize in more than one sensational act. Leoni Wybierala, brother of the human projectile Leinert, was also shot from a cannon. He told Adrian, the French circus chronicler,

> Eighteen people have left the muzzle of my cannon; sixteen have been wounded and two killed. I myself have suffered from a fractured skull, burnt face, broken knee and damaged vertebrae. Frankly, if I had known it was going to be so dangerous I'd never have started it. But you know how it is in the circus, once you start something. . . .

Leoni started at least two other daredevil acts. He himself drove a somersaulting car, and he had an act known as The Mast of Death, which a partner sometimes worked. A man climbs up an immensely high perch which is fixed at the bottom. At the top the performer stands on his hands and the pole sways to and fro. Just as the audience begins to feel that if it leans over any more it is bound to crack, they hear a loud report and the perch breaks in two. The man falls faster and faster as the top, to which he is still clinging, describes a semicircle in the air. But as the break is hinged a little above the center of the pole, he is not dashed to pieces but hangs swinging a few feet above the ground.

When this apparatus was set up for the dress rehearsal at Harringay, the performer asked Clem Butson, the circus director, when he would like to see the act. Time was short, and of the many new acts some had to be rearranged for the first night, so Butson told him that he had seen it on the Continent and was perfectly satisfied. The young man went away but returned a little later to say he thought he had better run through it just once before the opening, *as he had not done it for seven years.*

Many daredevils have used a spectacular fall as the basis of their act. At the Harringay Christmas Circus in 1950, Leon de Rousseau fell from a platform some forty feet above the ring, in a back somersault, to land feet first on a thick mattress. In the '90s, Zaeo used to fall from a "lofty platform" to the net, turning a back somersault in transit; but like the Ancillottis she was also an accomplished performer who could give a more elaborate act than just one simple thrill, and she was very conscious of her artistry. The *Daily Graphic* once sent its "Lady Commissioner" to interview her. "Now," said the reporter, "I want to hear from you something about the training of girl acrobats." "Then I am afraid," answered Zaeo, with a quick little laugh, "there is not much that I can tell you, for I am a gymnast."

Alois Peters fell from a great height with a length of rope fastened round his neck. Billed as "The Man Who Hangs Himself," he thrilled London audiences at the Agricultural Hall in 1936. Eight years later he killed himself while performing in America.

The high diver who falls from a great height into a small tank of water belongs to the same group of daredevils. While a male diver usually resorts to leaping in flames to a lighted tank, a female diver, such as Swan Ringens, will probably find that the contrast of grace and beauty with high courage is sufficient to hold the audience spellbound. It is difficult to look beautiful in an asbestos suit, and flames would merely detract from the femininity of the act. One of the most spectacular variations of this thrilling plunge is the Monte Cristo Dive, in which the performer is tied hand and foot, sealed in a sack and thrown from the high platform into the tank, where he escapes from his bonds and reappears wet but free.

This brings us to another type of act, that of Houdini and the escapologists. Houdini actually started his professional career in a small tenting circus in America. Although there is a risk of such acts being linked with conjuring, the sight of a man handcuffed, gagged and bound in a straitjacket, who is hoisted into midair and then proceeds to set himself free in full view of the audience, provides a much more interesting spectacle than someone who simply falls into a tank. Here dexterity is made more thrilling by danger, and the sense of danger helps the feeling of actuality. Up there the performer can have no accomplice; he must rely entirely on his own efforts.

When such tricks are performed in the ring one always suspects that things are not entirely as they seem. The possibility that a trick may be faked displeases the true circophile. For this reason yogis and fakirs are out of place in the circus. These artistes *appear* to hypnotize crocodiles, walk barefoot on the edge of a sword, roll on broken glass and remain buried in a coffin full of sand for ten minutes or more, and some of their tricks are indeed genuine. By pressing the jugular vein of an animal, anyone can make it lose consciousness until the blood flows back to the brain. Place your foot squarely down on a sharp blade and it will not be cut until you slide your foot *along* the blade or vice versa, and anyone can remain buried in a sand-filled coffin so long as there are enough folds in the shroud to hold sufficient air.

Conjuring has no place in the ring, yet in recent years the number of illusionists appearing with circuses has grown. In the early days of the circus conjurors might have filled out the programme because there were few artistes available. Barnum engaged Hoffman as a stunt, and the Davenport Brothers appeared at the Cirque Napoleon for the same reason. But it was Carmo who really started the fashion. Although he made his name on the music hall stage, he, like Houdini, had begun his professional career in the ring. He had toured Australia in circuses, and only turned to magic when an accident prevented him from showing his feats of strength. The circus was in his veins, and although he did not present an illusion in the ring of his first circus, he had shown that lions and even an elephant could be made to disappear on the music hall stage. He subsequently performed the disappearing lion act in the ring when he went into partnership with Ray Stott.

Whenever I see the quickness of the hand deceive the eye in a circus, I cannot help thinking that such dexterity would give more satisfaction in keeping a dozen plates spinning in the air. I would rather see fakirs, who may occasionally refrain from faking, than conjurors. But better than those who are buried alive or hypnotize crocodiles are acts like those of Professor Finney, who played cards under water, and Captain Wall, who wrestled with crocodiles. The Professor could actually hold his breath for nearly five minutes, but his act lacked the movement which is so essential to a ring. Captain Wall, on the other hand, was kept constantly on the move in trying to avoid the needle-sharp teeth of his animals.

Most daredevils, however, gain their effect from working at a great height; and they have done so since Herr Sanchez walked across the ceiling at Sadler's Wells early in the last century. Many have followed in his inverted footsteps, billing themselves as Human Flies. Laristo, in the 1860s, used large suckers attached to his feet, but most, such as Alois Peters, have preferred to put their feet into a series of loops rather than trust their weight to a partial vacuum. This act requires more than courage. One performer trained his children for seven months before he would let them appear ninety feet above the ground in a circus.

I had always imagined that the Wall of Death with its motor-cyclists speeding round the inside of a mesh or lattice cylinder suspended in midair had, like so many other acts, come from the fairground. Then I saw a circus poster of the Noiset Troupe pedaling round a vertical wall on bicycles, and discovered that the Davis family performed the same trick in midair, cycling round an inverted, truncated cone, which had nothing to stop them from falling into the ring except the speed at which they traveled. Both these acts were appearing in Paris in 1903. The bottomless cylinder is obviously more dangerous than the spectacular Globe of Death, in which motorcyclists hurtle in all directions round the inside of a latticework globe. In fact, during the 1951 season of Bertram Mills's Circus at Olympia, Arno Wickbold died after falling through the bottom of his cylinder, which was slung seventy feet up in the air. I saw this act at the opening performance when I was reviewing the programme for the *News Chronicle,* and I thought it exceptionally dangerous, not only because the bottom of the cylinder opened like a trap door once Wickbold was riding round the wall, but because he was wearing very flared trousers. A few days later the accident happened, and my news editor rang me to ask what I thought might have caused it. I told him the most probable explanation was that his bell-bottoms had got caught up in the machine and stalled the engine; and this was confirmed at the inquest. He might have saved his own life if he had let go of the machine, but this would have endangered the public.

The sensational acts of the daredevils always leave one a little dazed, which is why I would place them at the end of the first half of the programme. At this point the ringmaster announces, "My lords, ladies and gentlemen, there will now be an interval of fifteen minutes."

VIII

THE INTERVAL

The circus is a feast. The diversity of the menu tends to make us forget how much color and movement have met the eye, how many times the heart has leapt to the mouth or the belly been shaken by laughter, so it tends to give one indigestion. The interval comes as a welcome break, a pause in which one can relax. This is the time to stretch one's legs and meet old friends.

The intervals which I have enjoyed most were in the warm, sympathetic atmosphere of the Cirque Medrano. You could stroll past the photographs of famous performers, which lined the walls of the circular corridor under the seating, and come to the bar at the back of the ring curtains. Here there was always a clown or an auguste ready to pass the time of day, his prosaic small talk and matter-of-fact gestures contrasting strangely with the magnificence of his sequined dress or the grotesque pattern of his makeup. You could chat with a trainer, watch a troupe of acrobats limbering up, or pass on to the stables to inspect the horses. The setting had the same informality as a visit backstage; but while most people venturing behind the scenes in a theatre feel like intruders, here the public and the performers met on an equal footing, for there is no backstage in a circus.

It has gone now, that place where Degas painted Miss Lola,

hanging by her teeth high up in the cupola, and where Toulouse-Lautrec drew Louis Fernando, the son of the man who built it. Its slender pillars are said to have represented the quarter poles of the tenting circus in which old Fernando had been reared. It passed into the hands of his principal clown, Boum-Boum, whose real name was Medrano, and when Boum-Boum died, his son Jérôme took it over. He and his wife had a tiny flat over the stables, and between the Liberation of Paris and the end of World War II, I spent many, many evenings there, eating, drinking and talking circus, while the horses munched away in the stables below, and the performers changed into street clothes in the dressing rooms under the seating, before going to the café round the corner for a final nightcap. Although the Cirque Medrano has been pulled down, I shall never forget the delightful evenings I passed in that enchanting place.

In a tenting circus this atmosphere cannot be enjoyed in quite the same way. One has the feeling that the "backyard" is out of bounds, and that those members of the audience who do find their way there are privileged. In permanent amphitheatres and on tenting shows the real devotees of the circus always seem to wander round behind the ring doors in the interval. You will often see little badges in their coat lapels which stamp them as members of one of the many circus-loving societies. In America there is the Circus Fans' Association, a band of amateurs whose constitution starts, "We, who love the circus, and being ever mindful of the increasing problems with which the circus is confronted . . . bind ourselves together in the hope of forming fast friendships, and an organised effort to create an enthusiasm for, and interest in, the circus as an institution. . . ." This was followed by the Circus Fans' Association of Great Britain, the Club du Cirque in France, the Club van Circusvrienden in Holland, the Gesellschaft der Circusfreunde in Germany, the Amici del Circo in Italy, and the Amigos del Circo in Spain. Now there are also fan clubs in Belgium, Australasia, and South Africa. Then there are other organizations such as the Circus Historical Society in America, and groups devoted to circus model-making, the preservation of circus music, and acrobatics.

If one were to meet individual members of these societies separately in private life, one would never suspect that they had anything in common. Take, for instance, the unobtrusive little figures of Marthe and Juliette Vesque; they always seemed as fragile as the Sèvres porcelain which they once decorated so exquisitely. No one would have guessed that they shared their greatest interest in life with the urbane attorney-general of Haiti, Melvin D. Hildreth. But for years, unknown to anybody, these sisters used to sit in the cheapest seats of the Cirque Medrano and make sketches of every artiste who appeared there. When they were discovered and introduced to the people they had drawn, the delight of the two old ladies was only equaled by the pleasure of the performers at the meticulous accuracy of the sketches. And Melvin Hildreth, past president of the Circus Fans' Association of America, took the trouble to fly to England to attend the annual general meeting of the British CFA, then on to Paris and Holland to see the circuses and meet its devotees over there.

The circus is a disease which it is very difficult to eradicate. If you start collecting circusiana you rarely stop. Jacques Garnier's house in Orléans is full of prints, posters, programmes, china, glass, books, photographs, medals, tokens and toys, all dealing with the circus. It is one of the finest private collections in the world, but by no means the only one.

Once you get sawdust in your shoes you are a circus addict for life. Occasionally people will tell you that they have lost interest and don't go to the circus any more. Then one day they'll see the wagons pull on to the "tober" or hear a circus band in the distance, and all the old excitement will come surging back. They'll buy a ringside seat "just to see if it's the same as it used to be," and they'll come out as deeply under its spell as ever before. Some of these *aficionados* cannot rest until they have joined the circus professionally. Raymond Toole Stott, one of the founders of the Circus Fans' Association of Great Britain, became a circus proprietor for a time. Even when he gave up running his own show he did not give up the circus; he spent his time collating material for his astounding circus bibliography, which runs into four invaluable volumes, containing thirteen thousand entries. He is now working on the fifth volume.

The *Président-Bienfaiteur* of the Club du Cirque in France was Monsieur le Professeur Malladoli. His real name was Albert Raphaël, and he came from a family of famous bankers. But to him an aerial act held greater powers of attraction than high finance. Calling himself Mallodoli—his brothers with some difficulty prevented him from using the name *Pipioli*—he started a circus of his own, the Cirque Cocassien. And on his farm near Vernon he spent his time training animals, which in winter were stabled in the house while he slept in a caravan in the yard.

Monsieur le Professeur was an expert high school rider, and when his circus took to the road, the puzzled peasants of Seine-et-Oise were given a lecture on the various styles of *la haute école*, from La Guérinière to James Fillis. For this act Mallodoli insisted on dressing in a Louis XVI costume, with powdered wig and a bright green beard. Apart from his deep love of the circus, his passion was to shock the *bourgeoisie*. If, at one of his more outrageous acts, you looked aghast, or even taken aback, you would be subjected to horror upon horror. But if you took everything he said and did in your stride, you were his friend for life. He died in 1970, and I think the world is a little less colorful without him.

The greatest amateur circus was run from 1880 to 1933 by Ernest Molier in Paris. His manège in the rue Benouville started as a rendezvous for horsemen returning from the Bois de Boulogne and as a meeting place for those whose hobbies were boxing and fencing. The cult of gymnastics brought in the amateur acrobats, and it was not long before Molier decided to build a ring thirteen meters in diameter and give a little evening party at which his friends could show their skill. Here the comte Hubert de la Rochefoucauld appeared in a bar act—which was so good that he was offered a professional engagement—and other members of the French nobility appeared as animal trainers, acrobats, strong men and clowns. Molier himself worked in a jockey act and as a school rider, besides presenting the horses.

Only one performance was given in 1880, and the male members of the audience were as aristocratic as the company of artistes. But the female spectators were not, for in those days the ladies of *le monde* and *le demi-monde* could never meet, and to quote Molier, *"côté des grandes horizontales,"* were Cora Pearl, Reine Romani and others. In subsequent years this was put right. The circus became such a success that two performances had to be given, one for such leaders of fashion as the Duchesse de Grammont, the Duchesse d'Uzès and the Marquise de Castellane, and the other for the *"bataillon de Cythère."*

Year after year the dapper little Frenchman, who wore long, fierce moustaches and his hair *en brosse*, lured Paris society to his circus. Often his programme included acts of a type never previously seen. Much to the fury of her *maître de ballet*, Mademoiselle Violat of the Opéra was seen there as the first acrobatic dancer, and for thirty years she had no rival. In the privacy of a party—admittance was by invitation only—pantomimes were produced in which the girls appeared nearly naked, twenty-five years before nudity became the hallmark of French revue. A trained stag was presented there in 1887, and high school camels eleven years later. Performing cormorants, monkeys, hares and geese all made their appearance, every one trained by an amateur, while P. Hachet-Souplet showed his performing poodle driving a chariot drawn by sheep. Molier's greatest gentleman rider was probably Monsieur Desormont, an industrialist from the north of France, but his most famous pupil was undoubtedly Blanche Allarty, whom he married. Like many professionals she was a good all-round performer. She worked on a trapeze as well as in a pad act, and she was an excellent school rider, good enough to appear professionally in the United States with Frank Bostock.

In 1930 the circus celebrated its fiftieth anniversary, though owing to World War I it was only the forty-sixth programme. Three years later Molier died, a few weeks after appearing in the ring at his forty-ninth circus party. His obituary notices called him "the most sporting of sportsmen" and "the most Parisian of Parisians." During his life he remained faithful to four great loves and four great hates. The circus, horses, the theatre and women were what he adored, and the things he loathed were bicycles, telephones, the cinema and belly-dancing.

Others have followed Molier's example in running an amateur circus. Albert Menier, the chocolate millionaire, M.P.S. de Kroutikoff, a rich Ukrainian landowner, the Countess d'Oroszy in Hungary, B. van Leer in Holland and Alfred de Rothschild in England have all presented their own programmes in their own rings. All these amateurs were rich enough to run their circuses as a hobby. One Englishman went further; this was the Reverend Brother Gardner, headmaster of the Thomas More School at Frensham. Seeing parents watching the usual gymnastic display in the rain gave him the idea of producing a more interesting performance inside a tent, and from there it was a very short step to put on the first circus run by children for children. The experiment taught the boys more than riding and gymnastics; they learned patience, kindness, self-possession and the team spirit. They learned about England from touring the countryside, and zoology from training and caring for their animals. The finances of the circus taught them math; while making props, building up the big top and lighting the show gave them practical experience in carpentry, handicrafts and electricity. All these things were learned in a constructive way, not from reading books or doing prep., but by creating something of their own. The pity of it was that when the Reverend Brother Gardner died in 1947, no one else could be found to take over this fine enterprise, and the circus was sold.

America, too, has had amateur circuses. In 1930 the Little Theatre in Gainesville, Texas, was in a bad way. Talkies and the depression had put it three hundred dollars into debt. Someone suggested putting on a community circus to raise funds. Housewives, schoolchildren and businessmen threw themselves enthusiastically into the project. The Little Theatre was saved—and then soon forgotten, for the circus had got into Gainesville's blood. While still remaining amateurs, the townspeople hired retired performers to teach them professional tricks. Their circus visited a dozen or so different towns, sometimes playing to as many as 52,000 spectators a day. Although it remained Gainesville's hobby and professionals were barred from its ring, the annual expenditure —and receipts—amounted to some fifty thousand dollars. And today Dr. Charles Boas, professor of geography at a Pennsylvania university, sets out each summer vacation with a circus company consisting solely of college students to tour the eastern states of North America under the banner of the Circus Kirk.

People who run shows like this naturally have much to discuss with the professionals whom they meet during the interval, whether it is on their own show or on another's. Some overheads are equally burdensome for those who look upon the circus as a hobby and for those who run it as a business. Animals eat the same amount whether they belong to The Greatest Show on Earth or to a miniature circus in a fairground. One of the biggest changes the circus has seen in the last twenty-five years has been in expenditure. In many cases money that would have bought an animal's food for a week a quarter of a century ago now barely covers a day's supply. One used to allow £1 a week for a horse, £3 a week for a lion, £5 a week for a full-grown elephant. These days you can spend £1 a day on a horse. Lions will still eat between ten and fifteen pounds of horsemeat at whatever price you have to pay, and even young elephants will eat twice as much as a horse. When this book was first published an average English circus with, say, four lions, twelve horses, six ponies, six dogs, three monkeys, two bears and an elephant would have cost £60 a week, including the wages of the grooms and beast-boy. Today, Gerry Cottle's seven lions, four elephants, three camels, two zebras, four llamas, twelve liberty horses, six Shetland ponies, ring horses and chimpanzees, together with the trainers, grooms and beast-boys, cost £800 a week. It is only by bulk-buying, long term contracts and employing a full-time accountant who travels with the show that costs like this can be kept under control. And not even an accountant can force an Iranian general to pay the £70,000 that Gerry Cottle is owed.

The current wage of a groom is £35 a week, more than many a trainer was getting twenty-five years ago to present two wild animal acts in the ring. Now you will have to pay a trainer between £100 and £300 a week for an engagement, though obviously you will get the best terms for a long contract with no lay-off periods.

One cannot see the finances of the circus business in perspective if one only looks back a quarter of a century. Between the wars a tenting show such as Bertram Mills' would rarely pay as much as £250 a week for an act. Today the highest salary on a show such as Gerry Cottle's is £600, and that does not happen very often. Performers' salaries have not increased at the same rate as labor and feeding-stuffs.

It is interesting to compare these figures with the costs a century ago. When Powell & Clarke's Circus was tenting in Ireland in 1875, they would pay on average £2 a day for the "tober," that is, the field on which they pitched. Today local authorities in England have been known to ask as much as £1,000 for a week. A hundred years ago horses could be stabled for sixpence a night each, including the straw.

As for the salaries earned by the performers, Powell & Clarke were paying a top salary of £15 a week on their tenting show and the whole company cost £87. At that time the "take" could be as much as £87 a performance or as little as £6 17s. At Christmas they put on a special season in Belfast. Here they booked Lulu, the famous transvestite aerialist, on a percentage basis for a week. He cost them £82, but he brought in an extra £100 worth of business. That must have been big money in those days; and it came from tickets sold at three shillings, two shillings, one shilling and even sixpence.

If one considers the number of weeks a performer may be out of work in any one year, the comparatively short time for which he can remain at the top of his profession, the danger which so often accompanies his act, the long hours of training and rehearsal for which he gets no money, then one cannot say that the circus artiste has ever been overpaid. The Geraldos, who were reported to be getting £200 a week in 1949, when they appeared on the high trapeze at Harringay, told me that they gave themselves no more than another three or four years to do the act which made them famous; they were then twenty-six and twenty-seven years old.

Of course, these are average figures. In the United States higher rates may well apply. Behind the Iron Curtain they are certainly lower, and there the difference in wages between ring-boy and star is much less marked.

Though proprietors may not run into physical danger, they can very easily face financial disaster, and more than one director has been driven to suicide. The responsibility of taking a large company of human and animal performers around the country is heavy.

In America, Ringling once travelled with 1,400 employees and 900 animals, and gave performances to an audience of 15,000. The American magazine *Fortune* reported that the Ringling circus would lose money at the rate of ten thousand dollars a day if it stayed idle in Hartford, Connecticut, after a disastrous fire on 6 June 1944. That tragedy cost 168 persons their lives, the circus four million dollars in claims for damages, and five employees prison sentences for involuntary manslaughter. The Ringlings struggled on that season and for a time flourished once more with all debts paid and sentences served, but they later gave up tenting and worked only in big indoor arenas. In the end they sold Ringling Bros. and Barnum & Bailey's Greatest Show on Earth to the Felds, who have been running it in two units for the past decade.

Fire has often proved disastrous. In spite of Carmo's indomitable courage, the fire which quickly followed a snowstorm brought an end to his circus. Storms at sea, blow-downs, train wrecks and other acts of God have lost many other proprietors their shows. Fortunes have been lost in much milder weather conditions. Sunshine may keep people outside the big top just as rain will keep them inside their own homes. Then there are economic conditions to be studied. Sarrasani saved his circus by touring South America when inflation came to Germany. Today the labor market, harvest, and the condition of local industry must all be taken into consideration when planning a tour. The circus acts as an industrial barometer; it goes where money is plentiful. If times are bad in the cotton country or the wheat belt, it dare not risk a tour there. One can no longer afford to give people circuses if they also cry for bread.

In *The Lions Starve in Naples,* Johann Fabricius described the forced sale of a German circus in Italy. This book is based on the true story of Captain Schneider's Circus, which through sheer misfortune ended in bankruptcy. You could tell that Captain

Schneider was a showman from the moment he opened his mouth; his teeth were studded with diamonds, set in a pattern which is said to have resembled a butterfly. I have been told that he started in an architect's office, graduated to trick-cycling, and only took to training lions after looping the loop on his bicycle 999 times, because he had the feeling that the thousandth attempt would prove fatal. How much of this story is true and how much is showman's bluff, I cannot say. But I do know that he had a magnificent tenting circus, with a two-storied showfront whose Corinthian columns carried a classical pediment decorated with sculptured lions, and that at one time he worked with a hundred of these beasts in the ring. And I can also tell how the anti-performing-animal fanatics in Holland were invited to the performance and were so impressed that they stopped their propaganda. They afterwards published an article praising the conditions in which the beasts were kept and calling him *"a true friend of animals."*

On 17 April 1932, at Naples, Captain Schneider was forced to put £40,000 worth of material up for auction. The only items sold were two llamas, one bear, three goats, eleven monkeys and six geese; they fetched £60. Lot No. 1, which consisted of sixty-nine lions and two tigers, brought in no bid; the reserve was £5,027. A clown managed to save a performing pig from the butcher by saying it was his personal property. Schneider's own dogs were restored to him by a soldier, who, on hearing they were the Captain's pets, withdrew his bid of two shillings. Schneider was so touched by this gesture that he forced his way through the crowd to shake the soldier by the hand. A week later the sixty-nine lions were sold for £620, and all the equipment for £1,500. Captain Schneider's own end came in 1941, when he was killed by a lioness at Leipzig.

Nearly two hundred performers are known to have lost their lives while appearing in circuses and menageries during the last 125 years. Though nearly a third have been animal trainers, thirty-five of them died in the square wagon cages of the menageries. Lions have killed some thirty trainers, bears about ten, elephants and tigers more than half a dozen each. Next on the list of fatalities come aerial acrobats with almost three dozen, the parterre gymnasts with seventeen, riders with thirteen and wire-walkers with about a dozen. The remainder is made up of daredevils, sharpshooters and others. An average of 1.6 deaths per annum for all performers throughout the world is not high; one has only to think of the annual death toll on the roads.

Good luck has also played a part in the history of the circus. Although Astley's Amphitheatre was burnt down three times, Astley himself was able to make great improvements in the early days with the money he got from a diamond ring he picked up on Westminster Bridge. Abraham Saunders, on the other hand, not only had his circus destroyed by fire, he also lost his stud of fifteen horses in a storm in the Irish Channel. Although he was a good showman, Saunders, unlike Astley, was a bad businessman. If he disagreed with anyone he would fling a handful of gold and silver at their feet, saying "Damn you, take that!" After being thrown into the Fleet Prison for debt, he appeared before the magistrates in 1837—his ninetieth year—dressed in "a garment made of bearskin," having driven to the court in a sugar-box on wheels pulled by a Shetland pony. Whether his strange appearance should be put down to inherent eccentricity or to a flair for publicity is difficult to say.

Before World War II, poster space was limited in Germany, and Sarrasani used to employ nine bald men to sit on a tram-car. Each had a letter painted on his head, so that people passing between the seats read the name S.A.R.R.A.S.A.N.I. He would also send a party of men, dressed from head to toe in black, into the bars of the towns in which he was appearing. They never spoke a word until sufficient interest had been aroused—then they would chant in unison "Sarrasani is here!" turn on their heels and march out.

Barnum and Sanger both knew very well how to use such forms of publicity. In those days competition was fiercer and the public more credulous; wolves appeared to escape from their dens with singular ease, white elephants appeared from nowhere overnight, and once a small cart advertising "Lloyd's Circus" tacked itself on to the end of a rival's magnificent street parade, and the crowd followed the cart to the little show. One of the smartest pieces of improvised publicity was produced by George Wombwell, the menagerie proprietor. His only rival at that time was Atkins, and these two would always meet at St. Bartholomew's Fair. Once when Wombwell's show was in the north of England, he found that Atkins's advance billing was boasting that his would be the only wild beast show at St. Bartholomew's that year. Within a fortnight, Wombwell had travelled posthaste to Newcastle, packed up his menagerie and returned with fourteen wagons and more than fifty horses to open on time. Unfortunately, that night his elephant died. Atkins jubilantly proclaimed that he possessed the only live elephant at the fair, but Wombwell beat him at his own game, for he informed all and sundry that he was showing the only dead elephant; and he took the most money.

The greatest press campaign was the bluff worked over Jumbo. Jumbo was an elephant bought by Barnum from the London Zoo. A campaign was started by the press agents, who told the world that Jumbo did not want to leave England. Schoolchildren sent petitions, letters appeared in the newspapers, and questions were raised in the House of Commons. In all the excitement only Barnum sat back and said nothing, for he knew that the more England felt the loss, the greater would America consider the gain.

Elephants are still the press agent's joy. They are trundled out to publicize whatever commodity is made in the town where the circus is showing; and they have carried newly-wed couples from churches in England and France.

Weddings, births and deaths always make news. I have heard tell of a couple married in a lion's cage, a reception in the freaks' tent, an elephant's christening at which Josephine Baker and Maurice Chevalier were godparents,* and a funeral of a circus official which was attended by Red Indians, Circassians, Arabs, Hindus, Japanese, Chinese and Negroes, while six airplanes, flying long streamers of black crêpe, circled overhead.

It is from newspaper reports of such activities as these that the public learns about the ways of the circus. So it is not surprising to find that many people hold strange ideas about performers and their private lives. Yet the wildly improbable story recounted as fact and the inquisitiveness of the uninvited visitor are the two things which annoy circus people most. Time and time again I have heard an artiste mimic a nosey parker who has peered into a living wagon and made some remark such as, "Oh! Look, they've even got a little stove!" or "Do you suppose they can read and write?" George Sanger once gave me an even better example. Coming back from market one day with a roasting fowl under his arm, he heard a woman who was queuing up at the box office turn to her companion and say, "Gracious me, did you see that? They eat chicken!"

There is really nothing very extraordinary about circus folk, though they work harder, take more risks and travel further than most of us. Some neither drink nor smoke, but those that do can usually smoke and drink more, without suffering a hangover, than

---

* This was the first elephant to be born in a French menagerie. It belonged to the Cirque Amar, and was christened Auguste on the stage of the Empire, Paris.

most people, simply because they keep themselves in better condition. Clowns seem to have a penchant for fishing, but I suspect this is because they often have more time on their hands than other artistes. With animals to care for, rehearsals and traveling, most performers can do little more than snatch an odd half-hour. And then they love to play cards—nap, pontoon, poker, *belotte* or *loterie*.

A number of people think that all performers are Gypsies, and this annoys circus folk very much. You will still find quite a lot of Romanies on the fairground, but, as always, they keep to themselves, very much apart, and any drop of Romany blood which may possibly have found its way into the veins of a British circus family is now so thin as to leave little trace. Among performers there is probably more Jewish blood than Gypsy, though even this is rare.

On the Continent it is a different story. Many of the circus proprietors left the fairgrounds quite recently. Some of them have quite a lot of Gypsy blood—for example, the older generation of the Bougliones—and a few talk Romany to this day. There are also dynasties of performers such as the Salamonskys, Goldkettes, Strassburgers and Blumenfelds, who are obviously of Jewish origin. But the circus as a whole is a blend of most races and creeds. It is a microcosm which has already gone a long way to achieve the unity for which the macrocosm still strives.

Individually the people of the circus are very like you and me, though they often show more pride. They are less inclined to grumble about their own misfortunes, and when they describe the bad luck of others it is always with sympathy. They are, I think, the most courageous people I have ever met. I have known a performer who suffered agonies from a wound which had not healed for years to appear in the ring each night with the open gash covered only with a piece of sharkskin. I have seen another who was so lame that he hobbled to the ring curtains on sticks, but once on the sawdust went through his act without the trace of a limp. I have heard tell of a trainer who crawled from his deathbed to die in the circus. And the only reasons I can see for people doing such things is the pride they have in their work, and the love they have for their calling.

IX

THE BIG CAGE
and the Training of
WILD ANIMALS

Coming back to our ringside seat, we find that the big cage has already been built up for the wild animal acts. The business of erecting and dismantling the various sections is laborious to do and boring to watch, so you will find that cat acts usually come either just before or just after the interval. In this way the cage can either be pulled down or built up without interrupting the programme. In some tenting circuses the cage acts are presented as the last number of the first performance and the first number at the second. The time setting the ring each day is, in this way, cut by half; but though big cats may provide an excellent finale, they do not make a good opening number. The first number on the bill should stimulate one by its movement, and establish a sense of inevitability, on a domestic scale, rather than make us conscious of danger or show us the characteristics of exotic animals. In some permanent amphitheatres the cage is hidden below the ring fence and can be raised already set in one piece on hydraulic lifts. This allows a producer considerably more freedom in designing his programme, but it is, unfortunately, quite impracticable for a tenting show. Nowadays wire-mesh cages are gradually superseding iron bars. These are lighter, easier and quicker to put in position and, more important still, give a better view of the act.

To most people the word circus calls to mind a lion tamer with waxed moustaches, a befrogged uniform and Hessian boots, but such a character is never seen today. Although the uniform may linger on, the tamer has been replaced by the trainer.

Animal men, you will remember, were the third category of performers to join the circus by forsaking the fairgrounds, where the first wild animals to be put through their paces were shown in the traveling menageries. For a long time lions and tigers were merely exhibited, and neither tamed nor trained, for the animal men were always careful to keep the bars of the cages between them and their charges.

Elephants had been seen, to quote handbills and posters of the period, "taking kettles off the fire," "telling the time of day" and "lying down at the command" in menageries for many years before Manchester Jack dared to slip in amongst Wombwell's lions and sit astride Nero, or Atkins's keeper plucked up enough courage to lie down with the lion and the tigress who had produced a litter of hybrid cubs in October 1842. In France, also, the elephant appeared as a performer before lions and tigers. At Franconi's circus an elephant had driven nails into a plank, played upon musical instruments and tied a knot in a piece of cord some fifteen years before a horseman turned tamer, Henri Martin, entered a cageful of tigers for the first time. But, since the cage is up, let us consider the big cats.

There is really no difference in principle between training big cats and little cats. But principle is not everything, and although I would like to train the domestic variety again, I know I am much too slow to tackle big cats. You must be quick on your feet to be a trainer of lions or tigers. When I first started training Aubrey and Clovis I soon found that I had to wear leather gloves to protect my hands from scratches given unwittingly or in play; but leather gloves are hardly adequate protection against lions and tigers. However, the secret of training is again "a positively conditioned reflex," though the equivalent of Pavlov's phrase in circus language is "gentling." The Hagenbecks are usually given the credit for introducing the gentling system in the 1880s. But as Thétard once pointed out to me, the kind of act which the gentling system is supposed to have produced had been presented long before by trainers such as Martin, Van Amburgh and Carter. What really happened was that towards the middle of the century certain "tamers" tried to produce a more spectacular act by inciting the animals to roar, leap or strike out. Often they overdid this. The

MONS.^r MARTIN ENCOUNTERING THE LION.

London Pub.d by J.L.Marks 6 Worship Street Finsbury

A "penny-plain-tuppence-coloured" portrait of Henri Martin, the first modern animal trainer. (From the author's collection.)

Hagenbecks rediscovered the quieter act; and what is more important, presented it for the first time in a large circular cage. They, like Pavlov and the Behaviorists, also gave careful study to the underlying principles of training. But it should always be remembered that to scientists and psychologists training is never more than a means to an end, while to the trainer it is an end in itself.

129

The Bostocks worked along similar lines in England, and Frank Bostock, the Animal King, introduced the practice in America. It was he who summed up the difference between taming and training, saying, "The trained animal is a product of science; the tamed animal is a chimera of the imagination, a forecast of the millenium."

Understanding, based on scientific observation, is the very best basis for training. In the old days a wound inflicted on the tamer was repaid a hundredfold in order to show the wretched animal who was master. It was domination by force, and since the animal quite often came to realize that it possessed more strength than man, it did not always end happily for the tamer. Today an animal who wounds his trainer is very rarely punished, and furthermore the trainer makes every effort not to let the animal see the extent of the damage. This shows an understanding of two principles: the first is that the wound may well have been inflicted in play or by accident, or that even if it was made in anger it is no use judging animals by human standards; and the second is that an animal does not know, and should not be allowed to realize, its comparative power.

In the early days, animal men—and women—were all working in the dark. A few stumbled on the right idea, and even made some attempt to put it into practice, but most had no idea at all. One or two were so frightened that they had to take a stiff drink before entering the cage. They felt, as anybody who comes into contact with animals always feels, that beasts can tell when a man is afraid. Many people think that this comes from a smell exuded by the human which informs the animal of his fear. I am sure that it is derived from a sense of smell, but I am not entirely convinced that animals can reason: "This is Man putting up a protective barrier, like a skunk. What he really wants to do is run away, therefore this is the psychological moment to attack." I am more inclined to think that the animal cannot recognize fear as a smell, but that the smell causes an unconditioned reflex. Many trainers in the old days fortified themselves with the bottle. Although alcohol can give one dutch courage, it also slows down the reflexes, and that puts a trainer in the most dangerous position of all. Some, like Van Amburgh and Carter, died naturally in their beds—Polly Hilton lived to 104—others, like Macarthy (who worked under the name Massarte) and Lucas, were torn to shreds by the beasts they tried to tame, rather than train.

Those who died in the lions' den were not necessarily those who deserved such a fate; a fight amongst the animals themselves might get out of control, or their trainer might slip or fall. The only method of driving off the animals in those days was by using red-hot irons and sharp goads. Today a kitchen chair is used in training, and should that fail to keep the animals sufficiently far away, then a hose is turned on. A jet of water has broken up many a fight between the animals themselves. No one would be so stupid as to spoil the disposition, as well as the looks, of his valuable animals by burning them.

In menageries, animals have always been exhibited and presented in wagons which line the sides of the tent. Instead of the audience encircling the performers, the spectators are here surrounded by the beasts. The type of act that could be seen in the rectangular cage of a menagerie was worked against the back wall of the wagon. The Bostocks were the first to realize that this type of performance was not suitable for the circus ring, and to develop wild animal acts in the round. They did not build the first big cage —that came much later*—but they did open their cages on all sides and drag them into the center of the ring so that the act could be seen from every part of the house.

The size and shape of the cage determines the kind of act that can be presented. Square cages are still occasionally to be found, though they are no longer built on wheels. They are most often used by trainers who have worked the "gaffs" or fairgrounds, and the type of act seen in them is that known as *en férocité*. Walls set at right angles bring leaping, rampaging lions—generally known as bouncers—more easily under control, while at the same time making the act look more exciting.

Though there is only one accepted principle of training, it can be used in two different types of presentation: *en douceur*, or *en pelotage*, as it is more often called in the profession, and *en férocité*. The latter stresses the wildness of the animals and looks more dangerous than it really is, because the animals have been *taught* to snarl and strike out at the trainer. They have even been taught to appear to get out of hand; one of the most spectacular stunts is that in which a lion is trained to hurl itself at the cage door a split second after the trainer has made his exit. The audience is led to suppose that the

---

* It was not until 1888 that the circular cage was first brought into use by the Hagenbecks. Even then small shifting dens were used to bring the lions into the ring. It was Krone who first thought of connecting the beast dens to the big cage with a steel runway or tunnel.

The wild animal den in which lions performed before the invention of the big cage. (From the author's collection.)

trainer has had a narrow escape, little realizing that this happens twice a day in full view of the public throughout the season, and many more times during rehearsal.

Sometimes this type of number is accompanied by shouts, revolver shots and much whip-cracking. Clyde Beatty, who died in 1965, was the greatest exponent of this that I have ever seen. But, even with the *tour de force* that he presented, after one had seen it two or three times it began to pall. The connoisseur looks for more in an act than hullaballoo. It is, after all, a fake. An act *en férocité* may show off more of an animal's natural movements, such as the lightning quick stroke of a lion's forepaw. But the smooth spring of a tiger, or the soft, dangerous rippling run of a panther are equally well seen *en pelotage*.

Henry Thétard, who often presented groups of lions himself, once explained to me the difference between these two types of act from the professional point of view. "Fundamentally," he said, "a number worked *en férocité* is the easier; but the trouble is that it is extremely difficult to do well. The trainer must be a first-class actor. An act presented *en pelotage* is really more dangerous, because the trainer must work so near his animals. The beasts are always on top of him, and should they attack he has little chance of keeping them off. Therefore he must be sure of them."

Lions and tigers usually sit upright on small pedestals hooked to the bars of the cage. In an East German circus I saw an act, presented, I think, by Erhard and Christiane Samel, in which the cats lay stretched out on long pedestals, as indeed they do in the act presented by the Russian Nazarova. They looked much more relaxed than usual, but not bored.

There is a tendency in all cat acts for the tempo to slow down;

and this is more noticeable in a quiet act. Most cats, big or small, are lazy. In the jungle, where food has to be hunted, they are forced to overcome their lethargy in order to live. In a circus, where food is regularly provided, they naturally tend to become lazier still. When a lion or tiger appears sluggish, the easiest way to make the public realize that it is still dangerous is to wave something in front of its face as it sits on its pedestal. It will behave exactly like a pet cat confronted with a piece of string; it will stretch out a paw and try to pat it. When you see a lion crouched on its pedestal trying to knock aside the trainer's whip, it does not necessarily mean that it is going to attack him. In fact, as long as the animal remains on its pedestal the trainer is comparatively safe. But it should always be remembered that at no time is the trainer as safe as you are. At times he could be in grave danger, though you may not notice it.

In *A Showman Looks On*, C.B. Cochran described what happened when he booked Tommy Kayes and his lions to appear with Rosaire's Circus in 1942 for a special matinée before King Peter in aid of the Yugoslav Relief Fund. A ring-boy forgot one of the pedestals, and Tommy had to leave the cage to fetch it. This unsettled the lions, and Tommy momentarily wondered if he could continue the act. Of course he did go on, but afterwards his boots showed some unpleasant-looking claw marks as a result. Cochran thought that he was the only one who had noticed anything wrong. But later he received a letter from a man who had seen all the great trainers—Julius Seeth, Bonavita, Pezon, Sawade and the rest— which said that this was only the second time that he had seen a trainer in real danger. I happened to be at that show, and I went round to ask Tommy what had gone wrong. He told me that the unevenness of the ground had helped to complicate matters. Yet I am sure that most people in the audience had no idea of what was happening.

Besides their natural laziness, or perhaps because of it, lions and tigers are apt to grow sluggish through constipation, and so laxatives sometimes have to be given to keep the animals in good health.

One night at Olympia, Rajah refused to take his meat from the mouth of his trainer, Nicolai. The climax of the act was lost. When the lions returned to their dens, Rajah ate without interest, swallowing his meat whole. This is a sure sign of tummy trouble. A dozen or so incisions were made in a piece of horsemeat, and into each hole Nicolai put a well-known purge. The meat was then soused in castor oil and given to Rajah. The next day he was as lively as a kitten. Yet I would not have been a bit surprised to have heard someone, on seeing Rajah's lassitude, say "That animal must be doped!" The public does not realize that sometimes a trainer's greatest difficulty is to make the lions not less lively but more so. Liveliness, however, should not always be associated with danger—a sluggish liver can affect an animal's temper in the same way as it affects a human being's.

The teeth of carnivorous animals also have to be carefully watched. Pieces of meat get stuck in crevices around the gums and can cause abscesses.

Different animals naturally have different temperaments, and it is difficult to compare the training of one species with that of another. Animal men take more account of individual character than of common characteristics. Generalizations are always dangerous.

One of Frank Bostock's lions had only one fear: a whip, or even a straw, *held in the left hand*. Another whimpered, moaned, snarled and eventually roared in anger whenever a certain tune was played by the band. Knowledge of such things as these is more important to a trainer than the realization that lions are usually clumsy and that it is their clumsiness that adds to the danger, or that all big cats react to weather conditions, so a sultry atmosphere is likely to make them irritable.

Lions will gang up, and when one attacks its trainer the others will probably join in. As Thétard once put it,

> they are peasants with a touch of the wolf about them, and you must treat them as such. Tigers require more diplomacy. They are more catlike. One will attack you while the rest remain aloof; but they will pounce on you from behind, which lions rarely do.

Lions are slower and more deliberate than lionesses, which are easier to manage, yet at the same time more treacherous. Amongst tigers it is the quiet one that should be most carefully watched. Whether lions are more dangerous than tigers is a matter of opinion, but most animal men agree that polar bears are more treacherous than either.

It was Bostock's theory that the larger and stronger the animal the less need it has to use cunning to obtain its food in the jungle, and that the mental faculties of the smaller members of the cat tribe are much sharper. Yet it would be extremely dangerous to suppose that because an animal has cunning its muscles are weak. A jaguar can hurl a weight of one hundred pounds across the ring with a flick of the paw. It is only by living with animals and studying their mental as well as physical makeup that we can learn to understand them. We are not likely to reach any understanding if we attribute human feelings to them. When a group of lions refused to go through their routine because the orchestra would not play, they were not staging a sit-down strike in sympathy with the musicians' union; they were merely showing the trainer that he had conditioned their reflexes so successfully they they were lost without music.

A conditioned reflex, however, does not explain the following story. Once, when Frank Bostock's big cage was set up at Ocala, Florida, the lions behaved in the most extraordinary way. They not only ignored their trainer completely, but got off their pedestals and began sniffing around the arena. They refused to leave the ring, and in the middle of the night they started digging large holes, which is a very strange thing for any lion to do. With great difficulty the arena was cleared, the holes filled and the surface covered with clean sawdust. The next day the lions behaved in the same way again, and it became obvious that they were getting dangerous. The only reason that could be found for their behavior was the fact that the ground had once formed part of a graveyard, and although the human remains had supposedly been taken away, there could have been some bones left. When the tent was moved a short distance, the lions went through their paces in a perfectly normal way. That happened some seventy years ago, but so far nobody has discovered the link between death and the lions' behavior, any more than they have found out why it is that many wild animals seem to sense an impending tragedy, or why domestic animals appear to see ghosts.

Before any wild animals can be taught tricks, the trainer must get to know each one of his troupe intimately; all must be able to recognize their trainer immediately, by his personality, his appearance, his voice and his smell. I knew one trainer who, in spite of working the same act for several years, spent quite a long time each morning before rehearsal simply sitting in the cage with his tigers, talking to them as he mended the lanyard of his whip, or repaired a prop.

With a new group the trainer will first get to know his charges through the bars of the cage. Then, when he thinks the time is ripe, he will go in amongst them, taking an ordinary kitchen chair as his

A "penny-plain-tuppence-coloured" portrait of Isaac Van Amburgh, the famous American trainer. (From the author's collection.)

only means of defense. First he will teach them to sit on their pedestals when he gives them the cue. He will see that possible enemies are kept apart; he will not stand with his back to an animal of doubtful temperament; he will always give himself plenty of room to move around, so that he is not forced into a position with his back against the bars of the cage or hedged in by props. Many trainers prefer animals which have been born in the jungle. They are usually fresher, although F.C. Selous, the famous hunter, said that you could always distinguish the skin of a menagerie lion from that of a wild one because the former was healthier and had a longer and glossier coat. Jungle-born animals are difficult to get nowadays. Most of the animals that are seen in any country have been born there, although they may be billed as "forest-bred." When breeding lions one must be careful not to mate near relations. Inbreeding produces cubs that are susceptible to rickets and other diseases; occasionally it results in mental deficiency. Such animals should not be exhibited. The circus should always present the most magnificent specimens it is possible to find.

The tricks that can be taught lions and tigers are limited in number. The formation of various pyramids, jumping, balancing on a cylinder or a ball which runs in a groove, sitting up, lying down and taking meat from their trainer's mouth form the usual repertoire.

In an effort to provide originality, lions and tigers have been taught to walk a tightrope, or rather a double tightrope of two strands between eighteen inches and two feet apart. I find this act boring, because the animals lose their grace and look most ungainly as they lurch gingerly along the cords. More interesting to watch are those tricks in which lions or tigers have been taught to ride on a horse's or an elephant's back. Clyde Beatty achieved the difficult task of persuading a lion and a tiger to ride side by side on an elephant.

Another trick that cannot be said to come within the ordinary routine is to train a lion to draw a chariot which carries its trainer. But this has lost a little of its freshness, for nearly every great trainer from Carter to Kaden has done it at some time or other. A rarer spectacle today would be the revival of the act in which a lion drives two tigers harnessed to the chariot.

Other ways of obtaining variety are by producing a fast act with "bouncing" lions in a confined space, such as the one worked by Tommy Kayes, which was also seen at the end of the strange and exciting mixture of *férocité* and *pelotage* which Konyot presented. One can also achieve spectacle by sheer weight of numbers. No one has surpassed the grand total of one hundred lions which the unfortunate Captain Schneider presented before his circus was sold up in Naples. But the fact that an act contains spectacle does not mean that it shows great artistry.

The act which gave me most pleasure in the postwar years was Gilbert Houcke's presentation of his tigers. This number, suavely worked *en pelotage,* was a masterpiece of showmanship which brought out the character of the animals as well as their slinking beauty. At one moment the animals, flank to flank, wheeled round to face the trainer as he circled about them, and whenever he dropped to one knee the tigers sank together till their bellies touched the ground. The act had the speed and unity of a liberty routine, which may well have been due to Houcke's previous experience as a horse-trainer. The whole number was a triumph of smooth accomplishment and apparently effortless grace. But when one met Houcke after he had left the ring, one could see the sweat pouring off him and hear his quick breathing, for in reality such an act demands great concentration of effort. In 1961, Daisy, one of his tigers, wounded him so badly that he never completely recovered. A similar silk-smooth routine is now worked by Louis Knie with nine tigers.

Another European trainer who has become a circus superstar in America is Gunther Gebel-Williams, who, like Gilbert Houcke, also trained horses. He was adopted by Carola Althoff who married Harry Williams. Their real daughter, Jeanette, was married to Gunther for a while and has also appeared in the United States. In 1968 Carola Williams sent eighteen elephants, twenty-five horses, nine tigers, fifty pigeons and eleven parrots over to Ringling on a long contract. Gunther was in charge. He made his name presenting a superb group of eighteen tigers, and has since followed this up with leopards.

In Europe Gerd Simoneit had an act in which he caught a black panther called Onyx in his arms. It was part of a mixed group consisting of three lions, three tigers, three leopards, two pumas and Onyx.

The mixed group is an excellent way of bringing originality into an animal act. The number of combinations is almost limitless. One of the most effective collections was an act broken and presented by Alfred Court in which six lions, three polar bears, two black bears, two tigers and two leopards appeared. In the final tableau they all sat up on glass-topped pedestals floodlit from below. Another of this trainer's groups consisted of six leopards, three black panthers, one snow panther, four pumas and a black jaguar. According to Henry Thétard, Court broke and worked five mixed groups such as these—as well as one act of ten lions, another of eight tigers and a third act of black and polar bears—all within a period of fifteen years. Yet just as important to me is the fact that he taught other trainers such as Trubka and Damoo Dhôtre to follow in his footsteps.

Bears have been trained for many centuries, and yet they remain one of the species of animals which humans know least about, for they never show what they are thinking. In 1922 Sir Peter Chalmers Mitchell, FRS, for thirty-two years secretary to the Zoological Society of London, was called to give evidence before a select committee of the House of Commons. There he told the following story which showed how bears were sometimes cruelly treated *outside* the circus. An itinerant bear-leader, who wandered around the streets, was imprisoned for "gross cruelty," and Sir Peter was asked by the police to look after the unfortunate animal. All the time the bear remained in the London Zoo, in spite of the kindest treatment, it sulked and whined and became so thoroughly miserable that nothing could be done with it. When the trainer had served his sentence he went into the bear's cage, whereupon the bear went into transports of delight, licked his face and showed every sign of affection. It was obvious that if the trainer had not returned the bear would have pined to death. Street performers such as this were, more often than not, Gypsies, who usually managed to remain anonymous. Most circus trainers, particularly in Great Britain, loathe the Gypsy and any cruelty which he may employ. There is little chance of a circus trainer in England being confused with a Gypsy except in the minds of indiscriminating fanatics.

During the Middle Ages bears were frequently seen on the fairgrounds, and until quite recently they made an occasional appearance in London streets, where they were made to shuffle around in a pathetic lumbering dance. In the circus their best-known trick is that in which they ride a bicycle, but unless one has an act as good as Edith Crocker's—and many think hers the best bear act there has ever been—bears on bicycles can be rather dreary, though it does at least reveal their sense of balance.

Today Russians dominate the bear trainers. In 1975, we in the West saw Nelly and Rustam Kasseef with their football bears. Since then I have heard that Boudnidsky and a bear juggle on skates, and Mayorov's bears play ice hockey. The greatest name among Russian bear trainers is Valentin Ivanovitch Filatov, who presents a whole bear circus. And yet, excellent as all this may be, I find that after fifteen minutes or so of any animal act, I want to see something different.

Polar bears appeared early in the second half of the last century. By 1885 they could be seen in most traveling menageries. The most spectacular polar bears ever seen were probably the troupe of seventy which William Hagenbeck trained in 1895. Their tricks usually include such childlike thrills as seesaws and slides, and when seeing them at play it is difficult to realize that they can become dangerous, especially in rut. Some of the most beautiful specimens seen in England were those trained by Adolph Cossmy. Their good looks were largely due to the care and attention he gave them, even washing their coats with soap. It was just this that cost him his life. He stepped on the soap, slipped, and in falling inadvertently hit a bear on the muzzle. That was all that was necessary to bring about his most horrible death, for he was ripped to pieces in a few seconds, on 22 August 1930. A polar bear will not stop to reason that the cuff he has received was an accident, or remember the pleasure he gained from the shampoo. If he is suddenly hit his instinct is to strike back.

With wild animals the most dangerous position in which a trainer can find himself is on the ground. As long as he is on his feet he has a chance of being able to control even the most awkward situation. But once he has fallen this drops to zero.

The time it takes to break an animal group depends on the species, on the age of the animals, and on the tricks it is proposed to teach them. Big cats should start their training when they are fifteen to twenty months old. They are then able to concentrate, without yet being perturbed by questions of sex. It is possible to train them when they are older, but Togare once told me that he much preferred them to be under four years old. Sex naturally plays a great part in an animal's life, and a ten-year-old lioness or an eight-year-old tigress seems to experience the menopause in very much the same way as humans.

Once training has started it should be continued with regularity, then at the end of four months or so you may possibly have something to show for your patience. But no wise trainer will stop or even slow down at this juncture. A routine should be drawn up and strictly adhered to. The animals should always be fed at the same time for six days a week, and on the seventh they should fast.

The elephant is the only member of the animal kingdom, except the whale, to have a bigger brain than man; though if one were to compare the ratio of brain size to the size of the rest of the body, man would naturally be the winner. In spite of their huge bulk, the quickness with which elephants pick up a new trick will frequently amaze a trainer. Carl Hagenbeck had an elephant which in one day learned to lie down and sit up at a word of command. Within four weeks it was sitting at table ringing for a monkey-waiter, eating off a plate and drinking out of a bottle; "in short," says Hagenbeck, with almost justifiable exaggeration, "dining in the most orthodox human fashion."

During the greater part of the last century elephants were usually shown either singly or, very occasionally, in pairs. The first troupe to be presented was trained by the Englishman John Cooper, better known as a lion-tamer, who trained six elephants to appear with Myer's Circus. By 1876 he had increased the group to eight. Their routine included dancing the waltz and hornpipe. By 1882, when Myer's show was sold up, the number had fallen to four, and they fetched no more than one thousand guineas the lot.

Elephants seem to appreciate human behavior in a remarkable way, and it is not difficult to understand why such typical tricks as playing cricket and shaving so often form part of their routine. The animals most often seen in the ring are females—though in America they are always called "bulls"—of the Indian variety. Hagenbeck first succeeded in training African elephants, and today Gunther Gebel-Williams has two in his troupe, but comparatively few have appeared in the circus ring.

Darwin found that once an elephant was mated it often remained faithful to its partner and seemed to enjoy bringing up a family. This does not mean that they are "almost human." Although they often show remarkable cunning, particularly in escaping their tethers, and in spite of the fact that some appear to enjoy getting drunk, elephants should not be endowed with human attributes or feelings, any more than any other animal.

Their intelligent, humorous expressions and endearing ways have made them favorites with circus audiences all over the world. But nowhere do they form such a great attraction as they do in the United States, where they not only perform but are used to help in the build-up and pull-down of the big top. Although a good elephant act can show all the delicacy and precision seen in a troupe of Tiller girls, the beasts themselves can be extremely dangerous. Queen, alias Empress, alias Mary, killed nine human beings during her circus career.

Lockhart and Power are names which will always be associated with these animals. One of the most pleasing acts I have ever seen was presented by Madame Fischer at Olympia in 1950. From the curling tops of their ears you could tell that the animals were no longer young, but the sureness and deliberation with which they rolled a globe and walked along a line of bottles accentuated their character. The trainer stood back at the ring doors and the elephants did everything perfectly—but in their own time. An act which I watched on the Continent in which four elephants were prodded into position by four men *and* the trainer was probably the least impressive I have ever seen.

Schreiber's elephants hit the headlines in Germany about thirty years ago when the trainer stood on one end of a teeterboard and an elephant slammed its foot down on the other, thereby catapulting the man through the air in a somersault to land on the head of an elephant bearer. Actually this elephant was making the same movement as those which Rossi trained at the beginning of this century, when they struck the keyboard of a specially constructed organ. But the sight of a man being shot into the air is much more spectacular than a whole troupe of elephant organists. Even that trick has now been surpassed by Louis and Frank Knie with their partner Nikko Dobritch. Here the top-mounter is shot by the elephant to the shoulders of a middleman who stands on the elephant bearer's head.

Schreiber's Elephants. (Drawing by John Skeaping.)

Animals which are taught to "play" musical instruments seem to appeal to the public, and among the best-loved—second only to the elephant, perhaps—is the seal. Seals and sea lions are latecomers to the circus, and the credit for first training seals must be given to Captain Joseph Woodward. When this Englishman died in 1946, aged seventy-three, a memorial tablet was erected on which he was described as the "discoverer of the latent equilibrist power given to the sea-lion species." The Woodward family grave at Ramsgate is marked by a symbolic monument, the frieze of which depicts seals and sea lions working a circus act—and also helping to detect submarines in World War I.

Hagenbeck admits that Woodward was the first to train this type of animal, but in his book *Beasts and Men* (London: Longmans, Green & Co., 1912) he points out that Billy and Charlie Judge were the first to show "what really might be done with sea-lions."

Charlie Judge, who married Ida Sanger, afterwards became more famous as a trainer of chimpanzees. And although Billy Judge trained many different kinds of animals from cockatoos to lions, it was he who really developed the seal and sea lion acts, both at Hagenbeck's and afterwards on his own.

Sometimes calling himself Nansen or Alaska, Judge toured the world with his seals and had great success both in the circus ring and on the music hall stage. In England his act was better known on the halls, for although he knew practically every circus on the Continent, he only worked in four circuses in England.

Nansen's "Dressirte Thiergruppe" and Alaska's "Educated Seals and Sea-lions, including the only trained Walrus in the World," were not the only acts in which Billy Judge was interested. He also had a lot to do with "Mademoiselle Juliette et ses Phoques Savants," for Mlle. Juliette was really Madame Judge, whom Billy first met during a Battle of Flowers at Nice, where she was working as a nursery governess. Soon after they were married she found four baby seals for sale. She persuaded Billy to buy them, and reared them herself with a baby's feeding bottle.

Later Billy took to working with only one seal: Jackie and also the lovable Bichette were both starred at different times. In his contract with music hall proprietors Billy Judge always had special clauses inserted:

> The sea-lion is to be kept in the theatre and the management to provide water and drainage. The management to provide 17 lbs. best quality fish daily for feeding the sea-lion.
>
> The species of fish must be changed regularly, and salmon must be included in the meals at least twice a week.
>
> A special pool is to be built. . . .

Billy Judge was the first trainer to get one animal to balance another. One day he told me how it all started. He merely wanted to get a pet dog through the customs without having to send it into quarantine. The best way to accomplish this was to incorporate the animal in the act. For some time he could not see how this could be done. Then he had an idea: the champagne bottle which the seal balanced on its nose would suddenly break open and out would jump the dog. A *papier-maché* bottle big enough to take the dog was given to the seal to balance. When the seal managed to keep the bottle upright, it was gradually filled with sand until the weight equaled that of the dog. The dog then replaced the sand. Another original trick was added to Billy Judge's repertoire—and the dog escaped quarantine.

Since then the trainer Roland has taught one seal to lie down and balance another on its flippers.

The movements made by a seal in catching a ball on its nose, throwing it to a partner and catching another, are completely natural. If you watch a seal in a zoo you will see it catch a fish, first horizontally, then throw it up in the air so that it comes down vertically into its mouth.

Another act which shows the natural movements of an animal without any elaboration is that of the boxing kangaroo. Yet this act always seems too simple. It has no form or pattern. I have never seen this animal do anything in a circus ring but box; perhaps one day a trainer will think of showing off its ability to jump, just as seals demonstrate their powers of balance.

The search for originality has produced some very strange acts, and one of the strangest must surely have been that of Professor Langeneck and his ten performing eagles. These fierce birds fired off pistols, rolled cylinders and rode miniature bicycles, bringing a sum of forty pounds into their trainer's pocket every week at the turn of the century.

In the 1890s the wild animal business began to boom, and it was not long before sales were being held at Aix-la-Chapelle, Leipzig, Rotterdam, Hamburg, and Marseilles. In England, Jamrach, Hamlyn and Rice in London and Cross in Liverpool supplied animals to circuses all over the world.

In 1897 you could buy polar bears for £30–35 untrained, and £100 when trained. In France just before World War II, a cub cost 8,000 francs untrained, and by 1946 the price had risen to 100,000 francs. For a whole act of five lions, three tigers, one leopard, two bears and four boarhounds, all properties, one central cage and two

The reverse side of a hand-bill for Astley's in 1786 showing the tricks performed by General Jackoo, a monkey. (From the author's collection.)

new wagons, Hagenbeck was asking £2,730 in the 1890s.

When I was writing the chapter on training domestic animals, I had half a mind to include monkeys. They seem so human that I hesitated for some time before deciding to include them with wild animals. Their history, like that of the bears, is a long one, and monkey theatres have been popular on the Continent for centuries. At one time they were adopted as household pets, and in France the phrase *de payer en monnaie de singe* dates back to the reign of St. Louis, when a tax was imposed on all monkeys entering Paris, except those belonging to showmen, and these had merely to gambol in front of a tax collector to prove their authenticity.

As with bears, some species make better performers than others, but before long we may see monkeys which have hitherto been considered quite unsuitable appearing in the ring. It is only during the last eighty years or so—a period which coincides with the rise of sympathetic treatment and scientific training—that chimpanzees have been trained, yet these animals provide the most successful of all monkey acts.

Knie's chimpanzees, presented by Leon Smith (an Englishman who lived so long abroad that he could hardly speak his native tongue), brought the house down at Olympia in 1948. Reuben Castang's chimps, Max, Maurice and Akka, became Hollywood film stars, while those belonging to Charlie Judge were deservedly the most popular that England has produced. There have been other acts equally famous, and all have aroused a feeling of the warmest sympathy from the audience. The chimpanzee's love of applause, in which he often takes part, and his sorrow—which sometimes seems more like shame—at being scolded make him appear more human than any other kind of monkey.

As I have said before, monkeys seem to me the only animals in the circus which should be dressed in human clothes. Trousers and skirts look natural on them, and their gestures and grimaces persuade me that they like copying human beings. Flourens, a famous French physiologist of the last century, once went to the Jardin des Plantes in Paris with an aged acquaintance. One of the orangutans could not take his eyes off this old man. Just as Flourens's friend was leaving, the animal came up and took his walking stick. Leaning heavily upon it, with body bent and one arm held in the small of his back, the ape shuffled round in a perfect imitation of the old man, then, straightening up, handed him back his cane.

We have wandered some way from the big cage. Elephants, sea

lions, brown bears and monkeys are never presented behind bars. But the monkey imitating a man reminds me that in the circus men sometimes dress up as monkeys. Natal gave a very clever impersonation of a monkey. Such an act as his, performed high above our heads, can provide an admirable means of distracting the audience while the cage is being dismantled.

X

AERIAL ACTS

"My Lords, Ladies and Gentlemen! Michael of the Flying Angelos will now attempt the most daring feat ever presented in the history of the circus—a triple somersault from the bar of his flying trapeze to the hands of his partner! Ladies and Gentlemen, all eyes on Michael Angelo! I thank you."

The ringmaster retires, the slow waltz dies away, and the side-drums begin to roll softly. Way up above our heads the flyer sets up the extra high perch.* The catcher dusts his hands with powdered rosin and lowers himself into position, head downwards, his knees behind the bar and his hocks round the outside of the supporting ropes. From far away you hear a voice—a rather lonely voice—call "Prêt!" and almost before the answering "Hup!" we see the flyer grasp his trapeze and swing out from the narrow platform. At the top of the arc he lets go; over, over and over he turns, then hands meet wrists in a double grip and a great surge of applause envelops the performers.

---

* The small platform from which flights are made and to which the flyer returns is called a perch. For a triple, a higher swing is needed and so a narrow plank is fixed above the ordinary platform. This type of perch has nothing to do with the perch act.

In place of Michael Angelo read Ernie Clarke, Alfredo Codona, Arturo Concello, Don Martinez, Tito Gaona or any other name from that select band of aerialists—less than thirty strong—who have turned the triple somersault as a part of their trapeze act. The flying trapeze must count as the most romantic number in the circus. It has inspired many writers and quite a few film producers; yet I find a discovery made by Pierre Couderc some fifteen years ago more romantic than any novel or film. Circus historians and people in the profession had always believed that the first man to turn a triple from the bar of his trapeze to the hands of his catcher was Ernie Clarke, a cousin of John Frederick, the great jockey rider. He was performing the trick regularly in 1910. After him came Alfredo Codona, who, as even Clarke admitted, had more style. But the contents of an old trunk, hidden away in an attic, provided what to many is indisputable proof that a young girl of sixteen had regularly achieved this remarkable feat before the end of the last century.

The trunk belonged to Nellie Jordan. The Flying Jordans were an American act of great ability who traveled all over the world. In Russia they engaged a young girl called Lena as an apprentice. That trunk, full of photos, programmes and newspaper cuttings, revealed that Lena had turned the triple in 1897. Full descriptions appeared in newspapers as far apart as the *Johannesburg Times* and the *Sydney Mail*. Some may not believe these reports. It is possible that the newspaper accounts did exaggerate, but Pierre Couderc was a trapeze artiste himself and a man of great integrity, so I think the story of Lena is probably true.

Actually, Ernie Clarke performed the quadruple on a number of occasions in 1915, but only at rehearsal. Today, Don Martinez, who regularly turns a three-and-a-half, has also achieved this, but again only during rehearsal. Tony Steele, Vicente Ibarra and his brother Ignacio can all turn three-and-a-half somersaults, and Tito Gaona, who performs the triple blindfold, has often attempted the quadruple in front of the public.

Alfredo Codona was one of the greatest trapeze artistes, for he had the surest sense of style. Every one of his passes was exquisitely turned and some of them were more beautiful—though not more dangerous—than the "triple from bar to catcher."

It is the movement of the flyer after leaving the bar of his trapeze and before landing safely in the hands of his catcher which distinguishes a trapeze artiste. A really great performer should give one all the aesthetic pleasure that one gets from the lithe grace of a ballet dancer. Added to this there is the excitement of watching people work at a great height, the sense of birdlike freedom and the fascination of seeing the human figure in a new perspective. Of all the acts that can be presented in a circus it is the most satisfying, so let us study it in more detail. The flying trapeze was unknown 150 years ago. It was invented by a Frenchman named Léotard, and the singlet worn by trapeze artistes is called a léotard to this day. In the 1850s Léotard's father kept a gymnasium and swimming bath in Toulouse. Brought up in these surroundings, the boy became an excellent acrobat. One day after a workout in the gym he decided to have a swim. As he stood on the brink of the pool he noticed the cords which served to open and close the ventilators in the roof. He must have seen them a hundred times before, but this time they gave him a new idea. If he joined each pair with a wooden baton he could swing out, and if he fell he would only get a wetting.

This story was told me by the great circophile, A.C. McLachlan, who had heard it from Ted and Taff Volta—themselves exceptional aerialists—who in their turn had heard it from the director of Léotard's Gymnasium in Toulouse, fifteen years after young Léotard had first thought it out.

In the winter of 1859 Léotard arrived in Paris and appeared at the Cirque Napoleon. He became such a furor that everything from cravats to peaches had to be *à la Léotard*. Gradually the number of trapezes he used was increased until on one of his visits to Cremorne Pleasure Gardens in London he used five in a line, turning single somersaults from trapeze to trapeze. His success lasted ten years, then he suddenly died of smallpox while appearing in Spain.

Today trapeze acts can be divided into low trapeze, such as that used by Charlie Rivels in his comedy act, and high trapeze. They can also be divided into the categories of fixed or flying. Flying trapeze acts can be subdivided into bar-to-bar and bar-to-catcher.

In a bar-to-bar routine the flyer leaves one trapeze to catch another which has been released at the right moment by his partner, who stands on the opposite perch. In the bar-to-catcher routine the partner himself hangs from the second trapeze and catches the flyer. The catcher, by accelerating or retarding his movements, can counteract to some extent an error made by the flyer. In the bar-to-bar act it is up to the flyer alone. If he misjudges his distance he may get the twelve-pound bar swinging into his face and knocking out his teeth, or he may meet it wrong causing a wrench on impact, or, of course, he may miss it altogether.

Although it is less spectacular, some purists prefer this type of act because it is more difficult. The greater variety of releases, evolutions in mid-flight and catches which can be introduced when a catcher is used makes the bar-to-catcher routine a better spectacle. No one has turned more than a double somersault from bar-to-bar in public, and only eleven have regularly done that.

A straight pass. (Drawing by John Skeaping.)
A pirouette pass. (Drawing by John Skeaping.)

Normally a flyer hangs from his trapeze by his hands with his face to his objective and lets go at the top of the swing. He can also have his back to his goal, in which case he must turn a half pirouette in the air to face the catcher or second trapeze; or he can hang by his knee joints with his back to the direction of flight and let go by simply straightening his legs. Or again he can hang by his insteps. Lying across the trapeze with his hands gripping the bar, he can swing feet foremost and, on reaching maximum height, pivot about the bar by throwing the top half of his body down and his legs up, and then let go. This is known as the *passe en planche* or plange pass. In all these movements the body lies *under* the trapeze at the moment of release, but the flyer can also pass *over* the bar. Léotard used to stand with his feet on the bar and leap to the next trapeze, but since his day flyers have stood on their hands on the

A hock pass. (Drawing by John Skeaping.)
A plange pass. (Drawing by John Skeaping.)

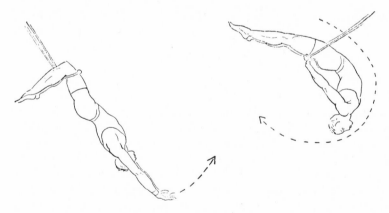

bar and plunged head foremost toward their catchers in the movement known as the *passe par dessus*.

While in midair the flyer can turn about his vertical axis in a pirouette, about his horizontal axis in a somersault, or by combining both movements perform a twister. If only one somersault is made you will probably see what is known as a lay-out back, that is a back somersault in which the body and legs are fully stretched and the back slightly arched. If more than one turn is to be made the flyer will hug his knees to his chest in the balled-up position.

The catcher has only two ways of holding his partner, by the wrist or by the leg. The leg catch is used when the flyer throws a one-and-a-half, a two-and-a-half or a three-and-a-half somersault. The way in which a flyer returns to his own trapeze depends to a large extent on the catcher, for he can give extra impetus. From these basic movements the routine is built up.

In America Ernie Clarke was announced as throwing a double somersault and twister. The movement was actually a double somersault and pirouette, which is much more difficult. In his book *Big Top Rhythms* (New York: Willett, Clarke & Co., 1937), Irving K. Pond explains that since the twister consists of turning the body in

Passe par dessus. (Drawing by John Skeaping.)

a somersault about its short axis at the same time as twisting it about its long axis, it is really one movement, although a complicated one. The double and pirouette, however, should be two separate and distinct movements, each turned around a different axis, yet they must both be made in the short space of time between leaving the bar of the trapeze and being caught by the partner.

In *Le Cirque dans l'Univers*, that splendidly named journal of the Club du Cirque, Alfred Court wrote that he had only seen the double and pirouette performed by three people. Each one did it differently. Clarke turned two somersaults balled up, and as he straightened out gave a sudden jerk with his shoulder to send his body into a pirouette. Rainat first turned a combined somersault and pirouette—a full twister—then turned his second somersault balled up in a bar-to-bar act. Concello turned a back somersault combined with a half-pirouette—i.e., a back half-twister—followed by a forward half-twister. But however it is made, the double and pirouette is an exceptional movement. Ernest Clarke fell into the net two thousand times before he accomplished it. Once he had succeeded, he and his partner rehearsed for three and a half years before presenting the act in public. There is another point of finesse which was well worth noting in this act. On the return flight Ernest Clarke caught the bar on its natural swing, which meant that there was no third partner holding it and letting it go at the right moment.

There are usually three or four performers in a flying trapeze act, one catcher and two or three flyers. Sometimes the flyers cross in midair, and one of the most beautiful movements is that in which one flyer, having made his first pass, returns to his trapeze as the second flyer leaves it in a *passe par dessus*. For an instant both artistes

A single somersault pass. (Drawing by John Skeaping.)

are seen flying through the air in opposite directions, one above the other. No one has surpassed the Majestic Leap of the Flying Melzoras in this movement. Here the first flyer returns to the flyer's bar under the second flyer, who has just left it to turn a back somersault to the catcher. According to Pierre Couderc, this has never been achieved by anyone else.

The Codonas formed what was perhaps the greatest flying trapeze troupe of all time. In the original act the male members, Alfredo and Lalo Codona, were Mexicans and the girl, Vera Bruce, was an American. She, it is said, was always in love with Alfredo the flyer, but he was unaware of this, and in 1928 he married Lillian Leitzel.

Leitzel had an act of her own. She gave a brilliant performance on the Roman rings, though she was better known as the girl who threw a hundred giant arm planges, swinging her outstretched body round her wrist, while she hung at the end of a rope fifty feet up in the air. This left her with a permanently open wound on her wrist.

Whenever he could, Alfredo would stand at the ring doors during her act, so that if there was an accident he could break her fall. But in 1931 she went to Copenhagen to work at the Valencia Music Hall, while he was touring Germany, throwing his blindfold forward somersault from bar to catcher. So, when on 13 February fatigue in the metal caused a part of Leitzel's apparatus to snap, he was not there to break her fall and she was killed.

Two years later Alfredo married Vera Bruce, but this marriage also ended in tragedy. After he had strained a muscle and found that he could no longer fly, he started to drink and eventually Vera Bruce asked for a divorce. A final attempt at reconciliation was made in a lawyer's office; when this failed, Alfredo Codona drew a pistol and shot first Vera and then himself.

Lalo Codona, the catcher, continued working with Clayton Behee and Rose Sullivan as flying partners. But after a time the strain of catching began to tell. On 12 November 1936 he wrenched his muscles and knew that the act known as the Flying Codonas was finished.

No one has equalled Alfredo Codona in style or sincerity. In spite of the fact that the routine of this act was designed as a crescendo, each single movement was so perfectly formed and executed that it was completely satisfying in itself. The first straight somersault from bar to catcher and the pirouette-and-a-half return were made with just as much beauty as the long-awaited triple and its two-and-a-half pirouette return.

A double pass. (Drawing by John Skeaping.)

Next to the Codonas one must place the exceptionally fine act of the Concellos, in which the girl justifiably played a greater part in the routine than in most other troupes. Antoinette Concello was one of the very few girls to throw a triple at that time, but it has since been achieved by Terry Lemus and Chetta Jarz. Terry Caravetta—her name before she married Ron Lemus—comes from Florida and started her career early. She turned her first triple when she was thirteen years old. With her sister Kandy, the twins Marleen and Maureen and brother Jim, the Flying Caravettas were the only teenage trapeze act in which all the flyers were girls. After she married, Terry and her husband formed the Flying Terrels. In 1976 Ron Lemus was killed in an air crash at Las Vegas, and since then other members of the Caravetta family have joined the act. The Flying Terrels appeared at Queen Elizabeth II's Silver Jubilee celebrations at Windsor in May 1977, where Terry turned her triple at the second attempt. Six months later they won the "championship" held on Clapham Common, London, and deservedly so, for this is an act in which an excellent routine is presented with great personality and charm.

In working on a flying trapeze care must be taken to examine the level of the ground beneath. Even if the apparatus is dead level in the air, the slope of the ground below exerts an influence on the swing. As Cleveland Moffett wrote in *Careers of Danger and Daring* (New York: D. Appleton-Century Co., 1901), "the swing of an acrobat's body will be accelerated over a downward slope or

The grip used by all trapeze artists. (Drawing by John Skeaping.)

retarded over an upward one." This curious fact has been checked with many of the great trapezists, including the Codonas, and all have confirmed not only its existence but also its danger.

Although in recent years flyers from Italy and the Americas have dominated trapeze acts, for a long time the great flying trapeze acts were French. Léotard started it, and the Rainats, the Alexes, the Algevols and others continued the tradition.

The double from bar to bar was first turned by Alex, secondly by a man called Evans who killed himself doing it, and then by Rainat who regularly accomplished this feat. This great aerialist died in 1957 at the age of eighty.

The French tradition was maintained by the Zemgannos (led by a journalist who took to the trapeze and was the first to make spectacular use of fluorescent lighting), the Méteors and the particularly fine troupe of Pierre Alizé. The Alizés worked a straight routine reminiscent of the Codonas and the Concellos, but it had a definite style of its own, and the catcher was one of the finest ever to appear.

The Condoras are said to have achieved the triple, but I do not think this was a regular feature of their act. They were content with a two-and-a-half somersault to a catcher who swung in a rigid frame, not a trapeze bar swinging on wires. This is too reminiscent of a pendulum, giving a clockwork effect to a movement which should flow freely. The little sideways tilt when flyer and catcher meet adds to the spectacle. With a rigid frame this is lost.

So far, the artistes I have mentioned perform on the *flying* trapeze. The French have also excelled on the *fixed* trapeze. In this act only one trapeze is usually seen, but when two are used they are not placed facing each other, but close together, side by side. Although the bars may swing, there is no flying. Those acts which are introduced to entertain the public while the big cage is being dismantled are often fixed trapeze numbers. For the most part the routine consists of various balancing feats, such as the head stand and hanging by the instep, the heel or the neck. These holds are alternated with turns and twists made about the ropes and the bar, and often for the climax the artiste sitting on the bar will make the trapeze swing higher and higher until suddenly she will fling herself backwards so that for a moment it looks as if she is falling, until instep and heel are locked in the angle formed by the bar and the supporting ropes. I once tried this trick myself. By flinging one's legs out sideways as one throws the body backward one brings the inside of each foot down the outside of the ropes until the heels hit the bar. It was not difficult, but it was painful, for the ropes scraped all the skin off my shins.

Barbette worked a technically excellent act with a surprise ending; few people seeing it for the first time realized that the graceful girl was really a man until he whipped off his wig when taking his call. He featured a single hock-catch and became a great success in France and America, where after retiring he became an aerial director. He died in Texas in 1973, aged seventy-three. Luisita Leers, whose routine included a remarkable neck-hold, Raymonde Marcoud, Maryse Begary and Mireillys were all excellent in this type of work. Today, Elvin Bale surpasses them all. His dive forward at the top of a giant swing to catch the bar in a heel-hold earned him the highest award—the Golden Clown—at the Third International Circus Festival at Monte Carlo in 1976.

The most beautiful act on the fixed trapeze that I have ever seen was that of the Geraldos. Madeleine and René Rousseau—for that is their real name—had such a love of their calling that they never ceased trying to perfect their technique, although to most of us it seemed already perfect. Theirs is the only act in which sheer beauty of movement has made me forget danger, and their act was very dangerous. Yet, when I first knew them, they would not use a net because, as they explained,

> If we did, there would be nothing to stop every Tom, Dick and Harry copying our act. They might not have our technique; with a net there would be no need for that. They would be cheaper to book and some people might think we had rivals. We must always be above competition. We must be technically perfect.

Sixty feet above the ring Madeleine edged back until the bar of her trapeze came half-way down her thighs. She stretched her legs apart, while René swung down from his trapeze alongside and seized the bar on which she was sitting. He swung back then forward and let go. Almost simultaneously he threw up his legs, his feet passed just inside those of his partner, and as his body fell he was left hanging, his instep hooked in Madeleine's. That was only one of the movements in a nine-minute act.

I came to know the Geraldos well when they appeared at Harringay in 1947 and 1948, and I found that their whole lives were dedicated to their work. Neither of them smoked nor drank spirits, though they liked red wine, and both slept for ten hours each night if possible. At that time René was sleeping badly and Madeleine was having occasional nightmares. Their one fear was cramp, and they would spend twenty minutes or more limbering up before each performance. Paul Boyle, the *Daily Graphic* columnist, got them checked over by a Harley Street specialist. He found that after the act René's pulse only increased from 72 to 78, while that of an ordinary person would have jumped to over 100. Blood pressure showed 160/110 compared with an average of 120/90. Reflexes were twice as quick as normal, and the muscles in Madeleine's feet were stronger than those in the doctor's hands.

After Harringay they went to work in America. It was their first visit to the United States, and in their early letters they described the strangeness of the New World in which they found themselves. "Time goes so crazily quickly here," they wrote,

> and the climate is tiring. . . . But our debut at Ringling's at Madison Square Garden was most successful and the people in the company are charming. . . . It's terribly hard work and we wonder what it will be like when we start tenting.

Soon after they started tenting they came to grief. It is difficult to say exactly how it happened. With a big circus, like Ringling's, one-day stands were not uncommon, which meant that the build-up of the tent had to be finished during the first performance and the pull-down started during the second. The audience is bound to react to this sense of restlessness; and the hawking of popcorn, programmes and pink lemonade tended to add to the confusion. Maybe this affected the Geraldos. Accidents have been caused by less: a blinding flash from a roving spotlight as its beam strikes the chromium surface of some prop, or a sudden cry, or just perspiration, any one of these things may prove fatal. Anyhow, the Geraldos fell, on 4 June 1949, in Baltimore, and why they were not killed remains a mystery. Looking back they put their chances at ninety-nine to one.

For eight weeks they lay in plaster cocoons. Stretched out on her stomach, Madeleine wrote me another letter:

> We fell, head first, hand-in-hand, from a height of fifteen metres. The extraordinary thing was that no-one uttered a cry, no-one stood up. And some of those who saw it happen said that we fell with such suppleness that many thought it was part of the act. Some even said, "It's lucky you rehearse those

falls, otherwise you might have been killed." Did you ever hear such an idiotic remark?

Her letter ended:

The doctor assures us that in 1950 we can work again just as before. Mercifully our courage has not been broken.

Nobody who knew the kind of injuries that could result from a fall of fifty feet thought they would ever work again. Yet they were back in the bill in 1950, though they were forced to use a net.

Most aerialists prefer to dispense with this precaution, not only for the reason given by the Geraldos, but because a net does not necessarily make an act safe. Ernie Lane of the Flying Wards was killed by falling into one when he was twenty-two years old; Genesio Amadori was twenty-five when he landed badly in the net and died shortly after. Some share the view of the Great Lothar, who once said, "If you force nets on aerialists, why not muzzle tigers?"

There is another safety device—the lunge, obligatory in the Soviet Union. Opinions differ on its merits. Many think that it denigrates the really fine accomplishments of the artistes. An audience can easily forget that a net is stretched below, but the lunge attached to the performer can usually be seen all the time.

Occasionally a number of ropes lead down to one long bar. The Five Varias appeared on a trapeze like this at Harringay in 1950. These girls worked together with amazing precision, and the crispness of their routine reminded one so much of Ida May's Midship Girls that I was not surprised to learn that the producer had appeared with this famous troupe.

Sometimes a ladder is used in conjunction with a fixed trapeze. It is laid across the bar like a seesaw, and the weight of two artistes performing at one end is counterbalanced by a third partner at the other. The Norbertys excelled at this, but while I admired their style, I could not help thinking that apparatus of a simpler design would give a greater effect of purely human achievement. Take this one step further and you have a tower in the middle of the ring with a beam balanced across it, with a motorcycle at the lower end and a trapeze at the higher. As the machine is driven around, the trapeze revolves over the ring fence. To my mind this is even more clumsy than an airplane circling over the sawdust, with a trapeze or perch hanging from its fuselage. Since it made its first circus appearance during World War I, this has been copied many times, the aircraft becoming a moon-rocket in the latest version. I find all such contrivances distract one's attention from the trapeze itself. It is a beautiful piece of apparatus, and needs no dressing up.

Some of the holds and balances made on a fixed trapeze can be performed with a fixed cradle, which, since it does not swing, provides a more rigid support. The bearer hangs head down with his hocks over one bar and his insteps under a second. He either grips the wrists of his partner or sometimes he holds two short ropes which end in rings or a bar on which his partner performs. At other times he uses his teeth to support his partner while the latter spins round like a top. But such acts are rarely so satisfying to watch as those in which the routine consists of planges and the more orthodox holds and balances. The Trio Dax and the Clerans used a cradle, and this type of act, presented without a net, can be almost as dangerous as the fixed trapeze. Charlie Clerans was killed this way in 1946.

If two cradles are set facing each other some fifteen feet apart, then one bearer can throw a flyer across the gap to another. This is called a casting act. The bearer becomes alternately a caster and a catcher. The strength and skill of such performers enables the flyer to make the most complicated movements in the air. I have even heard it said that the triple back somersault and half-twister have been accomplished this way, and this is an even more difficult pass than any of those achieved on the flying trapeze. Such tricks, however, require two casters to hurl the flyer high and far enough away. Yet this type of act can never be as spectacular as the flying trapeze because the radius of the arc a man can describe when hanging by his knees cannot be compared with the magnificent sweep of the trapeze.

Ropes can be used by aerialists in two ways, either stretched horizontally or hanging vertically. The routine which can be performed at the top of a vertical rope is limited and the artistes are usually women, for they best bring grace, charm and sex appeal into the act and so enhance its attraction. They are known as web acts in the United States, where a number of girls on individual ropes are introduced as an aerial *corps de ballet*. Antoinette Concello, after she had stopped performing on the flying trapeze, remained a celebrity as a producer of such spectacles for Ringling Bros. and Barnum & Bailey. There have also been solo acts of remarkable talent. Chrysis de la Grange, a French typist who learned her technique from an aerialist husband, became an excellent performer with a great sense of style. And yet, while watching her, I

162

found that I got just as much pleasure in watching her ascend and descend the rope as I did from her tricks at the top. Ropes are often used to climb up to a trapeze or cradle, and this has perhaps made it a means to an end and not an end itself. An amazing sense of muscular control is shown by the artiste who climbs either up or down slowly, hand over hand, with the legs and feet outstretched at right angles to the body. Another method of descent, which, although it requires considerably less effort, is pretty to watch, is achieved by the performer winding the rope round one leg and coming down to earth in a slow spiral called in France a *descente en ange*.

Of course the best known act in which a rope is used is the tightrope. The Greeks performed many tricks on ropes stretched sometimes horizontally and sometimes at an angle. They called the performers *oribates, neurobates,* and *schoenobates* according to the type of act. The Romans called them *funambulari,* which gives us the origin of the contemporary French word *funambule.* In the sixteenth century a performer slid head first down a rope stretched at a steep angle at the coronation of Edward VI and also at the festivities to welcome Philip of Spain a little later. Antony of Sceau imitated a drunken man on the tightrope in the reign of Louis XIV. Le Petit Diable—the first of the Paulos—lured all Paris to his performances at Nicolet's long before wire replaced rope and Blondin cooked an omelette high above Niagara. Today you will still find performers imitating drunks, sliding down ropes and treading the high wire as lightly as did their long line of predecessors. The Wallendas were not content with riding a bicycle along the wire; they linked two riders together with a steel bar on which was balanced a chair. On this chair stood a man and on his shoulders stood a girl. Even more spectacular, and to my mind more beautiful, was their famous pyramid of seven, which has never been equaled. Four men walked along the wire, linked in pairs by bars hooked over their shoulders. On each of the two bars stood a middleman. These were also linked in the same way. On their bar a girl top-mounter balanced on a chair. Originally performed by the Wallendas in 1925, this act was revived by Carl Wallenda's* cousins, the Omankowsky and Triska

---

* Carl Wallenda died after falling forty meters from his wire in San Juan, Puerto Rico, on 22 March 1978, when performing in the open air between two seafront hotels. That evening the rest of the troupe appeared in the circus as usual. It was not the first tragedy that this family had faced. In 1972, Carla Wallenda's husband, Richard Guzman, fell to his death, and ten years before that Dieter Schepp and Richard Faughman were killed and a third member was left permanently paralyzed when the pyramid collapsed.

families, in 1943. However, they considered it too dangerous to keep in their repertoire and the Wallendas took it over once again. One of Carl Wallenda's apprentices, a Puerto Rican called Gene Mendez, decided to work on his own, and for verve and panache his act is hard to beat today. It was he who took over from Alzana when he had his accident at Ringling's in 1958.

The Alzanas, who in private life were Harold Davis—the son of an English miner—his wife Minnie and his sisters Elsie and Hilda, put on one of the most thrilling acts to be seen in the circus. Down below, ready to break their fall should they slip, was Charles Davis, Harold's sixty-one year old father.*

The reason a Sheffield miner left the pits and took to the high wire is simple: he felt it was his calling. A natural aptitude, agility, muscle and daring are not enough. These things may produce a good circus artiste but never a great one, unless the heart is in the business as well. Harold Alzana was the right build, five feet four inches tall and broad in proportion. He was completely fearless— I have heard other circus artistes call him foolhardy—but most important of all was his love of his work.

One of the tricks in the Alzanas' act was the Human Wheelbarrow, where a girl, holding the spindle of the wheel in her outstretched hands, was trundled across the wire by the legs. The Weitzmann Brothers performed this on a two hundred foot rope, one hundred and ten feet high, at the end of the last century, but the Alzanas added an additional trick which, as well as enhancing the spectacle, also exerted a steadying influence. From the spindle hung a trapeze on which a third member of the troupe worked. While this obviously lowered the center of gravity, it also prevented the use of lateral stays; and most high wire acts today make use of these guy ropes, which, spaced at intervals of about ten feet, lead from either side of the wire down to the ground and so keep it steady. Sometimes it is impossible to anchor these lateral stays to the ground, as I found when organizing the spectacle of the first man to cross the Thames on a tightrope for the Festival of Britain in 1951. With a long walk—and the distance across the Thames was over one thousand feet—it is more important than ever to prevent the wire from whipping. In an effort to keep his balance a

---

* He did break their fall in 1947, when a tent hand allowed a rope to touch the end of a balancing pole and Hilda and Harold came tumbling down. For the 1950 season, André Pincemin, a trick-cyclist who married Hilda in 1949, took Charles Davis's place, waiting and watching in the ring.

wirewalker may easily make a sudden movement to left and right, setting up an oscillation which can be extremely dangerous. The lateral stays prevent this when they are anchored to the ground, because one has created a stable triangle the base of which is the ground itself. Over the water one must triangulate the stresses in midair. Two other wires, below and on either side of the walking wire, have to be rigged. The lateral stays lead out and over these, and are weighted. This reduces any tendency to whip.

Incidentally, although 130,000 people came to see Elleano on that occasion, few, if any, realized that although he was the first man to cross the Thames on a tightrope, a woman had done it ninety years before. Her name was Selina Young, the grand-daughter of a famous showman called Old Wild. She was nineteen years old when she first crossed the river from Battersea to Cremorne. Her first attempt was a failure, as someone had cut the lateral stays to steal the lead with which they were weighted. The rope started to oscillate and she had to slide down one of the stays to the safety of a boat. Repairs were made and she set off again, successfully accomplishing the 660-yard crossing in seven minutes. "To behold her," wrote an eye-witness, "as she stands midway between either shore, with Old Father Thames rolling sedately beneath her, is at once a grand and fearsome sight." Soon after this exploit she fell, and when she came out of the hospital one leg was three inches shorter than the other. Her professional career was over.

These lateral stays have other uses as well, for a performer can slip his foot under one and so anchor himself while he crouches down for another artiste to leap over him. And if at any time he should slip, these ropes may perhaps save him from falling to the ground. Blondin used them for fixing the stove on which he cooked his omelette. But for safety this artiste used a very long balancing pole which was heavily weighted at each end and was curved like a bow. This also lowered his center of gravity.

In spite of what some circus historians say, Chevalier Blondin was born at Hesdin, Pas de Calais, and not at St. Omer. His real name was Jean François Gravelet—not Emile*—but like so many performers he adopted the surname of the artiste to whom he had

* I am indebted to John Price for correcting the place of birth and christian name. His proof is given in his work *Some Details of the Life and Exploits of Blondin, the Ropewalker,* prepared for and distributed to members of the Union of Circus Historians, 1958.

been apprenticed. Although he took up his profession at an early age, it was not until he visited New York with the Ravel Troupe in the 1850s that he became well known. His real fame, however, came on 30 June 1859 when he crossed Niagara Falls for the first time.

All in all he made a series of crossings on six different occasions below the Falls, and several times above them in 1860, sometimes blindfolded, sometimes trundling a wheelbarrow. He balanced on chairs, turned a somersault, walked on small fork-shaped stilts and took passengers across pick-a-back at five pounds a trip. His favorite story was of how he asked the Prince of Wales if he might carry him across, and of Edward's reluctant refusal. It amused him to invite famous people to make the trip, particularly if he thought they were sure to decline. But he played this trick too often. After crossing the Seine, he invited Cham, the caricaturist, to return with him. "Certainly," said Cham, "I am perfectly willing, on condition that it is I who carry you." When Blondin started to argue, he added, "You see, it is you, not I, who refuse."

How much money he made from crossing Niagara is not known, but the publicity he got was enormous. On arriving in England in 1861, he received one hundred pounds a performance at the Crystal Palace. The management was delighted with the contract, since it netted over ten times that amount.

One of the most spectacular feats he is reported to have accomplished in London was to turn a somersault on stilts 170 feet above the ground. He astounded Paris by riding a bicycle along a rope at the Palais de l'Industrie in 1877. Even after he had retired he still took his "daily constitutional" along a rope he had set up in the garden of Niagara House, the villa which he had built at Ealing. His most famous exploit and the site of his house are commemorated today by Niagara Avenue and Blondin Avenue.*

Twice winner of the Clapham Common, London, "championships," the Great Doval is probably the finest high-wire performer today. Like Mendez he was apprenticed to a famous high-wire troupe—in his case that of Camillo Mayer in Europe. His spectacular routine includes a head-stand and stilt walking along the wire. Thrilling as this undoubtedly is, I find that stilts detract from the grace of the funambulist—what should be seen as a series of light, dancing steps too often becomes a hobble.

---

* The second person to cross Niagara was Mlle. Spelterini, who took eleven minutes to accomplish this. Farini and Harry Leslie also made the crossing.

Aerialists sometimes work on a slack rope. Cubanos, the Flying Dutchman, used a rope which hung in a great bight across the arena. Astride the rope he swung in giant arcs above the audience. With his ankles firmly fixed in short loops attached to the center of the rope, he performed some thrilling tricks. But the movements which can be achieved on a high, slack rope are limited, and for the climax of his act Cubanos forsook the rope and climbed up to a small platform from which he leapt to catch the bar of a trapeze. He missed it and fell—only to be caught by the ropes attached to his ankles. This was an exciting finale, but there was not so much artistry in this as there was in his performance on the swinging rope way up in the air.

Although this chapter is primarily concerned with aerial acts, one cannot write about the high wire and slack rope without mentioning similar acts which take place nearer the ground. Here there are three main categories: slack, tight and bounding.

The bounding rope, on which the little Indian, Bombayo, was the greatest performer in recent times, is held in tension by strong springs. By bouncing astride this rope the springs are made to give an extra lift for throwing somersaults. Bombayo threw a double back somersault, landing astride the wire.

In technique there is a fundamental difference between performing on the slack and tight wires. While walking the tight wire the performer must keep his center of gravity over the wire; on a slack wire the wire must be brought under the performer's center of gravity.

While high-wire acts may use balancing poles, which lower the center of gravity, the low-wire performer sometimes uses an open parasol. Here, pressure of air on its surface helps to keep one steady. But a reasonably efficient performer needs no such aid.

The greatest wire-walker the world has ever seen was Con Colleano. In fact, he was more than a wire-walker; he picked up the threads of the old tradition and, adapting them to the pattern of today, showed us what the term *rope-dancer* really meant. When, towards the end of the last century, Oceana started the fashion for "performing on the silver thread," dancing went out as well as ropes, and the new type of act was—and still is—referred to as wire-walking. But Colleano was a *wire-dancer*. His footwork was superb. His greatest feat was a forward somersault, which is much more difficult than a backward one. In turning forward through the air you cannot see where to put your feet as you land, while in throwing a back somersault the eyes can see both the feet and the wire as the head comes up.

The Colleanos, who came from Australia, and not Mexico as many would have us believe, were a great circus family. Con, Maurice and Winifred were all trained as acrobats. Maurice's delight was to work a series of flip-flaps, twists, somersaults and hand-springs across the ring and back, then across and back again, in one flowing movement. It has been said that he could throw a double somersault from the ground without a run. But Con was the star. In everything he did there was an integrity and style which is only found among the greatest performers. His work was every-thing to him. Like many great artistes, he tended to make his achievements sound simple: "If when I land," he told Dame Laura Knight, referring to his forward somersault, "I can feel the wire with my right foot between the ball of the big toe and the outer edge of my heel, I know I am all right."

Con Colleano's success had one unfortunate result. It set the fashion for wire-walkers to dress up in Mexican trousers. Not realizing that Colleano stripped his pair off and worked most of his act in the knee-breeches of a bullfighter, his would-be imitators shuffled along the wire, their floppy bell-bottoms hiding what little footwork they may have possessed.

There is, however, a definite Mexican school of wire-walking, and Colleano started by following in the tradition of Robledillo Mijares and Don Juan Caicedo. For years experts have said that Caicedo turned a back somersault on the wire in heavy riding boots and spurs. In the original edition of Thétard's *La Merveilleuse Histoire du cirque,* however, there is a photograph of him accomplishing this trick, and the boots, with spurs attached, are seen lying neatly on the ground.

Germain Aeros, who for many years enjoyed a notable success in France, presented a comedy act on the low wire in which he impersonated an elderly citizen befuddled with drink. Yet when he appeared in England he was not appreciated. More to the British taste was the clever fooling of Reco, the tramp on the wire, who, incidentally, became a successful English circus proprietor. The difference between these two performers was not so much in the technique of wire-walking, as in the sympathy which Reco inspired amongst his British audiences but which Aeros lacked.

Like other acts, wire-walking has been combined with different numbers in the endless search for originality. Juggling provides one of the best amalgamations, and in this the Reverhos excelled. Their hand-balancing while juggling on the wire was really remarkable, though it was a pity that such a fine routine should have been worked in one direction only, *à la music hall*. More recently, the Russian clown Popov, in the role of a comic chef, has combined juggling with working on the slack wire.

The low wire gives one an excellent opportunity for studying style. In a high-wire act, not only is one too far away to appreciate the subtlety of the footwork, one is also too conscious of the danger. After the performer has turned, let us say, a cartwheel, his efforts to keep his balance can be as graceful as the movements of a dancer or as ungainly as the fluttering of a frightened hen. On the high wire one is so relieved that the performer has managed to regain his equilibrium that one is apt to applaud a movement which, had it been made nearer the ground, would have produced a frown of reproof. At the same time, a finely executed recovery on the high wire often counts for nothing, because at that distance one is unable to appreciate the effort involved.

I never saw Con Colleano without being struck by his intense concentration and his sense of style. Style is a most difficult thing to define. Jacques Copeau once wrote that it was the perfection of technique, particularly muscular technique, used in the service of a sincere and spontaneous desire. This can best be seen in the circus by watching first the wire act and then the flying trapeze.

XI

LA HAUTE ECOLE

Although most of the acts seen in the circus can be traced back to those forms of entertainment which principally appealed to the masses, there is one act which has a more aristocratic origin. It is *la haute école,* or the high school of equitation. But among the professionals in England the word "high" is often left out; *écuyers* and *écuyères* are known as school riders.

Too many people nowadays seem to think that this exhibition of fine horsemanship is based on making a horse dance, and it is the circus proprietor who is largely to blame. After the traditional joke in which ponies are called "polonies," the clown will often say to the rider, "That's-a-very-fine-horse-you've-got-there-I've-seen-it-dance-the-waltz-and-the-polka-now-can-it-do-the-rumba?" Without waiting for a reply, he makes a hasty exit. The band breaks into "The Lady in Red," the rider raises his silk hat in salutation, but the horse—no matter what his actions may appear to be—does *not* dance the rumba. Horses cannot dance at all; they have no sense of time.

The high school act in the circus programme, which today has to be sold to the public as a ballroom accomplishment, is actually the last link in a chain which stretches back into the Dark Ages.

Paces such as the *lançade, courbette* and *capriole* are based on medieval movements of attack and defense, taught by knights to their war-horses. From the battlefields they passed to the tourneys. If one failed to unseat one's opponent at the first attempt, a *pirouette* or a *demi-volte* brought one back to the attack. If one wanted to change one's position without altering direction, then one moved obliquely *en deux pistes*. *Changements* and *contre-changements de main* were used for maneuvering and for feinting. Finally, when the victor approached his lady for his reward, he would make his horse move in the proud steps of the *passage*.

Movements or airs such as these still held their place long after jousting had given way to other pastimes. For centuries a king or general would not think of reviewing his troops except on the back of a horse performing a *piaffe* or a *passage*.

The French Revolution put an end to the famous riding school at Versailles. But even if the *sans-culottes* had not requisitioned the stables and beheaded the riding masters, I doubt that it would have continued for long. Highly trained horses had ceased to be of primary importance in warfare, and that is why a post-Restoration attempt to reopen the school failed in 1830.

A similar situation had developed in England. The increase of riding-masters found in the pleasure gardens during the eighteenth century has been traced to a lessening of interest in advanced equitation at home. It is not very surprising, therefore, to find that the decline of *haute école* in society coincided with its rise in the circus. Here its popularity reached its peak during the second half of the last century.

Two men stand out in this period of high school history, which also marks the heyday of the circus. The first is François Baucher, who was born in 1796 to the wife of a butcher at Versailles. He was a brilliant trainer of both horses and riders, and he revolutionized all preconceived theories. With him we find for the first time the name of the horse coupled with that of the rider. Those who remember the name Baucher will find that Partisan, Neptune, Buridan and Capitaine follow quickly in their minds. His career came to a sudden and unfortunate end in the midst of success. In 1855 he was crushed beneath a falling chandelier at what was then called the Cirque Napoleon, now the Cirque d'Hiver. Though his life was saved he never rode in public again; he died in 1873.

After Baucher came the Englishman, James Fillis, and his horses Markir, Germinal and Povero. He also founded a school of horsemanship which was based on rather different principles. This is no place to debate the old argument of lateralism versus diagonalism. It should be sufficient to say that whereas Fillis has been called a riding-master who broke with tradition, many now think that it was Baucher who renounced the old school of Versailles, and that it was Fillis who reconciled Baucher's technique to the more traditional methods.

At Clemenceau's request Fillis wrote his *Principes de dressage et d'equitation,* a technical work of great importance, which was published in 1890. From the English edition, *Breaking and Riding* (London: Hurst and Blackett Ltd., n.d.), I see that at least thirteen thousand copies have been printed. Very few circus performers have enjoyed such a literary success. Yet little has been written about the author; the most quoted phrase, that he was the son of a London barrister, I find totally inaccurate. Fillis is a famous circus name. There was a Fillis family on the bill at Astley's in 1857, and it was James Fillis's nephew Frank who took over one of the earliest circuses in South Africa. Furthermore, James Fillis himself tells us that he first appeared in the ring of the French circus proprietor Soullier, in 1844, at the age of ten. While he was making his name on the Continent, his brother Tom was earning £2 10s a week in 1875, with a circus in Ireland.

Fillis was often asked how it was that his horses were able to undergo such strenuous training without knocking themselves to pieces. He replied by likening them to gymnasts, who are gradually brought to such excellent condition that their muscles are as hard as steel and their whole physical fitness cannot be improved.

But, in the main, it was the *equestriennes* of the *haute école,* trained by such masters as Fillis and Baucher, who were responsible for the success of the circus. Although the two earliest *écuyères,* Phillipine Tourniaire and Constance Chiarini (afterwards Comtesse Rostopchine), were descended from circus stock, it was the otherwise unknown Caroline Loyo who became the original *diva de la cravache** at the age of seventeen, and it was she who trained the most famous of all school riders, her niece Emilie Loisset. Originally Emilie and her sister Clotilde appeared as pad performers with their uncle François Loisset. But after falling from her horse and injuring her knee, Emilie took up *la haute école.*

When François died in 1878, the circus was sold and Caroline Loyo retired. The two young girls then went to Paris to find their fortunes. There they got an engagement at the Cirque d'Eté, in the

---

*This phrase, first used in describing Caroline Loyo, is derived from the French word for a cutting whip, *une cravache.*

Champs Elysées, at a salary of three thousand francs a month. At the end of their first season Clotilde married Jean XXII, Prince of Reuss. But Emilie refused all offers of marriage. She concentrated on the perfection of her riding and achieved an even greater success than her sister.

Four years later she surprised everybody by becoming engaged to the Prince of Hatzfeld. But the wedding never took place. Rehearsing one morning at the Cirque d'Hiver, her horse, J'y Pense,* fell, and the fork of her side saddle caused grave internal injuries. As she lay on the tan she murmured, "Je suis brisée. Je sens que je vais mourir." She died two days later humming her entrance music, "La Valse des Gardes," in her delirium.

After they had carried her out of the ring, they picked up her little cutting whip; the silver band around the handle was engraved with the following words: "Princesse ne daigne, Reine ne puis, Loisset suis."

In a romantic age, such female centaurs as these found themselves the symbol of romance.

In the ring they nearly all wore the same dress: a top hat, an immaculate riding habit, cut by Redfern, a well-tied stock with a horseshoe pin, a veil and a buttonhole of violets. One or two women rode astride, however, dressed not *en amazone* but *en travestie,* wearing the uniform of Saumur or the costume of a court page. The Countess Fanny Ghyka was one of these, and it is said that she never wore the same clothes twice in the same season. This Rumanian beauty left her Serbian husband and ran off with the high school rider of a circus. She soon became more famous than her lover. But after topping the bill at St. Petersburg, Moscow, Milan and Vienna, she also met a tragic end. She was thrown on the last day of a most successful visit to Paris and died, aged twenty-four.

After a period of neglect, which was particularly noticeable in England, high school is coming back into favor. It provides a training for both horses and riders. Balance, coordination, suppleness, dexterity and strength are all improved. Furthermore, it is now realized that most of the airs, both on the ground and above the ground, are based on completely natural movements. Many can

---

*The Baron de Vaux gives the horse's name as Pour Toujours, and many writers have followed his lead. Tristan Rémy, a circus historian of meticulous accuracy, found this was not so.

Madame Phillipine Tourniaire, one of the first of the great écuyères. (From the author's collection.)

be seen by watching colts at play, or in the approach made by a stallion to a mare.

Although the elegance and grace of a school act makes it look easy, the discipline for both horse and rider is long and arduous. No one can appreciate this form of horsemanship if he looks upon it as dancing. Since it is only by distinguishing the various paces and

175

knowing when they are performed correctly that a high school act can be enjoyed to the full, it is appropriate to give a brief description of the movements.

1. *Passage.* A rhythmic trot in which the forelegs are picked up in the style of a hackney pony. When raised the forearm is held horizontally, and the cannon remains vertical, with the hoof turned in. The hind legs come well forward under the barrel of the horse.

2. *Piaffe.* This is a *passage* performed on one spot, without the horse moving forward—a *passage* marking time. There is also a movement known as the *piaffe balloté,* in which the off legs are raised and put down in the same place, while the near legs make a beat first to the front then to the rear, returning each time to the same spot.

3. *Pas Espagnol.* At each step in this walk the foreleg is raised and extended straight out in front. The whole leg should be as nearly horizontal as possible. Some horses, like some chorus girls, kick higher with one leg; both legs should reach the maximum. Watch the legs as they come back to the normal position; the knees should not bend.

4. *Trot Espagnol.* The forelegs reach the same position, but this is achieved at a rhythmic, springy trot.

5. *Pirouettes.* The basic pirouette is called the *pirouette ordinaire.* In this movement the hindquarters mark the approximate center of the circle, the circumference of which can be traced by the forelegs in a series of gallop-jumps. It can be made either

Passage. Galopade. (Eighteenth-century illustration in the author's collection.)

clockwise or counterclockwise, called a *pirouette à droite* or *à gauche* respectively.

In the *pirouette renversée* the hindquarters trace a circle around the forelegs at the center.

Pirouette en trois jambes is a variant of the *pirouettes* described above performed on three legs.

Volte à droite. Pirouette a gauche. (From the author's collection.)
Capriole. Piaffe. (From the author's collection.)

In the *pirouette à pieds croisés* the hooves at the center of the circle remain stationary, so that the legs become crossed as the horse turns about them. (A *pirouette renversée à pieds croisés* is much easier than a *pirouette ordinaire à pieds croisés*.)

6. *Travail de deux pistes.* The most common movement in this

work is called *l'appuyer,* or half-pass. Here, the tracks made by the fore and hind legs are separate but parallel, and form diagonal lines.

7. *Serpentine au trot.* This development of the *travail de deux pistes* is more effective. The direction of the diagonal is changed every four paces.

Croupade. Ballotade. (From the author's collection.)

Pesade. Courbette. (From the author's collection.)

8. *Changement de pieds.* This is a changing step. The step can be changed in several different ways. In a *changement de pieds de galop à temps* it is changed at every pace. The step known as the *pas de polka* is based on changing step.

9. *Galop sur trois jambes.* A three-legged canter in which a fourth leg remains extended all the time.

10. *Galop sur place.* In this the horse gallops without moving forward.
11. *Galop en arrière.* Here the horse makes all the movements of cantering and actually moves backward. This is a very difficult trick to teach a horse. It was performed with great success by James Fillis and his daughter Anna.
12. *Balancer de l'avant et l'arrière-main.* In these the forelegs and back legs are straddled out sideways.
13. *Levade.* A rear, developed out of a *piaffe,* in which the weight of the horse is taken on well bent haunches. A high *levade* is, for some unknown reason, called a *courbette* in France.
14. *Cabrade.* A high rearing position with forelegs outstretched.
15. *Ruade.* This is a high kick in which both rear legs are shot out together, the forelegs remaining on the ground.
16. *Capriole.* This is the prettiest of all the leaping movements. The forehand is raised as high as possible, the horse then jumps so that the quarters are raised and, with all four feet off the ground, the horse kicks out with both rear legs together while the forelegs remain tucked back under its belly.
17. *Croupade* and *ballotade.* In these positions all four legs leave the ground. In the former they are tucked under the belly of the horse, in the latter the rear legs remain vertical with the hooves turned back.
18. *Lançade.* A leap forward, with the forehand raised a little higher than the quarters.
19. *Pesade.* This is a rear in which the hind legs do not move,

Terre à terre. Mezair. (From the author's collection.)

while the lower part of the forelegs hangs vertically down with the hooves tucked back.
20. *Courbette.* In this movement the rear is maintained as long as

possible, while a series of short jumps are made without the forelegs touching the ground. (In France it means a different movement. See *Levade.*)

21. *Mezair* and *terre à terre*. These are varying degrees of the *courbette*. In the former the rear is higher than in the latter.

This is by no means a complete list of high school steps, but it should enable you to appreciate a good high school act in any circus in the world. It is fuller than the repertoire presented by *le Cadre Noir* at Saumur, which consists of *l'appuyer*, *le changement de pieds*, *le passage*, *la courbette (levade)*, *la croupade*, *la terre à terre* and *la capriole*. But at the riding schools in Saumur and Vienna you will find a sense of style which is unsurpassed.

Another point to be noted at Saumur is that the horses, performing airs above the ground, carry jousting saddles without stirrups and their hind hooves are not shod.

While *le Cadre Noir* does not specialize in any one breed of horse, at the Spanish Riding School in Vienna you will find nothing but Lipizzaners. They were originally Spanish, but during the eighteenth century Danish, Italian, German, Arab and English thoroughbred blood was introduced to the stud at Lipizza, near Trieste, where the breed became established. The foals are born brown but turn white between four and ten years old, and all can trace their ancestry back to one of six sires: Pluto, Conversano, Neapolitano, Favory, Maestoso and Siglavy.

Studying this form of riding at Vienna or Saumur is very different from watching a similar act in a circus. A manège is rectangular and a *school*, while the circus is round and, above all, a *show*. Therefore one should find more spectacle in the ring, but this should never be an excuse for bad riding or training.

Watch out for neatness and crisp execution. See that the animal works well with both off and near legs. And, above all, take note of the rider. If he slips about in the saddle, yanks at the bridle or appears in any way ungainly, he is downright bad. He should give one the feeling of watching a centaur, not only through his physical proximity to his horse, but also through their mental unity. Horse and rider must be so harmoniously balanced that the slightest movement of the rider causes such a quick reaction that it seems as if horse and rider think as one.

There are plenty of mediocre school riders about today, but few good ones, and it is only when you find a really first-class exponent of *la haute école* that you will realize what a beautiful act it can be. Before World War II Bertram Mills brought over Monsieur Cuyer, who was then the greatest *écuyer* in France. Julio Diaz de Valesco, Roberto de Vasconcellos, Charlie Hankey, Helmuth Barth and Arturo Manzano are others who gave excellent performances. Albert Schumann, following in the footsteps of his great-uncle, presented some perfect school acts at Harringay. On one occasion he worked a number on free rein, walking alongside or behind his horse, while on another he rode one horse and drove another tandem fashion. Toulouse-Lautrec depicts a woman accomplishing this feat. But in this kind of number there is a complexity of interest. What one wants to see is a horse and its rider as one entity, and then the correct formation of stylized movements. One's eye should not be distracted by anything else. I make one exception. I have never seen a more beautiful *capriole* than that presented on a free rein by the fine rider and trainer, Alexis Gruss. It is because of this distracting quality that numbers which include buggies pulled by the high school horses or acts which include a number of riders leave me unimpressed. Nor do I care much to see a girl dancing alongside a horseman. Mixing ballet dancing with high school riding seems to me rather like putting port in Stilton. If the cheese is really good it should not need port, while the port, if it is of fine vintage, should certainly not be used to doctor up a poor cheese.

Beween the wars *écuyers* were scarce and *écuyères* even scarcer. Baptista Schreiber, the wife of the Mexican wire-walker Jesus Mijares—who became a Scandinavian circus proprietor—Cilly Feindt and Regina Strassburger were for years the only ones who could be compared with the twenty or more who were living between eighty and one hundred years ago. Mary Chipperfield held the fort in more recent years. However good as riders these performers may have been, they all forsook the tradition of riding sidesaddle, dressed in a habit and top hat. For perfect dressing one had to go back to Thérèse Renz, who, in 1933, at the age of seventy-three, appeared at the Cirque Medrano with her horse Last Rose.

Now we have Katja Schumann, daughter of Max and niece of Albert, who has triumphantly proved that *la haute école* is far from dead and can still top the bill in any circus, given grace and fearlessness and above all that centaurlike quality which welds horse and rider into one. To me, a good high school act, more than anything else in the circus, has style. Today our way of living sadly lacks this quality. And yet the red curtains at the ring doors have only to part for the high school rider, and there, pacing proudly over the tan, comes the epitome of style.

XII

JUGGLERS
and Acts Based on
DEXTERITY

After the studied formality of the airs performed by the highly schooled horse, one needs to see something fast and scintillating, an act which appears to be almost, though never quite, out of control, a routine which is stimulating to watch, but which does not necessarily rely on danger. The flashing knives, tinseled clubs, star-spangled balls and spinning plates of the juggler, twisting and turning through the air, provide this.

Today jugglers frequently appear in the ring as if they were dressed for the gymnasium or the playing field. They often ask the audience to throw them a ball, to be caught on a stick held in the mouth. As they wait, they bounce about on their toes, frowning in concentration, very much like a tennis player waiting for a service on the center court at Wimbledon. Often their props consist of sporting equipment: tennis raquets, footballs, Indian clubs. All this contrasts well with such essentially traditional and formal numbers as *la haute école*.

There are two main movements in juggling: *showering*, in which objects follow one another round in a circle, and *cascading*, or *crossing*, in which the objects are caught and thrown alternately by both hands, so that their paths cross in midair. There is also the *double shower*, which is obtained by returning the object to the throwing hand so it traces a curve in the air, and of course one can throw and catch objects with the same hand.

A cascade. (Drawing by John Skeaping.)

It may at first be a little difficult to distinguish showering from cascading, particularly if the juggler works quickly. But if you look at the position of the hands, you will notice that in showering the hand which throws is held lower than the hand which catches and returns; while in cascading the hands are held level. The recognition of these two movements is important in appreciating a juggler's true worth, for, while cascading three balls is comparatively easy—it should be accomplished with five or more—it is difficult to play an even number in this way. In general the greater the number of balls, the harder the trick becomes; but a double shower of eight or a cascade of nine is actually easier than a straightforward shower of seven. Very few jugglers have managed to keep seven balls showering from hand to hand.

A shower. (Drawing by John Skeaping.)

Pierre Amoros juggled with nine balls, and this put him into a class which few others have reached. To play five balls in the movements I have described is good, especially if variety is brought into the act by changing the direction of the shower. Rapoli and Kara, for instance, could both shower five balls from right to left and left to right without breaking the rhythm of the movement. Juggling with seven or eight balls is extremely difficult, unless, in the latter case, small balls are used in couples and played four in each hand. Chinko, brother of Teddy Knox, the Crazy Gang comedian, worked with eight balls in this way when he appeared as the first boy juggler dressed in an Eton suit.

One of the Gee family, Charlene, who was lost to the circus in the middle of his career when he retired to run a hotel in South Africa, managed to play eight balls without throwing them in couples. But any number above five needs years of practice.

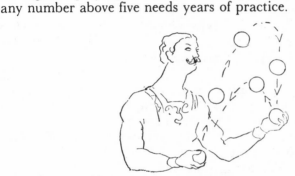

A double shower. (Drawing by John Skeaping.)

Plates are considered by some to be more difficult to juggle than balls. Severus Scheffer, who died in 1950 at Folkestone at the age of eighty-six, was one of the best plate jugglers. He came from a circus family which was famous both as a troupe and individually. All the members bore the initials S.S. The boys were called Sylvester, Severus and Sebaldus, while the girls' names were Sidonia and Suzanne. Besides dexterity, Severus also displayed great strength. He supported a live sentry in his box on his head, and at one time made his entrance in a dogcart which he subsequently balanced by one shaft on his chin.

But the greatest juggler of all time was Rastelli. He managed to get ten plates into the air at once; for this he used a belt with an attachment which held the last few plates he was to use in readiness. He also juggled with eight or nine balls. This would lead one to suppose that there are some at least who find that plates are easier to play than balls.

Enrico Rastelli was born in 1897, the son and grandson of a juggler. His mother was a trapeze artiste, who, when he grew old enough, also worked with her son in a perch act. Jugglers in those days were paid little, and Rastelli's father, who juggled on horseback, forbade his son to follow in his footsteps, thinking that he would do much better for himself if he continued as an acrobat.

Young Rastelli just had to juggle. He rehearsed in secret; and after six years he could play seven balls, compared with the five which were all his father could manage, but Enrico's ambition was to beat the record held by Amoros.

Then an Oriental troupe came to work in the same circus, and from them he learned foot-juggling and the use of a mouth-stick. After one year he is reputed to have been able to balance two balls on top of one another on a stick held in his mouth, and at the same time juggle with four others.

When old Rastelli found out what his son had been doing, he was furious; but since Enrico was already the better juggler of the two, his father could do nothing. And young Rastelli got a job at thirty roubles a day.

Six months later his father bought a circus of his own. The programme was made up of his son, who, apart from juggling, still appeared with his mother in the perch act, Stella Price as a wire-walker and her father as clown, a knife-thrower, a handcuff king, a contortionist and eight horses. World War I broke up the show. Enrico Rastelli married Stella Price and in 1917 left Russia.

By 1922 his act had become a star turn and at the end of the year he appeared in England at Olympia. In 1925 he was getting thirty pounds a day.

Dressed in shirt and shorts, he was the first great juggler to imbue his act with an atmosphere of outdoor sport. The act was lively, but he also contrasted movement with repose. In one routine he would sit on a stool with a football on each instep, another on each knee, two balanced one on top of the other on a mouth-stick, two more balanced in the same way on a stick on his forehead and one spinning on the forefinger of each hand. In another trick he stood balanced on his right foot while rotating a stick on his forehead, spinning a ball in his right hand, rotating a hoop on his left ankle and juggling three sticks in his left hand.

While playing against the Vienna football team he is said to have headed a football into the goal in spite of allowing them three goalkeepers.

He rehearsed regularly for eight hours a day. When he died, aged thirty-four, in 1931 at Bergamo from an abscess in his mouth, the circus lost another performer whose integrity, skill and devotion placed him in the front rank.

No one has yet come up to Enrico Rastelli, but Paolo Bedini, of the Bedini-Tafani circus family, followed not far behind with Eduardo Raspini hot on his tracks. However, it seems unlikely that anyone else will ever achieve the astounding feat of juggling with ten plates.

The number of objects used is not the only important point to look for. Bela Kremo played no more than three balls, but the variety of his movements, his finesse, his timing and his sense of style made him a great performer. Just as Rastelli became a better juggler than his father, so is Kris Kremo surpassing Bela. In a beautiful routine which brings into play top hats, balls and cigar boxes, Kris achieves the remarkable feat of turning a triple pirouette between letting go of three cigar boxes and catching them again.

Hats, balls and boxes are also used by Tolly M., a juggler of considerable promise who is the eldest member of the fine Risley act known as the Castors, *nom de piste* of the Moustier family.

Balls can also be played against a board, set either at right-angles to the ground—a method invented by L.A. Street—or on the ground itself. Not more than six balls have been juggled in this way.

Apart from the number of objects and variety of movements, interest can be obtained from widely. differing props, such as the cigar, open umbrella and mackintosh which were used in an act seen by a friend of mine at Ciniselli's Circus, St. Petersburg, in 1903.

The famous Cinquevalli made great use of strangely assorted equipment. He juggled with a teapot, a cup, a saucer and a lump of sugar, ending with the sugar in the cup, the cup on the saucer and the tea being poured from the pot into the cup. Once while picnicking at Marlow, the idea came to him of juggling with a bottle half-full of lemonade and an umbrella. The climax of this routine was to catch the neck of the bottle on the ferule and to open the umbrella as the lemonade poured out.

Cinquevalli was a German, who, like so many artistes, took the name of his tutor. In his case this was the acrobatic clown in the Chiese-Bellon-Cinquevalli Troupe. His act was a beautifully de-signed number in which speed and strength were contrasted with what appeared to be exquisitely delicate balances. His most difficult feat was to hold in his mouth a wineglass in which lay a white billiard ball; on this was balanced a cue; and on the upper, broader end of the cue, spot and red were poised, one on top of the other. But whatever you may read about Cinquevalli's feats of balance, never believe that they were accomplished without faking. Ask any juggler if it is possible to balance one sphere on another, and he will explain that this is only possible if one side is slightly flattened. I think that Cinquevalli was a man of such integrity that he must have hated stooping to such tricks. But professionals are all agreed that without some form of trickery his balances could never have been done. Other parts of his act, which required phenomenal strength, were not faked. He could spin a forty-four-pound washtub on a twenty-five-foot pole which he balanced on his shoulder. Then, dashing the pole away with his hand, he would catch the tub on the spike of a helmet which he wore, and still keep the tub spinning. Sometimes he might slightly misjudge the position of the center of gravity, and once when this happened at Lyons, he was thrown twenty feet by the impact of the whirling tub.

Holding a blowpipe, loaded with a dart, in his left hand, he would juggle with a knife, a fork and a turnip in his right. Suddenly, high in the air, the fork would be seen to stick into the turnip which at that moment would be pierced by the dart. As all three objects fell they were impaled on the knife.

The climax of his act came when a forty-eight-pound cannonball falling from a height of forty feet was caught on Cinquevalli's neck. People thought that it must be made of wood, so to show the audience that it was quite genuine it was first dropped onto an ordinary kitchen table—which it smashed to matchwood.

Another of his favorite tricks was a routine known as "The Human Billiard Table." In this act balls were made to run up his arms and over his body as he twisted and turned, until they landed in his pockets. This routine may possibly have been derived from the work of a Burmese called Moung Toon. He juggled with balls, made of glass or bamboo, which he never touched with his hands. From his instep he would throw a ball up and catch it on his raised knee. From there it would be thrown to his shoulder, then dropped and caught at the back of the knee, and so on.

Many Oriental jugglers came to the circus at the middle of the last century, and it was they who introduced the mouth-stick, plate-spinning and ribbon-waving. They also set the fashion for jugglers to appear dressed in kimonos.

By the beginning of this century Occidental jugglers had come to the fore. Amongst these was Hera, one of the first to work in evening dress. His routine, in which nine candles were sent flying into nine candlesticks by a flick of the wrist, was a forerunner of the trick performed by Gaston Palmer, which, in his broken English, he described as "all ze spoons into all ze glasses." There are others who also created a style of their own which has been subsequently copied by many others. You will often see, both on the halls and in the circus, a juggler who appears to let his props fall only to catch them at the very last minute with a minimum of effort. Rich Hayes made this popular more than fifty years ago. Other jugglers have built their act round a scene, such as a meal in a restaurant in which plates, bottles, fruit and cutlery have served as props. The Agousts became famous for such an act, and later the Perezoffs presented "A Supper at Maxim's." Most acts, however, relied on a purer form of juggling. Of these one must mention Kara, who, although he specialized in juggling with knives, managed to play seven balls and has been described to me by one member of the profession as "the greatest juggler's juggler." Very few performers ever tried to copy Bagessen, who broke an almost unbelievable quantity of plates at every performance with wistful regret, probably because he brought the genius of the clown into his work.

William Everhart, at the end of the last century, invented hoop-rolling, an act which Bob Bramsom performs to perfection today. Morris Cronin, like Everhart, was an American, and he was the first to juggle with clubs. The Swifts worked the neatest and quickest act of this kind that I have ever seen. But too often a mediocre routine using three clubs is dressed up in a dazzle of scintillating props and costumes.

I have seen very few jugglers on horseback. The first was Feroni, who stood on a pad, but Margot Edwards worked on a bareback horse. When she told me she came from circus stock, and had been performing since she was four years old, I was not surprised, for every attitude she took up and every gesture she made seemed to me to epitomize ring technique. No less an authority than Strehly in *L'Acrobatie et les acrobates* (Paris: Delagrave, n.d.) said that an equestrian juggler never played more than four balls, but when I saw Margot Edwards, she juggled beautifully with five, and was rehearsing with seven. Today the Brumbachs juggle from one to another on horseback.

Juggling is often incorporated with other acts. The combination of juggling and wire act performed by the Reverhos has already been mentioned. José Moreno was another juggling funambulist. Freddy Zay kept six hoops in the air while balancing a basket of flowers on top of a billiard cue on his forehead as he rode a high monocycle.

With diverse equipment such as this, a surrealistic element creeps in. Pictures of some of these acts contain all the irrational fantasy of Max Ernst or Salvador Dali. In Strehly's *L'Acrobatie et les acrobates* there is a drawing of a juggler balancing seven glasses and a carafe on his head, throwing three plates in the air with his right hand, spinning a hat with his left, and supporting a stool, which carries a parrot in a cage, on his raised left leg. In Zucca's *Acrobatica e atletica* (Milan: Hoepli, 1902) one can see two moustachioed men in knee-breeches sitting at a table on which stand a six-branched candlestick, an ice bucket, three bottles of champagne, two liqueur glasses, a box of matches, some knives and a cup and saucer. They are nonchalantly heading a large india rubber ball from one to the other, while one plays a guitar and the other a mandolin. Even in the writing of jugglers one can find a super-intensity and a strange fantasy. In describing the tricks which can be achieved with a top hat, Rupert Ingalese becomes almost vehement in his desire to see things done in what he considers to be a fitting manner. "Do *not*," he implores, "practice balancing it on the chin. It is not only inartistic, but useless from a practical point of view, to balance hats on chins. The correct place to balance a silk hat is on the bridge of the nose."

As most articles describe an arc through the air, juggling usually follows a flowing rhythm, but an odd, hestitating and staccato tempo is obtained by those who hold a rectangular cigar box in each hand and juggle with a third box which remains free. The music used in this act is often a slow rendering of "Pop Goes the Weasel"; the hollow knock, as the two supporting boxes are clamped against the third, punctuates the rhythm like a drumbeat. Kris Kremo's remarkable triple pirouette has already been mentioned. Sometimes at the end of this routine the center box is deliberately smashed. This produces a feeling of irrevocable finality which is strangely satisfying.

The Chinese seem to specialize in plate-spinning and waving flags and ribbons in intricate and dazzling patterns. Like the Russians, they also juggle with heavy porcelain vases.

Hats, candlesticks, umbrellas, balls, plates, knives, lamps, cigars, billiard cues, washing tubs, lemonade bottles . . . the list of props used by a juggler is almost endless. Yet some of the strangest are

A foot-juggler. (Drawing by John Skeaping.)

used by the foot jugglers. Gigantic playing cards, Maltese crosses, parasols, long cylinders, tables and even bedsteads occupied by dummy figures are thrown, twisting and twirling through the air, by those who lie on their backs and juggle with their feet. The cradle which supports them is known as a *trinka,* and the number is called an antipodist act. Levanda, who appeared at several royal command performances, came from a British circus family called Moxon which specialized in this kind of work. The neatness of her foot movements was as pleasing to watch as that of any ballet dancer. One of the difficulties of this act lies in trying to get variety into the routine. It is usually more spectacular when a trio of antipodists work together.

When, in this kind of juggling, inanimate objects are replaced by human beings, the act is known as a Risley act. Ask any knowledgeable circus enthusiast "Who invented the Risley act?" and nine times out of ten the answer will be "Professor Risley." But this type of act may well have been seen long before the Professor, whose real name was Richard Risley Carlisle, was born. Signor Colpi and his children appeared at Astley's in 1777, and a French print of this act shows thirteen different tricks, of which twelve might be performed by a Risley act today. However, none of the children is in midair, so he may have merely balanced them on his feet. Risley certainly made *les jeux icariens* popular, and he was their

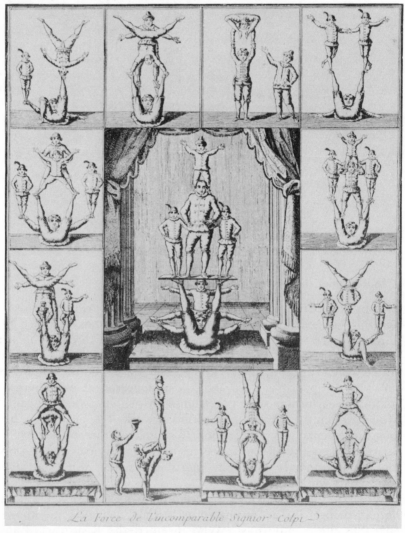

La Force de l'incomparable Signor Colpi

Signor Colpi's act in 1777, a possible forerunner of the Risley Act. (From an eighteenth-century print.)

most famous exponent. He formed the link between acrobatics and dancing; an Italian critic described him and his partners as "miracolosi saltatori-equilibristi-ballerini." It is surprising that a man so successful in his work and so dominating in his character should be dismissed in such a cursory manner by the historians of entertainment. No one but Marian Hannah Winter seems to have given him the position which he deserves; but she, perhaps, makes up for all the others in her fascinating essay, "The Theatre of Marvels" (*Dance Index,* vol. 7, nos. 1 and 2 [New York, 1948]), which is full of remarkable anecdotes.

Risley was an American, born in 1814, an amateur acrobat who joined a circus in his youth as "an athlete and performer on the flute." When exactly he started his Risley act is not known. Nor is it certain that he ever married, though throughout his career at least three Master Risleys worked with him, and these were always referred to as his sons. He achieved a great success in New York, London and the English provinces, but the wildest ovation was given him in Paris, where people flocked to see him in one of the stuffiest theatres in the city on the hottest nights of summer. Théophile Gautier, the first—and perhaps the most famous—serious French circus critic, was ecstatic in his praise. Fame followed him all over Europe. He topped the bill in practically every theatre from Drury Lane in London to La Scala, Milan, and in St. Petersburg he was decorated by the Czar.

Miss Winter tells how in London he also "found time to introduce a brilliant young equestrian named Young Hernandez, exhibit a panorama of the Mississippi some four miles in length . . . and open an American Bar and American Bowling Alley."* This must surely have been the first American Bar in England.

Risley certainly did not lack self-confidence. While in England he bet that he was the best shot, the best wrestler, the best billiards player and the best hammer-thrower in London. He won all except billiards. So the next time he visited England he brought with him an American champion to regain the honor for the United States. Unfortunately for the Professor, the Englishman won again, and he lost thirty thousand dollars.

Forming a circus company of his own, Richard Risley took his inimitable acrobatics to the Far East, and on his return brought

---

*James Hernandez's real name was Mickey Kelly. He was born in 1832, trained by John Robinson and died at Singapore while on a tour of the Far East, on 19 July 1861.

back one of the first troupes of Oriental tumblers to be seen in America and Europe. Risley's Troupe of Japanese Acrobats was soon followed by others, whose names at least provide a meeting place for East and West—perhaps the most delightful was "Bell's Oriental Gladiators."

I can find no proof of the story that Professor Risley committed suicide after one of his children had fallen during a performance and been killed. But his end was far from happy. Plagued by ill luck and rascally associates, he lost all his money, retired from the profession, and died in a lunatic asylum on 25 May 1874.

Here are the reserved and detached comments of the critic who wrote for the *Illustrated London News* in 1846:

> The very clever performances of Mr. Risley and his two sons continue to be nightly received with the loudest acclamations. Certainly nothing like it in the way of posturing was ever seen before. There is a graceful ease and precision in the manner in which all their evolutions are accomplished, exceedingly attractive; and the apparent absence of all painful contortions, or tottering overtasking of the ligaments, renders their gymnastics entirely free from unpleasant and unnatural postures. . . . The eldest boy has grown since he was last performing in England . . . but has lost none of that winning manner and prepossessing appearance which everyone must have remarked. Since the period just alluded to, the Risleys have been half over Europe, and their performances have everywhere been greeted with the warmest approbation. We can confidently recommend everybody to witness these clever evolutions.

The best Risley act I have ever seen is that of the Seven Ashtons, six brothers and their sister, who came from Australia. They represent a circus dynasty which can trace its history back nearly two hundred years and which ran the first tenting circus in Australia in 1852. Sometimes using as many as three *trinkas* in line, the bearers shot the lighter members of the troupe backwards and forwards from the soles of their feet in a remarkably fast and exciting routine. In this act one of the flyers somersaulted over another as they passed each other in midair. This trick has distinguished the acts of all great Risley artistes—the Lorches, the Bonhairs, the Grix Gregories and many others. The Kremos worked a Risley act at the end of the last century, and Anton Kremo turned a triple somersault, seat to seat, from the bearer's feet. Another member of the troupe managed to achieve a double, feet to feet, which is actually more difficult.

The presentation of a good Risley act means really hard work, and that perhaps is the reason the act is not seen as often today as it should be. Here the marked rhythm and dexterity of the juggler are combined with the suppleness and strength of the ground acrobat to produce a number which contains all the greatest qualities that one finds in the circus.

Ground acrobats form the subject of the next chapter; but as the juggler makes his final bow we might remember that here again is a character who has made a long journey down the aisles of history. His name is derived from *joculare,* to jest, but his story goes back beyond Rome. In the Tarot cards there are twenty-two major trumps, whose strange design is said to have been derived from the panels which lay between the columns on either side of an Egyptian temple. The first of these is *le Bateleur.* On the table in front of him lie his props—the balls, knives, cups and sticks which the juggler still uses today.

The juggler in the Tarot pack.

Professor Risley. (From a newspaper cutting in the author's collection.)

XIII

GROUND ACROBATS

Akrobatos, the dictionary says, means "walking on tiptoe," which suggests that the acrobat and the dancer have something in common. Dancing springs from a sense of ecstasy, and so do acrobatics; the child who hops and skips as he runs along may suddenly turn a cartwheel in sheer exuberance. However, once dancing is used to express other emotions than joy, the two part company. Love, sorrow, fear, triumph or revenge cannot be interpreted by purely acrobatic movements. After his first wild leap the acrobat forgot the cause and, impressed by its effect, became more interested in evolving physical variations than in trying to express different feelings by similar movements. Acrobatism is therefore more mathematical; it is primarily concerned with pattern. The body of the acrobat, like that of the dancer, is an instrument which expresses rhythm through motion; but this rhythm is the end in itself. The movements develop like a Bach fugue, creating a sense of satisfaction through their formal artistry rather than stirring the heart with hope or hatred or love.

Nor should acrobatics be confused with athletics. As Irving K. Pond wrote in *Big Top Rhythms,* "Athletics is the 'prose' of motion. Acrobatics is the highest form of 'poetry' in motion."

Although nowadays anybody who turns a somersault, swings on

a trapeze or performs a difficult feat of balance is called an acrobat, a hundred years ago the word had a more precise meaning. Those who worked on trapezes, ladders or any other form of apparatus were referred to as *gymnasts—aerial gymnasts* if they worked at height, *parterre gymnasts* if they worked on the ground. *Acrobat* was the name given only to a tumbler.

Tumbling provides the basic training for all circus artistes. No matter what they become afterwards, most of the greatest performers, from riders to aerialists, acquire their technique from being taught to tumble by some member of a troupe of acrobats who can teach as well as perform.

When I was traveling with Bertram Mills's Circus in 1937, I spent some time watching the young daughters of two Continental artistes having their first lesson in acrobatics. On a mattress spread in the "back-yard" behind the big top, two little girls, one two years old and the other three, arched themselves backwards and forwards over their fathers' arms till their hands met the ground. The fathers took their weight and also carefully guided their legs and arms into the right position. After a while they left the mattress and learned the rudiments of balance by standing on the palms of their fathers' hands. They enjoyed every moment of their lesson, and their occasional failure to accomplish some simple trick was always due to their laughter.

As they grow older circus children are taught more complicated movements with the aid of a safety belt to which a rope is attached, so that should they miscalculate time or distance they will come to no harm. But more important than any precautions to avoid danger is the child's own desire to succeed. Broken bones are bad enough, but broken nerves are worse. So lessons are given gradually. Serious training should start when the child is between six and nine years old; and the first lesson is the back bend. Bending, which has already been mentioned, makes a body supple. After this, muscle must be built up to perform more spectacular movements. Once a trick has been mastered, practice continues, first so that the performance becomes sure and polished, and then so that this brilliance can be maintained.

Unfortunately, today the necessity of earning one's living as soon as possible often means that a child appears in public directly the law will allow; and with so much time taken up at school, few young performers give such a finished performance as their parents did at the same age.

If the circus leaves you cold, you will probably think that the skill of the acrobat is confined to a facility for turning somersaults; but if the color, warmth and movement of the spectacle kindle a deeper interest, you will realize how much more is involved. In *Au Music hall* (Paris: Les Editions du Monde Nouveau, 1923), Gustave Fréjaville wrote:

> The work of an acrobat holds its own significance; it is an artistic achievement which develops like a symphony, and it contains the composition of a painting and the rhythm of a poem. In presentation every effort should be made to accentuate form, to throw into high relief the grace or difficulty of accomplishment, and finally to satisfy both eye and spirit with the triumph of human will, the secret of our pleasure.

To appreciate the art of the acrobat to the full one must know exactly what the performer is doing. In ballet the emotion which the dancer produces among those who watch is sufficient to give pleasure, though the connoisseur who knows something of how an effect is produced always experiences a deeper sensation. Since the acrobat is not concerned with expressing emotion, an appreciation of his technical skill becomes all the more important.

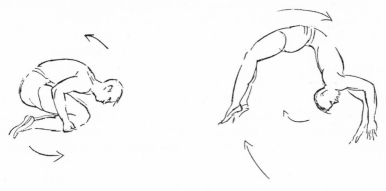

A back somersault. A lay-out back. (Drawing by John Skeaping.)

Let us start with the somersault. Everyone knows that this is a movement in which the body turns around a horizontal axis. Most of us know that it can be performed in two directions, backwards and forwards. But comparatively few realize that in turning even a basic somersault the body can take up one of two positions: balled-up, that is, with the arms hugging the knees to the chest, or in the

A handspring. (Drawing by John Skeaping.)

lay-out position; which means that the body and legs are fully extended. In describing a trick acrobats usually leave out the word somersault and use such phrases as a lay-out back or a double.

A simple somersault carries one in the direction of the turn. In a back, one lands behind the starting point; in a forward somersault, one lands in front of it. But one can also turn spotters to land exactly where one started; and, most difficult of all, one can even throw a back to land in front of this point, a somersault which is know as a gathering back.

A forward somersault is more difficult to do well than a back. And, in spite of the name given to it in France—which is *un casse-cou*, a "break-neck"—it is less dangerous.

In a somersault the hands never touch the ground; in the handspring and the flip-flap they do. To do a handspring the body is flung *forward* onto the hands and the legs are then thrown up and over the body. But the hands should push the body upward and leave the ground before the feet land. The flip-flap is the same movement performed backwards. With arms upstretched, the head and body are thrown *back* on to the hands, and the legs are brought

A flip-flap. (Drawing by John Skeaping.)

A round-off. (Drawing by John Skeaping.)

over the body to jack-knife down behind the arms. If the legs leave
the ground before the hands land, then the movement is called a
monkey, which is short for monkey-jump. It really is a jump, for at
one brief moment the whole body, arched back, is clear of the
ground. But one must have extremely good eyesight to distinguish
this difference.

In the lion's leap the performer jumps up in the air before
throwing himself forward on his hands, as in a handspring, but the
movement is usually completed by the acrobat tucking his head
down, bending his arms so that his body is lowered on to the back
of his neck, and then rolling over, with legs drawn up, and so on to
his feet.

Next we come to three more complicated movements: the round-
off, the brandy and the butterfly. In the round-off the body is
thrown forward on to the hands, but these are not placed side by
side as in the handspring; they land one in front of the other. The
body therefore turns through an angle of ninety degrees as the legs
come up. As they fall, the back hand is raised and the twisting
movement is completed so that by the time the feet reach the

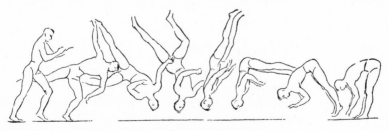

A Borani or brandy. (Drawing by John Skeaping.)

A butterfly. (Drawing by John Skeaping.)

ground the body has turned through an angle of one hundred and eighty degrees. Some people say that a round-off is the same as a cartwheel, but a cartwheel is turned with the body facing front all the time and moves to the side. In a round-off the performer starts facing the finishing point and ends facing the starting point. The movement known as the full round-off consists of a round-off quickly followed by a flip-flap and a back somersault. Irving K. Pond has likened this to a musical composition, in which "the action, starting in the major, flows through the minor, back again to the major, and finishing on the tonic chord, gives contrast of tone and a sense of completed melody." It is an ideal movement with which to end an acrobatic act; if the performer makes his exit with a full round-off, he lands at the ring doors, facing the audience, ready to make his bow.

The brandy—a corruption of Borani—is a cross between the round-off and the forward somersault. The body twists in the air so that on landing it faces the starting point, but, as in the somersault, the hands must never touch the ground. It is made from a running start and the legs follow one another round over the head instead of moving together, though they should both meet the ground at the same time.

Maurice Colleano—brother of Con and Bonar—was an adept at these movements. He would take a short run and then turn a series of flip-flaps, brandies, round-offs and somersaults, including the double, back and forth, crossing the ring four times without a break.

Finally we come to the butterfly. From a standing position, with legs straddled wide, the arms and body are swung slowly to the left, then thrown with as much impetus as possible over and behind the right leg. The left leg has helped this swing by pushing the body off the ground, and now the right leg does the same, so that, with the movement half completed, the body is upside down in the air, but facing the same direction in which it started. In landing the left leg meets the ground first and the right leg follows.

The dozen movements described here by no means form a complete list of the ground acrobat's tricks. The expert can pick out nearly twice this number and, if one were to include the various bends and limbers which are often seen in the gymnasium as well, the total would run into hundreds. I have tried to steer a middle course, ignoring purely elementary work and concentrating on those movements most often seen in the circus which can be elaborated and combined with others. Obviously a double somersault is a greater achievement than a single, but even more important than one particular trick is the way in which a series of movements are made to flow and contrast in rhythm.

There is always some danger, even in ground tumbling, but for those who want more sensational thrills one has only to introduce

A one-hand walk-over. (Drawing by John Skeaping.)

a hoop of knives. The Dutchman, Kees Kalmar, for instance, could leap through a sixty-five centimeter circle of thirteen daggers, held vertically in the air. Besides bringing an extra touch of danger to the act, this hoop of blades stressed the accuracy of the performer's movements.

The tricks so far described can be accomplished unaided. More complicated variations can be achieved with the help of a spring-board. Springboards are of three kinds. There is the small wedge-shaped sort, know as a cushion, which is most often used to help a rider leap to the back of a horse; there is the seesaw or teeter-board, which has led to a particular form of act, to be described later in this chapter; and there is the *batoude*.

This apparatus consists of two parts, first a long board which slopes down to the ring, and then a short spring plank which is supported at either end on trestles of different heights so that it slopes in the opposite direction. It is used for a type of act which is rarely seen in England though still popular in other parts of the world; it is known as The Leaps. The performer runs down the first slope, lands with both feet on the center of the resilient upward-sloping plank and so gains extra lift to clear a series of obstacles; and the effect is enhanced by adding one more obstacle after each leap. While in the air the leaper complicates his flight by turning somersaults and various twists.

Many an artiste has been killed in trying to turn a triple somersault in this act. In a triple, a man is apt to find himself out of control and there is a serious danger of his falling on the back of his neck. A double somersault over four elephants, topped by a pyramid of men, was regularly performed by an American, Artressi, some years ago. This meant a flight of thirty feet from *batoude* to mattress. Leapers always land on a mattress because without it there is too great a risk of the jolt ultimately causing stiffening of the joints. Circus proprietors in Europe might well revive this act. The apparatus is simple, horses and elephants are generally available to serve as obstacles, and there must surely be some performers left who, even if they could not rival Artressi, could give an interesting and original display.

The extra impetus provided by the *batoude* is obtained simply from the resilience of the wood. If instead of supporting the plank at both ends one balances it in the middle, thereby forming a seesaw, one can obtain even more lift. By allowing the heaviest member of the troupe to drop from a pedestal on to one end, a light acrobat standing on the other end can be catapulted high into the air, particularly when the teeter-board is made of a tough springy wood such as hickory. This apparatus would be no use to the leaper, for he has to combine height with distance, which is why he runs down the long sloping board before making his jump. But for vertical flights the teeter-board is unsurpassed, and has given us the springboard act.

In this act an acrobat, known as the top-mounter, is shot into the air to land on the shoulders of a bearer who stands a few feet behind him. His place on the teeter-board can then be taken by another, and the one who weighs most can again climb up on to the pedestal to drop on the raised end and so send a second mounter to the shoulders of the first. The process can be repeated again and again so that a column of four, five, and now even six men high is built. Just as I had corrected that last sentence for this revised edition, I read that the Bulgarian Kehaiovi Troupe have reached seven men high, but not without a perch, and the members do not all stand on their partners' shoulders.

As in the leaps, variety is obtained by turning twists and somersaults during the flight. In 1904, the Picchiani Troupe was the first to turn a back somersault to form a column four-men-high, a feat emulated today by Leana Staneck of the Seven Stanecks. She also turns a back somersault to land on the middleman's head—not shoulders—while he is standing on the bearer's head.

In the climax of this type of act the last top-mounter may turn a double somersault before landing on the shoulders of his partner. The final man is often a child. I believe that when the Ortans first appeared in England, the top-mounter was fourteen years old. It is comparatively rare to find this feat achieved by a fully grown person, although it was included in the routine of the Allisons.

In a springboard act, as in all acrobatics, it is the pattern of movement that counts. And if it is the difficult build-up to a four- or five-men-high that gets the biggest round of applause from the public, the enthusiast will also obtain satisfaction from watching the neat come-down that follows. Irving K. Pond describes the beautiful movements of the Montrose Troupe when they broke their column of three men high. "Suddenly," he writes,"we see what appear to be three somersaults turned simultaneously in the air. The top-mounter has turned and landed on the shoulders of the under-stander, who himself has turned and recovered in time to receive the top-mounter, the middle-man having turned to the shoulders of the fourth, in waiting." The movement finishes with both top-mounters somersaulting to the ground. But, as Pond points out, the first three somersaults are not simultaneous, because each man must have a firm base from which to spring, and so they are turned consecutively—which demands even more concentration and coordination.

In some acts the bearer supports a chair secured to the top of a perch. The flyer, having turned his somersaults, flings himself into the seat. This cannot be compared with the formation of a column. The chair stuck up on the end of the perch is an ugly piece of apparatus; the top-mounter lands bottom first, which is not a very graceful position; and, finally, it is obvious that the bearer can correct any error made by the top-mounter much more easily by moving the chair than by moving three men balanced on his shoulders. The chair is only for the second-rate. One should also notice if the four- or five-men-high is a true column or a pyramid. The Yacopis' five-men-high was formed as a pyramid with three under-standers, then three lower middlemen bearing a "cradle" on which stood a middle middleman bearing a top middleman ready to receive the top-mounter.

The Great Alexanders, who sometimes appeared as the Great Hungarian Troupe, were one of the best springboard acts to be seen in recent years. They were formed out of the troupe which, before World War II, was known as the Magyars, an act originally created by M. Gondor, who became director of the state circus in Budapest. Another excellent act was the Hortobagy Troupe. The best springboard acrobats were often Hungarian or, if not of the Magyar origin, frequently wore Hungarian costumes. Nowadays many other nationals also excel, including the Bulgarian Boytchanovis, who, like the Yacopis, build up a five-men-high pyramid, but without using the middleman's "cradle."

Today Russia and other countries behind the Iron Curtain bring variety into traditional acts by amalgamating two different types of apparatus. The Solohkin Troupe catapult their top-mounter from the springboard to form a three-men-high column, *standing on a wire*. According to Pierre Couderc, the Tokoyas, who are Hungarian, combine a springboard with a Risley act.

A variation of the springboard act which has recently appeared is known as the Russian swing. The principle is that of a child's swing, but the seat is enlarged to become a platform and the ropes are replaced by four rigid bars which lead down to each corner. I find this apparatus too stiff and cumbersome. It reminds me of those old-fashioned steam yachts one used to see on the fairground. It lacks the crisp snap and catapulting effect of a springboard.

Rumania and Bulgaria have provided the greatest bar acts. In its simplest form the apparatus consists of four posts, some eight feet high, set about eight feet apart to form a square. The tops of the posts are joined at either side by wire and at either end by wooden bars on which the gymnasts perform. It is, in fact, an open cube, and this shape makes a perfect framework for a display of acrobatic skill. The word *cubist* was used by the ancient Greeks to denote certain acrobatic movements, and some people may be tempted to try to trace a connection between the contemporary bar act and the classic school of gymnastics. Unfortunately, no such link exists. The bar act was invented by two Americans, Lauck and Fox, in 1875.

Today, three bars set up in the form of a double cube are more often seen than two bars, because this allows for a greater variety of passes. The Poppescus used an apparatus based on the double cube, but by replacing the wires, which usually join the bars at each side, with rigid wooden struts, they brought seven bars into play. The Luppus and Dimitrescus are other Middle Europeans who have excelled at this work. Though Bulgaria and Rumania are renowned for their bar acts, France, Germany and Spain have also produced outstanding performers. Before he turned to animal training, Alfred Court was an amateur gymnast who became a professional *barriste*. He would never think of flying away from the end bar to the ground without turning a somersault, and usually it was a double.

The routine of a bar act consists of circling round the bars, passing from one bar to the other and flying off to the ground, the last two movements being enhanced by various leaps and somersaults. It looks much easier than it really is, for a performance on the bars is one of the most grueling forms of all acrobatic work.

One of the movements which looks most simple is the giant swing, in which the acrobat circles round the bar at arm's length. Yet few people realize that, owing to centrifugal force, when the body reaches the bottom of the circle the drag on the performer's hands is equal to four and a half times the weight of his body. One of the prettiest movements consists of a pass from an end bar to the center arriving in a handstand, and from there passing to the last bar in a *blavette*, which is a jump made from the hands but in which the body and feet swing down, so that the performer hangs from the third bar in a normal position, having left the middle bar with his head down and his feet in the air. Sometimes a pass is made from one end bar to the other straight over the center bar. This is dangerous, and more than one acrobat has been killed when his head hit the middle bar. Contrary to popular belief, this movement is less difficult if the acrobat turns a somersault during his flight over the middle bar than if he does a straight flight. Pierre Couderc says that a straight pass without a somersault "requires such formidable 'counter-timing'. . . that only a few *barristes* such as Enrico Diaz and Alfred Court were able to execute it perfectly."

When two bars are used the act often includes a large proportion of comedy. Jix, Jax and Max, who were really members of the Gridneff troupe of performers on unsupported ladders, dressed up as Searle-ish schoolchildren and presented a comic routine. Amusing though this may be, I prefer to see more straight work; the double and triple bars provide too fine an opportunity to be dismissed as props for clowning.

In the Silaghis' act, I remember, the comedy work was confined to a dwarf, and they obtained variety by setting a catcher at one end, hanging from a bar which was higher than the other two, so that some of the movements were reminiscent of the flying trapeze. Another bar act which gave me great satisfaction was that of the Ibarras, who forsook this work for the flying trapeze.

Some of the bar acts which I have mentioned were performed at a great height. One of the first to work an aerial routine was Avalo, who got his name from being called *un diavolo*—a devil—by the King of Italy. The Avalos afterward produced an act in which the bars were set vertically instead of horizontally, but I do not think anyone else followed in their footsteps.

Bar acts were often combined with others. The Soviet Zementov Troupe used a set of four bars, of which the two in the center were slightly higher, rigged above a trampoline. A trampoline, like a springboard and *batoude*, is also used to give an acrobat extra impetus in making a jump. It is rather like a wire-spring bedstead. Canvas, stretched tightly on laced elastic or steel springs, provides a resilient platform. It looks like a game for children, but it can be surprisingly dangerous. The Zementov trampoline must have been thirty-five feet in length, for it stretched nearly across the ring, but I have seen others which are no more than ten or twelve feet long.

Sometimes a trampoline is set up with two uprights at one or both ends which support a catcher. On such an apparatus Tito Gaona can throw a triple somersault to the shoulders of his brother just as he does from bar to catcher on the flying trapeze.

The tempo of a trampoline act is slower that that of an ordinary ground acrobat. The extra spring which the trampoline gives to the performer allows him to turn beautiful, slow somersaults and pirouettes in the air; it therefore provides an excellent means of studying the turns and twists of various acrobatic movements. It frequently gives one the impression of watching a slow-motion film. The acrobats seem to hover at the top of their flight, which introduces a fascinating hesitation into the rhythm. It lends itself especially to comedy, for when anyone falls flat on his face he immediately bounces back to an upright position. Sometimes members of the audience are invited into the ring to try it out. It looks much easier than it really is. And anyone not used to standing on a trampoline will find it so difficult to balance that the effect is bound to be ludicrous.

The jargon of the trampoline performer contains phrases which are incomprehensible to other acrobats. Pierre Couderc tells how a friend referred to a certain performer's "right and left double arabs" only to be corrected by a trampoline artiste who said: "Those are not side somersaults, sir. They look like it to you, but each is really a brandy, out of a fliffis." This last word is how a trampolinist describes a forward double somesault with a half-twist on the second turn.

The real comedy turn of the ground acrobat is the Humpsti-Bumpsti act. A few chairs, a table, a ladder, perhaps a plank of wood, a butter slide, two men—and the fun begins. Never for one moment is the chair under the man who is about to sit down, nowhere else can one find a table with such a slippery surface, no one but the most experienced *cascadeur* could fall so hard and so often. Often such acts end with each man grasping his partners ankles, head to feet, and rolling like a crazy wheel up and over the table, then back between the legs and underneath, and so out through the ring doors.

Though primarily a comedy number, the Humpsti-Bumpsti act usually contains a great deal of highly skilled work, and the timing and muscular control are often much more difficult than in many straight acts. Anyone can appreciate the crazy inevitability of such a knock-about number, but the speed at which the routine is taken allows little time to grasp the effort which is involved, unless, as sometimes happens, a short contrasting sequence of slow-motion acrobatics is introduced. One of the best variations of this is "the man who deflates himself," gradually subsiding to the ground like a pricked balloon.

At the beginning of this chapter I pointed out that the acrobat is not concerned with expressing emotions or sentiments. Yet there is one act which, as well as demonstrating physical skill, seems at least to symbolize a state of mind. It is not merely a play upon words that has made the British refer to psychiatrists as trick-cyclists, and there is a psychological appeal in the act of the man who rides, or tries to ride, a bicycle in the ring. In Joe Jackson's exquisite clowning we could see a tramp being tempted by an inanimate object which only became alive when touched by the hands of man. But as soon as this happened it seemed to be possessed by a thousand devils. The duel between Joe and his bicycle was the epitome of the old fight between man and machine. When, in the ring, man loses the battle, the audience feels intensely sympathetic; when he triumphs, they are delighted.

In a straight act we see the trick-cyclist either completely subordinating his machine, sometimes forcing it to accomplish the almost unbelievable, or we see him working in such harmony with it that the characteristics of both the rider and his bicycle are presented in a fresh and stimulating way. The outstanding effects gained by the trick-cyclist are thrown into high relief by being contrasted with the inevitable rhythm of his pedaling. The bicycles used in the circus have no free-wheel and are low-geared, so the rider's legs move steadily up and down but faster than normal. Suddenly this quick rhythm is broken, when, with a deft back-pedal, he stops and raises the front of the machine to balance it on the rear wheel. The extreme smoothness of the bicycle's movement as it circles round and round the ring complements this rhythm and also provides a contrast to the sudden spectacular tricks.

The earliest trick-cyclist was a man named Ancillotti, who is said to have introduced this type of act in 1868. His son, Ugo, led the Ancillotti troupe of nine performers, whose routine at one time included a backward leap from the shoulders of one rider to land in a handstand on the shoulders of another following, both bearers being mounted on penny-farthings.

Since then there have been many excellent troupes of trick-cyclists, and among the best I can remember was the Klein Family. I have never seen a better designed act than theirs. It had a strong element of comedy backed up by some remarkable tricks. Once again the principal performer was a tramp; however good the supporting company, he always managed to go one better. His one-wheel waltz was most satisfying to watch, and he also proved to be a brilliant clown. Other acts, such as the Brockways, rely on comic bicycles for their effect. This can be overdone; comedy props should never dominate an act, they should always be subservient to the human performers.

With monocycles, the higher the saddle, the more spectacular the act becomes. But the effort required to keep one's balance makes the routine appear jerky. This type of machine is best used in comedy numbers, such as that worked by the Dormonde Brothers, who, although they appeared mostly on the music hall stage and in the cabaret, were admirably suited to the circus.

Today the Russian Pekouline Troupe presents a routine in which two monocyclists, facing each other, carry a bar on their shoulders. On this a third monocyclist balances, bearing a top-mounter on his head.

One might think that a monocycle is the lowest cycle denomination, but in the 1890s a Frenchman appeared on a semicycle, a half-wheel. This freak machine was not a success and he went back to the bicycle on which he specialized in looping the loop.

Serge, the son of a proprietor of a bicycle shop in the suburbs of Paris, achieved some remarkably fine hand balances on a bicycle which was placed on top of a high pedestal. But good as this act may have been, one cannot compare it with one which keeps on the move all the time. After all, a bicycle is first and foremost a means of locomotion, and it is a pity not to use it in this way. Of the solo performers, the best I have seen is Lily Yokoi. Her technique is faultless, her sense of style impeccable, and both are imbued with her own compelling personality.

Another act which can be seen on the Continent combines trick-cycling with a perch act. I find this a rather unhappy union. In the perch act, strength is allied to balance; by setting a perch on a bicycle, the weight of the top-mounter is taken by the machine, and half the effect is lost.

This chapter deals primarily with acts which contain movement, and it always amazes me that a piece of apparatus as small as a pair of roller skates should produce an act of such speed. At the end of the last century Harry French, having completed his routine on a monocycle, without a saddle, would finish his act by appearing with a small wheel strapped to each ankle; since then roller-skating in the circus has been closely allied to the work of the trick-cyclist. Roller skates do not allow one much variety in routine, but by introducing a mouthpiece with which the skater supports his partner as she spins round in a horizontal plane while he revolves in a small circle, a short sharp act can be built up to a thrilling finish.

There is one other type of circus performance which comes into the category of ground acrobatics. Arab tumbling makes no use of props, but its character is so individual that it deserves a place to itself. The act usually consists of building up and breaking down a series of human pyramids. The climax often consists of one member of the troupe supporting all the other members, and since these may number eight or nine, this feat requires prodigious strength. Such an act always ends with a display of whirlwind tumbling. One after another the Arabs leap across and around the ring in a series of somersaults, cartwheels, flip-flaps and twisters. For the most part the tricks are familiar, though the bounding sideways somersault is a particularly Arabian leap. The technique by which the ordinary movements are accomplished, however, is very different from that employed by a European. Arabs seem to hang in the air. There is a hesitation in the wildness of their action. Where an acrobat trained in the Western school leaps, the Oriental seems to bound. Irving K. Pond has noted this difference and taken it a stage further. He has traced a similarity in the Eastern approach to music, architecture and tumbling, and he contrasts this in each case with its Western counterpart: "Where in the West the composition is expressed in a long gradual sweep, in the East it is demonstrated by a succession of brilliant chromatic runs."

No Arab has equaled the amazing work of Bracco or Iñas, who did as much straight off the ground as many now attempt with the help of a springboard. But perhaps it is a little unfair to compare two such different schools. Just as one can appreciate the architecture of a mosque as well as of a cathedral, so can one derive pleasure from the tumbling of the Arab as well as the performance of a Western acrobat.

XIV

CLOWNS' ENTRÉE

So we come to the clowns. I have left them to appear at the end of the bill partly because I wanted the final act to give those of you who are still sitting in a ringside seat something you could view with tolerant amusement, and partly because I wanted to show how much of the appeal of the circus is gained from purely physical displays before coming to the one turn which is based on thought.

Like a wire-walker, the clown treads a narrow path; he walks the knifelike edge which divides humor and pathos. He holds the balance between action and repose, between the clearest madness and the cloudiest sanity. He plays with situations, characters and words as the juggler plays with his clubs, knives and rings. He can appear as eccentric as any contortionist, yet underneath his grotesque buffoonery one is always conscious of a dignity as great as that of the high school rider. And his spontaneous grace and spiritual daring are the complement of the grace and daring of the aerial acrobat. He is the soul of the circus.

He is both iconotect and iconoclast; for though no one else breaks our images with such thoroughness, neither does anyone else first build them up with such skill. He projects himself into the noblest role, only to drag forth the fool lurking within. André Suarès once said, "He holds the tragic mirror to comedy and the comic mirror to tragedy."

Down through the ages man has always been sentimental enough to etherealize "he who gets slapped." It is this which has kept clownship moving. M. Willson Disher has described this in his stimulating and comprehensive study *Clowns and Pantomimes* (London: Constable, 1925). Arlecchino started his career in rags and tatters, as the butt of every jest. From there he moved through the rôles of knave, parodist, magician and dancer, until his rags and tatters became stylized in the lozenges of his present dress. Even the colors he wears have become symbols: red, fire; blue, water; yellow, air; black, earth; and these have somehow come to be called elemental *humors*. The character as a whole has become the symbol of romance.

Meanwhile, Pierrot had taken his place as the butt. Soon he too changed, first to knave and finally to mystic, the symbol of sentiment. The butt then became Clown, who likewise graduated through the stages of knavery and bullying to achieve the symbol of a kind of cunning wisdom. His place was taken by Auguste, who, also being the one who gets slapped, is now almost etherealized into the symbol of pathos.

While it took several hundred years to bring about the metamorphosis of Harlequin, in Charlie Chaplin we saw the process accomplished in a lifetime.

Who will be the next butt? There are signs that it may be the crazy zany of the American hokum act. In the world of today he may well develop into the symbol of erudition.

A Frenchman once said, "Clowning is a particularly English speciality, because it personifies the Englishman's extraordinary penchant for eccentricity, the dominant symptom of Anglo-Saxon melancholy." History has disproved this; although it has shown that during the last century a considerable number of the greatest clowns were English, and that most of them received more recognition in France than in their native country. Price, Boswell, Bibb, Sandy, Grice, Hayden, Foottit, the Hanlon-Lees . . .

On their sentimental journey, some pierrots were diverted from their route and found themselves cavorting in the circus ring. Here, under acrobatic and equestrian influence, they became what we know as clowns, though they were then billed as "grotesques." At first they could hold the ring alone. But when "Mr. Merryman," in exchanging pleasantries with the ringmaster, made that august person look too foolish, it became apparent that the clown would have to find his own butt.

These early equestrian and acrobatic clowns became crystallized in the great French clown, Jean-Baptiste Auriol. Born in 1806 at Toulouse, to a family of gymnasts, Auriol was first trained as an acrobat. After touring the French provinces with his family, he traveled through Spain, Prussia, Bohemia, Switzerland and Holland with Loisset's Circus. In 1835 he appeared for the first

AURIOL
Le premier Clown français
Lithographie de THIERRY Frères, à Paris
1841

Auriol, the first great French clown. (From the author's collection.)

time in Paris, and he caused a sensation. This "dainty Hercules," as Théophile Gautier called him, leaped over eight mounted horsemen and twenty-four soldiers firing their rifles. His favorite trick was to put on a pair of slippers, then turn a somersault out of them and land in them again. He was also a brilliant rider. But first and foremost he was a clown.

In England the great clown was Joseph Grimaldi, who was a pantomime artiste. The nearest he came to the ring was when his father composed a dance which was produced at the Royal Circus; yet he left his Christian name as a legacy to all clowns, who are still called Joey to this day.

Men like Decastro filled the comic roles at Astley's. They gave place to others such as Dickie Usher, who once traveled from Westminster to Waterloo Bridge in a tub drawn through the water by eight geese, and from there set off in a carriage pulled by eight cats. A similar feat was performed by Tom Barry, who sailed from Vauxhall to Westminster in a washing-tub drawn by four geese in 1884. In both cases it would be more accurate to say *appeared* to be drawn by geese, because the tubs, in fact, were towed by rowing boats some distance ahead.

Although trained animals—other than horses—appeared with clowns in small traveling circuses, such a combination did not become popular in the resident circuses for some time. It was not until the end of the last century that an outstanding success was achieved by a man with an animal partner. That happened when the Englishman Tony Grice introduced his performing pig Charlie to Paris.

Many of the traditional gags were invented in this era. Some time ago, when putting on an exhibition of circusiana in a London store, I came across the descendant of a clown famous a hundred or more years ago, The Great Little Huline. This clown's son had also entered the profession, and I acquired his reminiscences. They are written in a fine copperplate hand upon six sheets of paper, which measure twenty-four by fifteen inches. The first sentence runs: "I was born in Dundee in 1842, where my parents were playing with Cooke's Circus." After describing various circuses all over Europe, he goes on: "We were the first to make an entertainment of the hat-throwing business. In 1883 we were [employed] in Paris at £36 a week for our hat-throwing."

As I read, I remembered that only a few days previously I had seen a clown sending a series of white conical hats spinning through the air, to land, one on top of another, on his partner's head. I had a look at the hats afterwards, and found that they made use of the same device that Huline had thought of nearly seventy years before: a rubber stiffener hidden in the rolled brim which keeps the hat open as it sails through the air.

I have heard it said that the Russian clown Durov, whose trained rats are described in an earlier chapter, was the first to mock the failings of the bourgeoisie. Certainly he caused several officials of the imperial régime to lose office. He also deflated the pomposity of the Prussian military caste when he taught his pig to ridicule the *pickelhaube*—a gag which nearly caused an international incident. He and his pig were expelled from Germany in 1907 for *lèse-majesté*. He was fined a greater sum for poking fun at those in authority than any other Russian clown, and I believe he had a street named after him in Moscow. But Foottit and his negro partner, Chocolat, had satirized class-consciousness at the Nouveau Cirque in Paris during the final quarter of the last century.*

Foottit was the son of an English circus proprietor. His mother was Sarah Crockett, whose brother married "Lord" George Sanger's sister. The boy first appeared in the ring when he was three years old. Thirty years later he was the idol of Paris, making 1,200 francs a month.

In 1867 the clown's father was, for a short time, a partner in Powell and Clarke's Circus. From that almost forgotten enterprise came not only the great Foottit himself, immortalized by Toulouse-Lautrec, but John Frederick Clarke, champion jockey-rider of the world, and Ernie Clarke, the first man to turn a triple somersault on the flying trapeze. Even the Powells achieved more than average renown. Though their riding was overshadowed by the Clarkes, they joined the Henglers, both in marriage and in highly successful management.

Suddenly, in the midst of his success, Foottit left the French capital without a word and turned up in St. Petersburg, where he earned twenty-five thousand francs in six months. Perhaps it was after watching his performance here that Durov found the technique which he later put to such good effect in the service of—and occasionally in opposition to—the new ideology.

Acrobatic clowns were still in vogue in the 90s. Their development began in the middle of the century, when the Prices excelled,

---

* In Spain Ramper was fined so often for poking fun at the Franco régime that the first thing he would do on entering the ring was to hand over his money, saying, "There's my fine in advance. Now I can speak my mind!"

and reached an even higher level with the Hanlon-Lees, whom D.L. Murray has described as "the cynic philosophers of the *fin-de-siècle* —the unconscious prophets of the crash of its civilization." But the main trend in circus clowning then took the form which we know so well today—the clown and the auguste.

According to some authorities the auguste was born in 1864, when a jockey-rider, called Tom Belling, stumbled drunkenly into the ring and grinned foolishly at the audience of Renz's Circus in Berlin. The audience called "Auguste—idiot!" and the next day he reddened his nose and, wearing a suit several sizes too large, deliberately stumbled and smiled fatuously at the public. They took this new character to their hearts. He was introduced to Paris by Guyon fourteen years later, but it was not until the end of the century that the auguste found his rightful place as the partner and butt of the clown.

So Foottit found Chocolat, and in their train came Cyrillo and Busby, Alex and Porto, Ilès and Loyal, Antonet and Beby, Pipo and Rhum, the Cairolis and many others—always the elegant, clever white-faced clown and the outrageous auguste, in the baggy trousers and grotesque makeup.

In Russia and America the tendency seems to have been for clowns and augustes to work alone. Oleg Popov, Karandash, Emmett Kelly and Lou Jacobs, for instance, are all individual performers.

Although the clown has long forgotten that he was the one who once got slapped—and though there have been signs in the last fifty years that the auguste is also becoming etherealized—the clown is not yet ready to move on. So the duo in some cases has become a trio or a quartet, such as the Zacchinis, the Fratellinis, the Albanos, and the Dario-Barios—always the one clown, but with two or even three foils.

I remember an old clown saying to me, in 1950:

> Things aren't what they used to be, you know, not for clowns. Take the Christmas shows. Run in, run round, run out. That's all it is. As for tenting! Why, they get the tent hands to clown now. Labourers at £6 a week, grub and a doss down in the horse tent, appearing in the ring as clowns!

There was a lot of truth in that, and there still is. Between the wars most circuses billed a whole gang of clowns; but the only ones that were remembered were the entrée clowns, who had a place in

the programme to themselves and appeared as an act. As the old
pro said, the others—fill-in clowns—"ran in, ran round and ran
out," while the props were being set for the next number. And it
happens today. The quicker the ring is set, the slicker the production—and the less time there is for clowns.

To "get across" to an audience, six to nine thousand strong, in
forty-five seconds means that the clowns must produce an immediate visual impact. In this the Sloans excelled. They realized
that the alarm clock strapped to the wrist as a watch, or a wooden
beer-barrel tap used as a cigarette-holder, were all right for an
English tenting show, but no good for Ringling Bros. and Barnum
& Bailey in America, where three rings and four stages were
surrounded by a hippodrome track. Here the old school of clowning
is dead and even the traditional masks of white-faced clown and
red-nosed auguste are being lost in a less subtle makeup which
blends both. Bigger audiences mean broader effects; so the Sloans
specialized in stilt-walking. And if you looked in the professional
newspapers you could find advertisments nearly as long as their
legs.

In the old days all clowns who were looking for a job would insert
a discreet "card" in the professional press. It would read:

> AT LIBERTY
> CABERNET AND PINOT
> International Clown and Auguste
> All coms., 73 Aïda Avenue, Brixton,
> London SW9

All that has changed. I remember reading an advertisement in
The World's Fair which ran to more than six column-inches,
inserted by the Sloans, whose real name is Yelding. Starting with
"The NAME should be sufficient. VACANT FOR THE SUM-
MER SEASON," it went on to list the many effects and props
which the leader, Harry, "the champion high stilt-walker of the
world," could produce. "Comedy stilt walk-rounds" included "Fat
Policemen, Evening Dress Drunks and Female Crinolines." Coming off their stilts the Sloans offered "comedy novelty walk-
rounds," of which Three-headed Clowns, Upside-down Women,
Rubberneck Women, Female Dwarfs and Giant Cockerels were
but a few. They went on to offer with pride their Comedy Horse
Entrée, listing the circuses in which it had achieved an outstanding
success. The advertisement proceeded to point out that they were

willing "to work in conjunction with others in any entrées for which we have, without fear of contradiction, the finest array of sequin spangle satin clown dresses, with which we combine deportment and speak the King's English." The Sloans deserve their success both in England and abroad. There are very few English fill-in clowns and even fewer entrée clowns who have achieved an international success in recent years. Old Regnas is one exception, and if you read the name backwards you may see the reason why. He is the great-great-grandson of John, brother of "Lord" George Sanger. Perhaps Regnas should be classified as a comedy animal act, but in that case Durov would also have to come into the same category, and he is always counted as a clown. The other exception is Don Saunders who is very definitely a clown, although in recent years he has forsaken the bald wig which, like Grock and Noni, he used to wear.

The situation which faces the clown confronts many other circus artistes in England. But while the skill of the acrobat, the juggler or the rider cannot be learned in half an hour, too many circus proprietors seem to think that funny business can; so they dish out the old threadbare gags to the tent-hands, together with a pot of clown-white and a stick of carmine, telling them to get on with it.

Clowns often start their careers as riders, acrobats, wire-walkers or jugglers. It is difficult to say, for instance, whether the French clown Beby will go down to history as an auguste or as the middleman in the unique three-men-high on horseback of the Fredianis. Such clowns only turn to the more ephemeral talent of laughter-making when broken bones, stiffening joints or chance prevent them from working their usual act. Many of them, therefore, are middle-aged or unfit for other work. It is not surprising that when times are bad a number of proprietors of small tenting shows feel that they can do without them and employ tent-hands and lorry drivers instead.

What these proprietors forget, however, is that the professional clown is always thoroughly grounded in ring technique. They also forget the importance of personality and individuality. In attempting to teach the amateur to call ponies "palonies," and other traditional gags, they forget the power of Grock's "Sans blague!" of Pimpo's eager "Let me have a go!" and of Charlie Rivels's ecstatic "Acrobat-oh!" If they remembered these things, they might produce clowns who were at least adequate.

The most important aspect in the appearance of a clown—

particularly an auguste—is his silhouette. That is why the nose is so often exaggerated and often the feet as well. Emphasis is given to features that protrude. This basic principle was completely ignored by the man who thought the individual makeup of each clown and auguste should be painted on an egg shell to form a sort of register. The one thing an egg can never show is a different silhouette.

To tell a good clown from a bad one is easy—either you are amused or you are not. But to distinguish a great clown from a good one is more difficult. A great clown will never give anyone the impression that he is playing a part. He never appears to have learned his lines or studied his gestures. He seems to be a fathomless source of perfect improvisation. One is conscious of a power which appears limitless because it reverses our preconceived ideas; to quote André Suarès again, "the clown's greatest cry is silence; stupor is his eloquence."

A great clown will not stoop to caricature. We caricature only those things we despise. To ridicule the things we love demands the higher art of parody. Just as the Greeks would parody a sacred drama immediately following its first performance, so the clown in the modern circus will parody the things we hold most sacred today. To do this he must be a great clown.

One of the finest tributes paid to any artiste are the words which Jacques Copeau wrote in his introduction to Pierre Mariel's *Histoire de trois clowns* (Paris: S.A. d'Editions, 1923), the life story of the Fratellinis, who were made *Officiers de l'Académie*. He tells them to remain content with simply being clowns, who, after all, are the heirs of the exquisite commedia dell'arte. He explains that they have already exerted a marked influence on this age and that as time goes on they will doubtless have more and more imitators, but that they will always be distinguished by two inimitable qualities, purity of style and what he calls *gentillesse*. "By purity of style," he says, "I mean your perfect technique . . . particularly in giving expression to sincere and spontaneous sentiment." He describes *gentillesse* as that quality which, throughout history, has always been found in the truly great clown, for no matter how low he stoops in his buffoonery he never forgets the dignity of man.

The Fratellinis, like all great clowns, worked an entrée and never filled in between turns. Entrées are mainly traditional plots such as *The Barber of Seville, The Living Statue, William Tell, The Bull Fight, Hamlet,* and now there seems to be an epidemic of comic motor cars. Some entrées provide a greater chance to study a clown's technique than others. One which accentuates the necessity for perfect timing is The Broken Mirror,* and I have never seen this better presented than by Pipo and Rhum, both alas! now dead.

The plot is simple. The clown explains to M. Loyal, the traditional blue-coated French ringmaster, that he has just been given a leading part in a new play and would like to rehearse in front of a full length looking glass. The auguste is told to fetch one while the clown goes off to change into his theatrical costume.

There is a crash of breaking glass, then the auguste reenters in so nonchalant a manner that it obviously hides extreme embarrassment. *No, no, no, there has been no accident. . . . The crash? . . . A mere bagatelle . . . a small hole . . . nothing. . . .* But he is forced to get the looking glass, and he brings in the huge frame with a few jagged splinters of glass sticking to the corners. There is only one way out: the auguste must act the part of the clown's reflection.

It is fortunate that the clown's costume is a smart version of his partner's rags. He may not notice the difference, especially as he has been celebrating his good luck. Mistily he sees his reflection in the mirror. He advances, and the auguste also steps up to the frame. Together they breathe heavily on the imaginary glass that separates them, together they remove an imaginary speck with a forefinger and together they polish its surface. Then the clown must have a raw egg for his voice; his throat is a little sore. But since only one egg is forthcoming, the auguste has to hide it in his trouser pocket. And so the pantomime goes on. . . .

The auguste, thinking everything is too easy, gets overconfident. The clown sweeps off his hat in a low bow. Quite naturally the auguste follows suit. But when the clown regains his upright position he sees that his reflection has the hat in the opposite hand. Really puzzled, he moves his hat from his right hand to his left. He sees the hat move across the mirror from left to right. He tries again, and the auguste, oblivious to the implication, again reverses the movement. The clown, astounded, slaps his thighs. The auguste mimics the gesture . . . and then the game is up. He has forgotten the egg in his trouser pocket.

That is all. It is the simplest plot imaginable. And yet when Pipo and Rhum worked together, their timing, their sure knowledge of

---

* Lupino Lane, in his informative and entertaining book *How to Become a Comedian,* says that this was invented by his grandfather, George Hook Lupino, and first performed by him and Fred Evans at the City of London Theatre in 1862. Tristan Rémy, however, traces its origin to the popular theatre in eighteenth-century Spain and says it was introduced to the circus by the Scheffers.

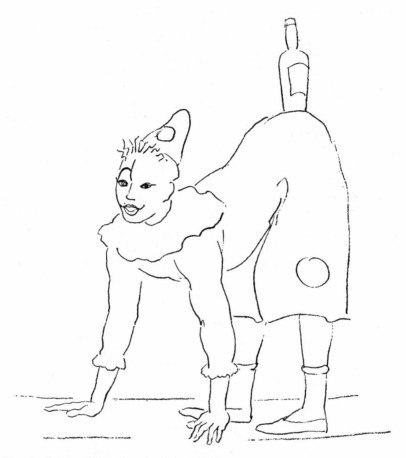

Circus clown. (Drawing by John Skeaping.)

the psychological moment and their artistry in that one short scene was worth more than three long acts at many a London theatre. The scene is still performed today, and among the best to include it in their repertoire are the admirable Swiss Chickys. It was Rhum —or was it Porto?—who started the fashion of using the name of a drink as a *nom-de-piste*. Anyhow, Porto, Rhum, Whisky, Cognac and Pastis have all appeared in the ring.

To most of us the old story of the clown who rushes into the ring to make others laugh, while behind his painted grin a sob is stifled, must seem the epitome of Victorian sentimentality. Yet, on several occasions I have known clowns step onto the sawdust with a heavy heart. Bobino—my old friend Bob Beasy, who gave me such help in training my cats—was told that his wife Bertha had died in hospital only a few minutes before he appeared in the ring. And an even greater shock came to Lulu, the daughter of that grand old clown Joe Craston. On the eve of opening at Ringling's Circus at Madison Square Garden, she and her husband were broadcasting. "He does such funny things," said Lulu of her husband. "Yes, I do," replied Albertino, and at that moment fell down dead. But within half an hour Lulu was on the hippodrome track at the final dress rehearsal.

Just as often, a clown, after hearing good news, enters the ring with a dancing heart. Of course the public never hears about it. People are sentimental enough to prefer to link sorrow with the clown. They like to identify themselves with "he who gets slapped." Children love him for a simpler reason. He expresses, loudly and eloquently, the bewilderment they feel when they find themselves in an adult world. In showing up the ridiculous foibles of mankind he provides the young with the confirmation of their suspicions that it's pretty silly being grown-up anyway, and for that they adore him.

XV

FINALE

The programme is over. But in much the same way as all the artistes gather together in the ring to take their final bow and thus sum up the performance as a whole, so I would like you to think back on the performers who have appeared before you in these pages and to see if they provide any evidence to substantiate or disprove the principles of the circus which were outlined during the Overture.

Wherever circus enthusiasts forgather you will always hear someone say that such and such an act "is not circus." Nine times out of ten the reply will be, "Not circus? What do you mean? It was done at Astley's." Astley's has come to be regarded as a standard, but it is a false standard, because soon after its opening it got mixed up with the theatre. To find out what is and is not "circus," we must go back to first principles.

You will remember that in looking at the empty ring we saw that the circus could be seen from all sides, and that because of this it gave us a stronger feeling of the third dimension than any other entertainment—the feeling of solidity which one gets from looking at sculpture, instead of its two-dimensional representation seen in painting or on the stage. This business of being able to see things from all sides made the circus the spectacle of actuality. Pierre Bost once wrote, "In an age when women wear jewellery made of glass and wood, when houses are built of strawboard and when silly couplets after being sung by the whole world for six months, are forgotten the next day, it is pleasant to think that the circus remains the one domain where one cannot build without wisdom, and where diamonds are never rivalled by paste."

Conjurors should find no place in the circus, for as Edouard de Perrodil said in *Monsieur Clown!* (Paris: Dalou, 1889), "trickery and the ring cannot be reconciled," and the artiste who deliberately fakes his trick is despicable. Even the props should never look other than what they really are. The apparatus of a bar act which is disguised as a pergola or the perch which is made to look like a palm tree is ridiculous in the ring, though it may seem quite suitable on the variety stage.

Although the same acts appear both in variety theatres and circuses, a clear distinction must be made between these two entertainments. The apparatus may be the same, but the methods of production which the stage imposes forbid the establishment of actuality. Pierre Bost pointed out that in a variety theatre the curtain rises on a scene in which the apparatus is already set up. It bursts upon us in all its glory. How are we to be sure that there is no fake? In the circus each piece is brought in separately and assembled before our eyes. The wires and struts are tested in full view of the audience by the performer, who slips into the ring in his dressing-gown before he makes his proper entrance in tights and spangles. The music hall romanticizes the circus, and this is gilding the lily, for if truth is sometimes stranger than fiction, then actuality can be more enchanting than romance.

The facts that the circus audience holds the spectacle in its midst and that this spectacle is one of actuality both lead us to the third principle: that those who watch are a part of the show. In the circus there is a stronger tie between the public and the performer than there is in any other entertainment.

These attributes must give one certain principles of production. The shape of the ring demands movement; and movement is also required by the practical needs of the audience, for an act must be worked in the round. Though it is possible to put a circus act on a music hall stage, a variety act should not appear in the ring because it is played in one direction. The fact that in the circus one can always see what is going on behind a performer's back helps to establish the feeling of actuality. The acrobats, jugglers, gymnasts and horsemen who find the ring the ideal place in which to perform are still those who rely entirely on their own physical skill and dexterity, who actually do exactly what they appear to do, who can and should be seen from all sides because they have nothing to hide and everything to show.

Sculpture is not seen at its best in a picture. The fact that the circus is essentially three-dimensional makes it impossible to present it at its best on a two-dimensional screen, whether on the large cinema screen or the small television screen. When busts or statuettes are filmed or televised they are usually shown rotating on a turntable. This might be done with some individual numbers in the circus, but with others a revolving ring would merely negate the movement of the act. Even if the camera were to track round and round the ring fence it would hardly enhance a liberty act. There is another reason why the camera can never satisfy the circus devotee. The eye that watches the spectacle is the lens of the camera, and what it looks at is selected by the director. It does not necessarily focus on what you or any individual member of the audience wants to see.

On the other hand, given a knowledgeable and enthusiastic director, it can teach the tyro a lot. By zooming in to a certain hold, by showing, say, footwork in close-up and, above all, by replaying acrobatic moves in slow motion, the camera can teach one to appreciate what is really involved in a beautifully explicit way.

Circus acts must also be produced with the utmost simplicity and with purity of style. The more complicated the turn, the simpler its presentation must be, so that the audience can appreciate more readily exactly what effort is involved. But simplicity must not be confused with the simple. A simple act contains little spectacle, and spectacle is another essential quality, though it must be kept under control. Sheer weight of numbers can provide spectacle, but more often than not there will be no room, then, for recognition of artistry. The artistry of the act should come first; its spectacular features should either enhance the craftsmanship or be derived directly from it, never destroy it.

In the chapter on liberty horses I pointed out that it was better to see four beautifully trained animals in a meticulous routine than forty tossing manes and a hundred and sixty flying hooves. Circus publicity often ignores this point and proudly proclaims, "twenty-five acts, fifty elephants and two hundred horses!" This probably makes the public think that it is getting wonderful value for its money, just as most people will think that a man who has a dozen suits must be better dressed than a man with only two, until it is explained to them that it is the cut that counts. As soon as you begin to know something about the circus, you will look for names on the posters, not numbers. And you will soon find that in the best acts, color, lighting, costumes, music and tempo are all used to enhance movement, style and the feeling of actuality.

Have the greatest artistes and directors always provided us with the proof of all this? On the whole I think that the performers have, though the proprietors have not. The outstanding acts of the circus, such as those of Colleano, Frediani, Codona, Rastelli, and more recently the Geraldos, the Schumanns, Gunther Gebel-Williams, Kris Kremo, Lily Yokoi and the Flying Farfans have all been distinguished by these things. Of course they have other qualifications as well. A star has to have personality, ability and, more important still, the power which enables him to sell his act. How often has a really excellent trick misfired because it has not been presented with the panache, the verve and that touch of justifiable arrogance which links the performer to his audience and holds the two in sympathy? But these assets are not confined to the circus artiste alone, and it is the distinguishing qualities of his act with which we are concerned.

The public and the proprietors have been less fastidious. The public has not discriminated between the real hard work of the tumbler or bar performer and the easier, more showy routine of the springboard. The directors and proprietors of permanent circuses replaced the tan with coco-matting, which ruined voltige and jockey acts—and the public let them. In the tenting shows these aspects of horsemanship also went into decline, for the American system of one-day stands does not always allow one to build the perfect ring. When Henry Thétard was travelling with the Radio Circus in 1950, he found that for this reason Gruss had to cut out his riding act in one town out of every four.

The directors have often dressed their house numbers to look pretty instead of to show movement or enhance the characteristics of an act. A high school number should be dressed so that the unity of the horse and rider can be appreciated; it should also echo the stateliness which the act shows above all others. I was interested to find that this had long been appreciated by the French Army. The uniform of *le Cadre Noir* has remained the same since the creation of the cavalry school at Saumur in 1825. It is a severe and simple design, and as *l'Ecuyer en Chef*, General Blacque-Belair, pointed out in 1909, "It is dark to show the silhouette to advantage."

Hungarian peasant costumes with frills and bows and ribbons, with baggy trousers and exotic headdresses, take the eye away from the very points that should be accentuated. The fluttering color and form of these costumes would be excellent for an act of dashing horsemanship—but not *la haute école*. I have yet to see the riding clothes of the last century bettered for this act. But there is no need for them to be black. Thérèse Renz wore a white riding habit, and there are still people who think that no one has looked better.

Music is being treated in much the same way. All the really great directors from Cuzent to Sarrasani have taken meticulous trouble with their music. Just as tights and leotards help an act because they are of good design, so do such tunes as "Under the Double Eagle" by Wagner, Sousa's "Washington Post" and Strauss's "Radetzky March." Why today production numbers featuring pop singers or groups should be introduced, I do not know. It seems to show the theatrical influence of make-believe, the invasion of musical comedy and cabaret. The Cirque Medrano went through a bad period only when variety artistes and cabaret performers entered its ring. In the heyday of the circus, Paris could boast of five permanent circus buildings. London, alone of all the great European capitals, found that it could not support one amphitheatre, but London is the only city that time and time again built circuses which included a stage. Ask the ordinary circus-goer which act he found least satisfactory in a performance, and nine times out of ten he will name an act lacking in one of the true characteristics of the circus which I have described.

Circus proprietors have often complained of the difficulty in finding first-class acts, and of the expense involved in adapting an existing building to a circus for a limited season. At Blackpool, the circus became so popular that an extra matinée had to be introduced each morning. Perhaps if there was a small permanent building, such as the Tower Circus in Blackpool, it would still be possible to put on an excellent programme and make it pay in London, in spite of a limited seating capacity. Perhaps one day the circus will find a permanent home in the place where it was born.

Because the American public has come to expect three rings, I doubt that this could ever be accomplished in New York, and yet I am not entirely convinced. America has drawn many original acts from Europe, and recently a circus school has been founded in New York City which presents its students in a single ring. In Paris today the Conservatoire National du Cirque, run by Alexis Gruss junior and Silvia Monfort, present *Le Cirque à l'Ancienne*. There is also the Ecole Nationale du Cirque run by Annie Fratellini and

Pierre Etaix. Let us hope that these innovations herald a return to true circus traditions.

Twenty-nine years ago, when this book was first published, I wondered about the future of the circus. I thought it would survive, but I could not visualize a growth in discernment amongst the public in general, nor could I see performers raising the standards of the acts they presented in the ring. It also looked as if television might indeed become a rival. I hoped that appreciation would not deteriorate and that bureaucratic legislation—always negative, *against* this and *against* that—would not prevent children from training at an early age or animals from appearing in the ring. I also hoped that frontiers between countries, at least in Europe, would no longer be a barrier, and that labor problems and economic crises would not inhibit progress. I hoped, but I was anxious.

Today my hopes have risen and my anxiety has slightly diminished. As I said in the foreword to this edition, the growing interest in zoological gardens, nature reserves and safari parks (not all of them as good as they should be), the growing popularity of riding, including dressage, and the acclaim given to the gymnasts in international sporting events could all lead to a regeneration of the circus.

So much for the public, on which the circus, no less than the theatre, the opera, the ballet and the cinema, relies. On the performers' side we have seen well-established records broken and the achievement of feats hitherto thought to be impossible. We have also seen an upsurge in originality of production and in combining various acts. Under the patronage of Prince Rainier III, the Festival International du Cirque de Monte Carlo has become an important annual event, and its Golden Clown a most coveted award.

Are these the first signs of a renaissance? I hope so, but in the end it is the public which will decide.

Why do people go to the circus? It may be partly due to the fact that in these unsettled times when the future of a sorry world looks black, they find consolation in watching the fulfillment of their wish that "It really will be all right in the end." The basic reason, however, is that they love to watch feats of dexterity and balance and strength, they like to see fine animals in the peak of condition, and they are interested in what animals can be persuaded to do by man's ingenuity. Above all they love the directness of the circus spectacle, whether it sends a shiver down their spine or a laugh which shakes their diaphragm.

In the circus, the work of the animal trainer is an end in itself, not a means of persuading dogs to retrieve game; the acrobat and gymnast leap and turn in the air for the sake of the movement, not to express emotion, as does the dancer; and the rider mounts his horse to show you the art of riding, not to win a race or hunt a fox.

There is one point which both the public and the circus proprietor should remember, and of which one is reminded when one sees the whole company assembled in the ring at the end of the final performance. It is that the circus always has been and must always remain international. Throwing quota barriers across national frontiers makes the circus turn inwards. This means no fresh blood and no new ideas; little variety can be introduced to keep the circus alive. Not only should indigenous acts travel abroad and foreign acts visit us, but leading circuses, of no matter what nationality, should tour the world as they have done in the past. The circus, as we have seen, has no barrier to separate the public from the performer. That principle should not only apply to the spectacle which is presented in the ring, but to every phase of its existence, everywhere.

As the artistes make their final exit from the arena, the last to leave the trampled sawdust is the ringmaster, who has introduced each act to the audience, as I have done in this book to the reader.

If some feel that I have not given enough space to the glamor of the circus, the lure of the red wagons, the romance of spangles and sawdust, I make no apologies. I have tried to strip the circus to its essentials, to get back to why and where and how things came to be, and what is involved in doing them today. The circus is like a rococo carving; it has been gilded and painted so often that the sharp edges of its original form and the skill of its craftsmanship are becoming lost. If I have stripped it down to the bare wood, I am sure that your very next visit will cover it with all the color and gold leaf that you could want. But if you now find its outline more incisive, if its pattern and fine workmanship are more clearly defined, then this book will have done something to sharpen your appreciation as well.

I have never left a circus completely satisfied. No programme that I have ever watched has contained all the things I wanted to see. Often I have wished that this act had been cut or that one elaborated. I should have liked to have seen different lighting here, heard other music there. . . .

Some of you may feel the same way now. In some respects I hope you do, for at least it shows that you also can be critical while in a seat at the circus.

231

Glossary

A century ago circus people were much addicted to slang. Most of it was *parlyaree,* that strange Italianate language which somehow got called *lingua franca.* Although "bevvy" still lingers on as a word meaning a drink, I have only heard one man say that he had "scarpered his letty with the fillia of the donah of the carsey," by which he meant that he had run away from his lodgings with the daughter of the lady of the house. Showman's slang is gradually becoming lost in the general colloquialisms of the day. Horses are no longer called "prads," and I have actually been reprimanded for calling a trailer caravan a living-wagon. However, as some professional terms may still puzzle the layman, I have compiled this glossary. Where a fuller explanation is to be found in the text, the page number is given. Strictly American words are followed by (Am.).

Acrobat. This should really be confined to tumblers. *See* Gymnast. Plain acrobatics consist of somersaults, flip-flaps, boranis etc. Stand-up acrobatics cover hand-to-hand balancing, forming pyramids and so on. Lie-down acrobatics include Risley acts.
Advance agent. On a tenting circus "the advance" travels ahead

of the show to book grounds, order fodder, arrange publicity etc.

After-show. (Am.) The concert which in the old days followed the circus performance in the United States of America.

American riding machine, or **Mechanic.** A cranelike device used in training trick-riders. See pages 53–54.

Antipodist. A foot juggler.

Auguste. The grotesque partner of a white-faced clown.

Back. Short for "back somersault"; usually qualified by another word, e.g. "a lay-out back" or "a gathering back." See pages 199–200.

Backyard. The area behind the performers' entrance in a tenting circus.

Baggage stock. (Am.) Heavy draft horses.

Baguette. A cane hoop over which a bareback rider jumps.

Bale ring. The iron ring to which sections of the big top are hitched and hauled up to the top of the king pole.

Balloons. Paper-covered hoops through which performers jump.

Ballerina act. A name erroneously given to bareback riding. It should be applied only to a high school act in which a ballerina dances alongside the horse.

Banners. Broad strips of cloth over which a trick-rider jumps. In America, they are also painted cloths outside sideshows depicting the various attractions within.

Bar act. A performance on horizontal bars, usually set about eight feet apart; one of the most strenuous acts in the circus. See pages 207–8.

Bar-to-bar. The routine of a trapeze artiste who dispenses with a catcher and flies from one bar to another. See pages 151–52.

Bar-to-catcher. Here the flyer leaves the bar of his own trapeze to be caught by his partner.

Batoude. A plank sloping down to a short springy board inclined upward; this is used to give more lift when leaping over obstacles.

Bearer. One who supports his partner or other members of a troupe, with or without apparatus such as a perch.

Bender. A contortionist who specializes in bending backwards. See page 69.

Big top. The main circus tent; originally American.

Blow-down. The demolition of the big top by a high wind.

Blow the stand. (Am.) To miss a town on the itinerary.

Blues. (Am.) Cheap seats, usually at the ends of the big top, far from the center ring, named for their color. *See* Reds; Starbacks.

Bull. (Am.) An elephant, regardless of the sex.

Borani. An acrobatic movement often corrupted to "brandy." See page 203.

Bouncer. A lion which has been trained to bound off the walls of its cage.

Brandy. *See* Borani.

Butcher. (Am.) Seller of candy, popcorn, lemonade etc.

Butterfly. An acrobatic movement. See page 203.

Calliope. A steam organ used in American street parades.

Carpet act. An acrobatic act worked on the ground, often on a carpet.

Cascade. A juggling term. See pages 183–84.

Cascadeur. A tumbler who specializes in knockabout comedy, especially falls.

Casting act. An aerial act in which the flyer is thrown from one performer to another.

Cat act. Performing lions, tigers etc.

Catcher. Member of a flying trapeze troupe who catches the flyer.

Charivari. A collection of clowns all doing something different, now usually at the beginning of a programme. Eighty years ago in Germany it was applied to a liberty act.

Clem. (Am.) A fight, usually between the circus company and local inhabitants.

Clown. In Europe there is a difference between a clown and an auguste. The former is always dressed in satin or spangles, has a dead-white makeup and is, essentially, elegant. His butt is the auguste, q.v.

Clown alley. (Am.) Dressing tent reserved for clowns.

Concert. (Am.) The entertainment which followed a circus programme in America.

Courier act. A riding act invented by Andrew Ducrow. See pages 59–60.

Cradle. A rigid frame on which aerialists sometimes work.

Cushion. A wedge-shaped platform sometimes used in leaping to a horse's back.

Da capos. The finale of a liberty act in which the horses return to the ring singly to perform individual tricks.

Day and date. Appearance at the same place on the same day as a rival show.

Dog and pony show. (Am.) Derisive description of a small circus.

Double staking. Extra tent stakes driven in as a storm precaution.

En douceur or **en pelotage**. A method of presenting wild animals so that they look tame.

En férocité. A method of presenting wild animals so that they appear very fierce.

Entrée. A comic scene played by clowns.

Equestrian director. Ringmaster. Americans are particularly fond of the term and equip their equestrian directors with whistles, which very few ringmasters in Europe use.

Feet-to-feet. A somersault turned from the feet back to the feet, in contrast to feet-to-fork.

Feet-to-fork. A somersault in which a rider takes off from a standing position but lands astride.

Fill-in clowns. Those who rush in between acts, but do not work an entrée.

First of May. (Am.) A novice; derived from the opening of a tenting season when experience is lacking.

Flip-flap. An acrobatic movement. See pages 200–201.

Funambulist. A wire-walker or rope-dancer.

Gaff. A fairground booth.

Garters. Narrow ribbons over which a bareback rider jumps.

Gathering back. A back somersault which ends in front of the starting point.

Gentling. A word coined by Hagenbeck for training animals solely by patience and bribery.

Gilly. (Am.) A light wagon hired for odd jobs around the lot.

Grease joint. (Am.) A hamburger or hot dog stand.

Grouch bag. (Am.) A purse carried under one's clothes.

Gymnast. Technically, gymnasts work on or with apparatus, while acrobats do not. This applies to both parterre and aerial gymnasts, though the difference between acrobats and gymnasts is not now strictly observed.

Hand spring. An acrobatic movement. See page 200.

Hand-to-hand. A type of balancing act. See pages 63–65.

Haul. (Am.) The distance from the railway to the tober or lot.

Head-to-head. A type of balancing act. See page 66.

Hey Rube! (Am.) The battlecry of the American circus.

Hook-up team. (Am.) Those who load and unload the circus wagons at railway stations.

Humpsti-bumpsti. A knockabout acrobatic act.

Jeux Romains. A riding act. See page 58.

Jockey act. A riding act. See pages 48–50.

Joey. A clown, derived from Joseph Grimaldi, a pantomime clown.

Joint. (Am.) A concession stand.

Josser. A member of the public, not one of the profession.

Jump. (Am.) The distance between the lot in one town and the next.

Kid show. (Am.) A side show.

Kiester. (Am.) A wardrobe trunk, or in England theatrical basket.

King poles. These support the canvas of the big top at its apex. They may be set in line or in squares. A simple three-ring circus has four in line.

Kinker. (Am.) A circus performer; originally an acrobat.

Klischnigg. A contortionist's act. See page 68.

Knockabout. Comedy acrobatics in which falls and slaps predominate.

Lay-out. A kind of somersault in which the body remains straightened out instead of tucked or balled up.

Lay-out man. (Am.) The person who arranges the positions of the tents and wagons on the lot.

Leotards. Skintight singlets worn by acrobats; named after the inventor of the flying trapeze.

Liberties. Horses presented "at liberty," i.e., with no rider. See pages 93–104.

Lion's leap. An acrobatic jump. See page 201.

Lot. (Am.) The circus ground or tober.

Marinelli bend. A position taken up by a contortionist. See page 68.

Mechanic. *See* American Riding Machine.

Middleman. A performer between the bearer and the top mounter.

Mixed group. A wild animal act of several different species.

Monkey jump. An acrobatic leap. See page 201.

Mud show. (Am.) A circus traveling by road rather than rail.

Pad. A flat platform strapped to a horse's back.

Pad room. (Am.) Dressing room, so called because the pads were usually kept there.

Paper. Free tickets; and, in America, circus posters.

Parade. This can refer to a procession, either across the ring or through a town. Alternatively, it can mean the show-front of a fairground booth; those who work there to attract a crowd are known as paraders, while the verbal exhortations are made by a spieler in England and a barker in America.

Pas de deux. A riding act. See page 58.

Pass. The flight from one trapeze to another. See pages 151–54.

Pedestal. The tub or stool on which an animal sits.

Perch. A pole of steel or bamboo up which a performer climbs. It can also refer to the launching platform of a trapeze artiste.

Pirouette. A turn made by the body in midair about its vertical axis.

Plange. From the French *planche;* a position in which the body is fully extended.

Posturer. A contortionist who specializes in front bending. See page 69.

Principal. Short for "Principal Lady (or Gentleman) Rider."

Props. Short for "properties"; the word used throughout the entertainment world for accessories.

Quarter poles. The poles which support the canvas between the side poles and the king or queen poles.

Queen poles. These are found between the king and quarter poles.

Razorback. (Am.) A man who loads or unloads the wagons at the railway.

Red. (Am.) An expensive seat; hence "a red one" means a profitable stand.

Ring fence. The low barrier which surrounds the ring. In small circuses this was once a strip of canvas. On the bigger shows it is of wood, painted white inside, and sometimes it has a red matting top. In America it is called the ring curb or ring bank, reminding one that once it was a bank of earth.

Risley act. An act in which one or more performers, lying on their backs, juggle the smaller members of the troupe with their feet. See pages 191–95.

Rosinback. (Am.) A ring horse, from the rosin which prevents a trick-rider from slipping.

Round-off. An acrobatic movement. See pages 201–3.

Roustabout. (Am.) A general laborer.

Running ground mount. A run across the ring ending in a leap to the back of a cantering horse.

School. Short for high school.

Scissors. A movement in voltige. See page 49.

Smoke wagon. (Am.) Two small wheels joined by a low axle, used to maneuver king poles.

Splits. In stride splits the legs are stretched out before and behind the body; in center or straddle splits they are stretched out on either side.

Spotter. A somersault in which the performer lands exactly where he took off.

Springboard. A see-saw or teeterboard used to give extra lift to an acrobat.

Stand. In England usually qualified by the length of the stay, e.g., a two-day stand; in America it means any place the circus visits.

Starbacks. Expensive seats, from the design on the back.

Staubs. (Am.) Tent stakes.

Straw house. An audience so big that some have to sit on the ground.

Sway-pole act. (Am.) A high perch act in which the base is fixed and the top sways to and fro.

Three-men-high. A column of three men, the bearer supporting the middleman on his shoulders (or, more rarely, head) and the middleman carrying the top-mounter in the same way.

Tober. The circus field or pitch; known in America as the lot.

Top-mounter. An acrobat supported by a bearer or middleman.

Trampoline. A canvas sheet stretched on springs. See pages 208–9.

Trapeze. There are two kinds of trapeze act. In the flying trapeze, the performer leaves the bar of one trapeze for either another trapeze or the hands of a catcher; in the fixed trapeze, although the bar may swing, the performer does not fly. In America "trapeze" is often shortened to "trap."

Trinka. A small cradle in which antipodists and Risley performers lie while juggling with their feet.

Twenty-four-hour man. (Am.) The person who inspects the lot and checks the arrangements made by the advance agent the day before the circus is due to arrive in a new town.

Twister. An acrobatic movement, combining somersault and pirouette. See pages 153–54.

Voltige. A riding act. See pages 47–60.

Walkaround. (Am.) Parade of clowns along the hippodrome track which surrounds the rings.

Wardrobe. All costumes, headdresses etc., and the wagon or tent in which they are kept.

Web act. Performance on a vertical rope. In America the assistant who attends to the bottom of the rope is called a "web sitter."

Western pastimes. An act which includes rope-spinning, whip-cracking, knife-throwing and sometimes sharpshooting.

White wagon. (Am.) The main office on the lot.

Bibliography

In the original edition I listed 101 volumes; now there are 125. They are not the only ones in my collection which amused or instructed me. They have, however, contributed more to this book than the others. Some have provided facts, others have stimulated thought, and in a few of them you will find an elaboration of those aspects which, for reasons of space, I have covered in a rather cursory way.

Adrian, (Paul). *Attractions sensationnelles*. Bourg la Reine, 1962.

Anonymous. *Le Cirque Franconi, par une chambrière en retraite*. Lyons: Perrin & Marinet, 1875.

Anonymous. *The Russian State Circus, 1918–1938*. Moscow: Iskusstvo, 1938.

Amiel, D. *Les Spectacles*. Paris: Les Editions du Cygne, 1931.

Barnes, Al G. *Master Showman*. London: Cape, 1938.

Barnum, P.T. *Struggles and Triumphs*. Buffalo: The Courier Co., 1889.

Beatty, Clyde (in conjunction with Anthony, E.). *The Big Cage*. New York: D. Appleton-Century Co., 1936.

Beatty, Clyde (in conjunction with Wilson, Earl). *Jungle Performers*. London: Hale, 1946.

Bidel, J.-B. F. *Les Mémoires d'un dompteur*. Paris: Librairie de l'Art, 1888.

Bilboquet. *Mes Souvenirs*. Paris: Félix Alcan, 1933.

Birkby, Carel. *The Pagel Story*. Cape Town: Howard B. Timmins, 1948.

Borassatti, G. *Il gymnasta in practica ed in teorica*. Venice, 1743.

Bost, Pierre. *Le Cirque et le music hall*. Paris: Au Sans Pareil, 1931.

Bostock, E.H. *Menageries, Circuses and Theatres*. London: Chapman & Hall, 1927.

Bostock, Frank. *The Training of Wild Animals*. New York: The Century Co., 1903.

Bradna, Fred (and Spence, Hartzell). *The Big Top*. New York: Simon & Schuster, 1952.

Campardon, Louis E. *Les Spectacles de la foire*. Paris: Berger-Levrault, 1877.

Cervellati, A. *Storia del circo*. Bologna: Poligrafici Il Resto del Carlino Editore,1956.

Chindahl, George. *A History of the Circus in America*. Caldwell, Idaho: The Caxton Printers, 1959.

Chipman, Bert. *Hey Rube!* Hollywood: Hollywood Print Shop, 1933.

Clarke, John S. *Circus Parade*. London: Batsford, 1936.

Coco. *Coco, the Clown*. London: Dent, 1940.

Cooper, Courtney Riley. *Lions 'n Tigers 'n Everything*. Boston: Little, Brown & Co., 1925.

——————. *Circus Day*. New York: Farrer & Rinehart, 1925.

——————. *Under the Big Top*. Boston: Little, Brown & Co., 1923.

——————. *Boss Elephant*. Boston: Little, Brown & Co., 1935.

Conklin, George. *The Ways of the Circus*. New York: Harpers, 1921.

Coup, W.C. *Sawdust and Spangles*. Chicago: H. Stone, 1901.

Coutet, A. *La Vie du cirque*. Paris: Arthaud, 1948.

Dalsème, A.-J. *Le Cirque à pied et à cheval*. Paris: La Librairie Illustrée, 1890.

De Bussy, C. *Les Forains à travers les âges*. Avignon: L'Intermédiaire Forain, 1930.

Decarpentry, General. *Baucher et son école*. Paris: Lamarre, 1948.

Decastro, J. *Memoirs*. London: Sherwood, Jones & Co., 1824.

De Cordon, Paul. *Instants de cirque*. Paris: Chêne, 1977.

De Vaux, Baron. *Ecuyers et écuyères*. Paris: J. Rothschild, 1893.

Dembeck, Hermann. *Manege Frei!* Berlin: Buchmeister-Verlag Gmbh., 1937.

Depping, Guillaume. *La Force et l'adresse*. Paris: Hachette, 1871.

Disher, M. Willson. *Clowns and Pantomimes*. London: Constable, 1925.

_____. *Greatest Show on Earth*. London: Bell, 1937.

_____. *Fairs, Circuses and Music Halls*. London: Collins, 1942.

Duroff, V.L. *My Circus Animals*. London: Routledge, 1937.

Dworschak, Franz X. *Circusroem*. Naarden: Rutgers, 1943.

Eipper, Paul. *Circus*. London: Routledge, 1931.

Fellows, Dexter, and Freeman, A.F. *This Way to the Big Show*. New York: Viking, 1936.

Fillis, James. *Principes de dressage et d'équitation*. Paris: Flammarion, 1892.

Foster, Frank. *Pink Coat, Spangles and Sawdust*. London: Stanley Paul, 1948.

Fournel, V. *Le Vieux Paris*. Tours: Mame, 1887.

Franconi, V. *Le Cavalier et l'écuyer*. Paris: Calmann Lévy, 1891.

Fréjaville, G. *Au Music hall*. Paris: Les Editions du Monde Nouveau, 1922.

Frichet, H. *Le Cirque et les forains*. Tours: Mame, 1899.

Frost, Thomas. *The Old Showmen and the Old London Fairs*. London: Tinsley, 1875.

_____. *Circus Life and Circus Celebrities*. London: Chatto & Windus, 1881.

Gallici-Rancy, Henri. *Les Forains peints par eux-mêmes*. Bordeaux, 1903.

Garnier, Jacques. *Théodore Rancy et son temps*. Orléans, 1975.

Gasch, Sebastian. *El circo et sus figuras*. Barcelona: Barna, 1947.

Gillespie, T.H. *Is It Cruel?* London: Herbert Jenkins, 1934.

Ginisty, P. *Mémoires d'une danseuse de corde*. Paris: Fasquelle, 1907.

Gomez de la Serna, Ramon. *Le Cirque*. Paris: Kra, 1927.

Grock. *Grock raconté par Grock*. Paris: Attinger, 1931.

Grock. *Sans blague!* Paris: Flammarion, 1948.

Hachet-Souplet, P. *Les Animaux savants*. Paris: Lemerre, n.d.

_____. *Le Dressage des animaux*. Paris: Firmin-Didot, n.d.

Hagenbeck, Carl. *Beasts and Men*. London: Green & Co., 1912.

Hartsberg, Hiler, and Moss, Arthur. *Slapstick and Dumbbell*. New York: Lawren, 1924.

Hediger, Dr. H. *Studies of the Behaviour of Captive Animals in Zoos and Circuses*. London: Butterworth, 1955.

_____. *Wild Animals in Captivity*. London: Butterworth, 1950.

Holm, A. *Saaden et Liv*. Aarhus: Gravens Andersens Forlag, 1946.

Hubler, Richard. *The Cristianis*. London: Jarrolds, 1967.

Ingalese, R. *Juggling*. London: Gaskarth Press, 1921.

Keith, Charlie. *Circus Life and Amusements*. London: E.W. Allen, 1879.

Kilmer, Joyce. *The Circus and Other Essays*. New York: Gomme, 1916.

Kober, A.H. *Circus Nights and Days*. London: Sampson, Low & Co., 1928.

———. *Star Turns*. London: Noel Douglas, 1928.

Lang, Heinrich. *Circus-Bilder*. Munich: Ackermann, 1879.

———. *Voltigeurs, jongleurs et saltimbanques*. Paris: Goupil, n.d.

Le Roux, Hugues. *Les Jeux du cirque*. Paris: Plon, 1889.

Lijsen, H.J. *De Hooge School*, Zwolle: La Riviére & Voorhoeve, 1943.

———. *Achter het Gordyn*. Deventer: Kluwer, 1949.

Lloyd, James. *My Circus Life*. London: Noel Douglas, 1925.

McKechnie, S. *Popular Entertainments through the Ages*. London: Sampson, Low & Co., n.d.

Manne, E.D. de, and Menestrier, C. *Galerie historique de la troupe de Nicolet*. Lyon: Scheuring, 1896.

Marcossan, I.F. *Autobiography of a Clown*. New York: Dodd, Mead & Co., 1931.

Mariel, P. *Histoire de trois clowns*. Paris: S.A. d'Editions, 1923.

May, Earl Chapin. *The Circus from Rome to Ringling*. New York: Duffield & Green, 1932.

Moffet, C. *Careers of Danger and Daring*. New York: Appleton Century, 1901.

Molier, E. *L'Equitation et l'athlétisme*. Paris: Baudinière, 1925.

———. *Le Cirque Molier*. Paris: Dupont, 1904.

———. *L'Equitation et le cheval*. Paris: Lafitte, 1911.

Orlando, Henning. *Cirkus*. Stockholm: Wahlstrom & Widstrand, 1944.

Perrodil, E. de. *Monsieur Clown!* Paris: Dalou, 1889.

Pichot, Pierre A. *Les Mémoires d'un dompteur*. Paris: La Revue Britannique, 1877.

Pond, Irving K. *Big Top Rhythms*. New York: Willett, Clark & Co., 1937.

Reichmann, William. *Arthur Konyot: The White Rider*. Barrington, Ill.: The Hill & Dale Press, n.d.

Rémy, Tristan. *Les Clowns*. Paris: Grasset, 1945.

Rendle, T. McDonald. *Swings and Roundabouts*. London: Chapman & Hall, 1919.

Renevey, Monica, ed. *Le Grand Livre du cirque*. Geneva: Edito-Service, 1977.

Rivels, Charlie. *Akrobat-oh!* Stockholm: Norstedt, 1934.

Robinson, Gil. *Old Wagon Show Days*. Cincinnati: Crockwell, 1925.

Saltarino, Signor. *Artisten-Lexicon*. Düsseldorf: C. Kraus, 1891.

————. *Pauvres Saltimbanques*. Düsseldorf: Ed. Lintz, 1892.

————. *Fahrend Volk*. Leipzig: J. Weber, 1895.

Sanger, "Lord" George. *Seventy Years a Showman*. London: Dent, 1926.

Saxon, A.H. *Enter Foot and Horse*. New Haven and London: Yale University Press, 1968.

————. *The Life and Art of Andrew Ducrow & The Romantic Age of the English Circus*. Hamden, Conn.: Archon Books, 1978.

Sevrette, Gaston. *Les Animaux de cirque, de course et de combat*. Paris: Colin, 1924.

Sherwood, R.E. *Here We Are Again*. Indianapolis: Bobbs-Merrill & Co., 1926.

————. *Hold Yer Hosses!* New York: Macmillan, 1932.

Spalart, R. *Baucher et sa méthode*. Fécamp: Cauchois, n.d.

Strehly, G. *L'Acrobatie et les acrobates*. Paris: Delagrave, n.d.

Thétard, Henry. *Coulisses et secrets du cirque*. Paris: Plon, 1934.

————. *Les Dompteurs*. Paris: Gallimard, 1928.

————. *La Merveilleuse Histoire du cirque*. Paris: Prisma, 1947. (A revised edition, brought up to date by L.-R. Dauven, was published by Julliard, Paris, in 1978.)

Toulouse-Lautrec-Monfa, Count Henri de. *Au Cirque*. Monte Carlo: Editions du Livre, 1953.

Tyrwhitt-Drake, Sir Garrard. *Beasts and Circuses*. London: Arrowsmith, 1936.

————. *My Life with Animals*. London: Blackie, 1939.

————. *The English Circus and Fairground*. London: Methuen, 1946.

Vail, R.W.G. *Random Notes on the History of the Early American Circus*. Worcester, Mass.: American Antiquarian Society, 1934.

Van Doveren, J. *Hoogeerd Publiek*. Amsterdam: Elsevier, 1948.

Van Doveren, J. and Nesna, H. *Circus*. Maastricht: N.V. Leiter-Nypels, 1950.

Van Hare, G. *Fifty Years of a Showman's Life*. London: Sampson, Low & Co., 1893.

Verne, Maurice. *Musées de volupté*. Paris: Editions des Portiques, 1930.

Walker, "Whimsical." *From Sawdust to Windsor Castle*. London: S. Paul, 1922.

Williamson, S.S. *On the Road with Bertram Mills*. London: Chatto & Windus, 1938.

Zora, Lucia. *Sawdust and Solitude*. Boston: Little, Brown & Co., 1928.

Zucca, A. *Acrobatica e atletica*. Milan: Hoepli, 1902.

Index

Abilio, 67
Accidents, fatal. *See* Circus, death in
Acrobats, 30, 34, 35, 63, 197–212. *See also* Training, for acrobats; names of individual acrobats
Adams, Spike, 65
Aeros, Germain, 168
Agousts, 189
Agricultural Hall, 110
Albanos, 218
Albertino, 224
Alberty, 71
Alex and Porto, 218
Alexander Serges Troupe, 52
Alexanders, Great, 206
Alexandrini, 62
Alexes, 158
Algevols, 158
Alizé, Pierre, 158

Allarty, Blanche, 119
Allisons, 205
Althoff, 96
Althoff, Adolph, 101
Althoff, Hermann, 50
Alzanas. *See* Davises
Amadori, Genesio, 161
Amars, 42
Amoros, Pierre, 185, 186
Ancillottis, 106, 110, 210
Angelo, Henry, 28
Animal acts, 35, 75–104, 127–47, 171–82; cruelty in, 75–85, 89–91, 96, 123, 139. *See also* Training, for animal acts; names of individual trainers
Antonet and Beby, 218. *See also* Frediani, Aristodemo
Arnold, Tom, 40. *See also* Tom Arnold's Circus

247

Artistes: doubling as ushers and programme sellers, 24; irritated by lack of public understanding, 125-26; proud of their calling, 35, 126
Artressi, 204-5
Ashtons, Seven, 194
Astley, John, 30
Astley, Philip, 28, 29, 30-31, 32, 124. *See also* Astley's Amphitheatre
Astley's Amphitheatre, 31, 33, 39, 50, 53, 60, 124, 173, 192, 216, 225. *See also* Astley, Philip
Atkins, 124, 128
Atlas, Miss, the Strong Woman. *See* Rogge, Gerda
Audience of circus, 24, 25-26, 224, 226, 228, 230
Augustes, 56, 214, 218-22. *See also* Clowns; names of individual augustes
Auriol, Jean-Baptiste, 215-16
Avalos, 208
Aymar, Mr., 53

Bagessen, 189
Baker Boys [pseud. Corinthians, Cumberlands], 57
Balancing acts, 64-67, 70, 73. *See also* names of individual artistes
Bale, Elvin, 73, 159
Bales, 73
Bar acts, 207-8. *See also* names of individual artistes
Barbette, 159
Bareback acts. *See* Jockey acts
Barnum, Phineas Taylor, 111, 124, 125. *See also* Ringling Bros. and Barnum & Bailey

Barnum & Bailey. *See* Ringling Bros. and Barnum & Bailey
Barry, Tom, 216
Barth, Helmuth, 181
Bates, 29
Baucher, François, 172-73
Beasy, Bob [pseud. Bobino], 81-82, 223-24
Beatty, Clyde, 132, 137
Beby. *See* Frediani, Aristodemo
Bedini, Paolo, 187
Begary, Maryse, 159
Behee, Clayton, 156
Beketow, 44
Bell, Billy, 50
Belling, Tom, 218
Bells, 38
Bell's Oriental Gladiators, 194
Bertram Mills' Circus, 40, 73, 103, 112, 121, 198. *See also* Mills, Bernard, Bertram, and Cyril
Bibb, 214
Blondin, Chevalier. *See* Gravelet, Jean François
Blumenfelds, 126
Bobino. *See* Beasy, Bob
Bombayo, 167
Bonavita, 133
Bonhairs, 194
Bostock, Frank, 119, 130, 134, 135
Bostocks, 130, 131
Boudnidsky, 139
Bougliones, 41-42, 126
Boum-Boum, 116
Boytchanovis, 206
Bracco, 212
Bradbury, 50
Bramsom, Bob, 189
Brockways, 211
Brown, Frank, 39
Bruce, Vera, 155-56
Brumbachs, 189

Buffalo Bill. *See* Cody, Colonel

Bunte, Captain, 71

Butson, Clem, 40, 110. *See also* Tower Circus

Caicedo, Don Juan, 34, 168

Cairolis, 218

Cannonballs, human, 107–9. *See also* names of individual artistes

Capelli, Signor, 79

Caravettas, Flying, 157

Carlisle, Richard Risley [pseud. Professor Risley], 191–94

Carmo, 111, 122

Carmo's Circus, 62

Carolis, 56

Carré circus, 101, 102. *See also* Carrés

Carrés, 42, 101. *See also* Carré circus

Carter, 128, 130, 137

Castang, Reuben, 146

Castors. *See* Moustiers

Chessington Zoo Circus, 101

Chiarini, 29

Chiarini, Constance (Comtesse Rostopchine), 173

Chickys, 223

Chiese-Bellon-Cinquevalli Troupe, 187

Chinko, 185

Chipperfield, Dick, 40

Chipperfield, Mary, 181

Chipperfields, 40, 41

Chocolat, 217, 218

Chotachen-Courtauld, 51

Ciniselli's Circus, 84, 187

Cinquevalli, 34, 187–88

Circus: death in, 28, 36, 50, 62, 66, 108, 109, 110, 112–13, 122, 123, 126, 130, 140, 141, 156, 158, 160–61, 162, 163 n, 174, 204, 208; financial aspects of, 34–35, 39–40, 50, 108, 120–23, 144–46, 166, 173, 174, 186, 216, 217, 218; in Austria, 31; in Eastern Europe, 31, 43–44, 122, 206–7; in England, 24, 28, 32–33, 37, 38, 39–40, 130, 139, 168, 174, 193, 214, 219, 229; in France, 30, 32, 33, 41, 42, 67–68, 85, 101, 104, 128, 158, 168, 193, 214, 217, 229; in Germany, 32, 34, 35, 39, 42, 44, 132, 217; in Italy, 158, 193; in Latin America, 39, 168; in Russia, 31, 43–44, 48, 52, 84, 139, 161, 190, 193, 207, 217, 218; in Spain, 31, 217 n; in United States, 31, 35–36, 38, 52–53, 108, 120, 122, 130, 141, 158, 160, 193, 207, 218, 219, 228, 229; international character of, 27, 31, 126, 231; mergers in, 36; physical specifications for, 24, 40, 43, 57–58, 127, 131; unlike the theatre, 24–26, 27, 115, 225–26

Circus, amateur, 118–20

Circus, Roman, 28

Circus Corporation of America, 36

Circus Kirk, 120

Circus Schreiber, 101

Circus Schumann, 102. *See also* Schumann, Albert; Schumanns

Circus Strepetow, 50

Cirque Amar, 125 n

Cirque Cocassien, 117

Cirque de Paris, 42

Cirque d'Eté, 33, 41, 173

Cirque d'Hiver, 33, 41, 42, 111, 151, 172, 174

Cirque Franconi, 85, 128. *See also* Franconis

Cirque Medrano, 51, 115–16, 181, 229. *See also* Medrano, Jérôme

Cirque Napoleon. *See* Cirque d'Hiver

Clarke, Ernest, 150, 154–55, 217

Clarke, John Frederick, 50, 150, 217

Clarkes, 50

Clerans, 162

Clermont, 85

Cliquot, Chevalier, 74

Clowns, 44–45, 56 n, 74, 213–24. *See also* Augustes; names of individual clowns

Cochran, C. B., 57, 133

Coco, 81

Codona, Alfredo, 150, 155–56

Codona, Lalo, 155–56

Codonas, 158, 228

Cody, Colonel [pseud. Buffalo Bill], 42, 74

Cognac, 223

Colbergs [pseud. Crystal Wonders], 65

Coleseu de Recreios, 102

Colleano, Con, 167–69, 203

Colleano, Maurice, 168, 203

Colleanos, 168, 203, 228

Collins and Elizabeth, 73

Colpi, Signor, 192

Concello, Antoinette, 157, 162

Concello, Arturo, 150

Concellos, 154, 157, 158

Condoras, 158

Conjuring, 111–12, 226. *See also* names of individual conjurors

Conklin, George, 37

Conservatoire National du Cirque, 229

Contortionism, 65, 67–70. *See also* Training, for contortionists; names of individual contortionists

Cooke, Hubert, 50

Cookes, 31, 38

Cooke's Circus, 216

Cooper, John, 141

Corinthians. *See* Baker Boys

Corty-Althoffs, 57–58

Cossmy, Adolph, 140

Cottle, Gerry, 40–41, 120–21. *See also* Gerry Cottle's Circus

Cottrelly, 38

Couderc, Pierre, 150, 155, 207, 208, 209

Courier acts, 59. *See also* names of individual artistes

Court, Alfred, 138, 207, 208

Craggs, 34

Craston, Joe, 224

Crazy Gang, 185

Cremorne Pleasure Gardens, 151

Cristiani, Belmonte, 51

Cristiani, Lucio, 51

Cristiani, Mogador, 51

Crocker, Edith, 139

Crockett, Sarah, 217

Cronin, Morris, 189

Crystal Palace, 166

Crystal Wonders. *See* Colbergs; Spurgats

Cubanos [pseud. Flying Dutchman], 167

Cumberlands. *See* Baker Boys

Cuyer, Monsieur, 181

Cuzent, 229

Cuzent, Paul, 60

Cyrillo and Busby, 218

Dario-Barios, 218

Davenport Brothers, 111

Davises [pseud. Alazanas], 112, 164
Dax, Trio, 162
de Kroutikoff, M., 94
de la Grange, Chrysis, 162
de Rousseau, Leon, 110
de Thiers, Mademoiselle, 107
de Vasconcellos, Roberto, 181
Decastro, 216
Desormont, Monsieur, 119
Desprez, Marcel and André, 105–6
Dhôtre, Damoo, 139
Diable, Petit, 163
Diana, Mademoiselle, 74
Diaz, Enrico, 208
Diaz de Valesco, Julio, 181
Dimitrescus, 207
Divers, high, 110–11. See also names of individual artistes
Dobritch, Nikko, 142
Doksansky, Sylvia, 57
Dormonde Brothers, 211
Doval, Great, 166
Ducrow, Andrew, 48, 50, 59–60, 62
Durov, Anatol, 84
Durov, Vladimir, 84, 87–88, 217, 220
Dwarfs, 68, 208

Ecole National du Cirque, 229
Edwards, Margot, 189
Eldred, Frank, 39
Electricity in the circus, 37
Elleano, 165
Escapologists, 111. See also names of individual escapologists
Etaix, Pierre, 230
Evans, 158
Evans, Fred, 222 n
Everhart, William, 189

Fan clubs, circus, 116–17
Farfans, Flying, 228
Farini, 166 n
Fat ladies, 68
Faughman, Richard, 163 n
Feindt, Cilly, 181
Felds, 122
Fenyes, 44
Fernando, Louis, 116
Feroni, 189
Filatov, Valentin Ivanovitch, 139
Fillis, Anna, 179
Fillis, Frank, 38, 173
Fillis, James, 118, 172–73, 179
Fillis, Tom, 173
Finney, Professor, 112
Fischer, Madame, 141
Flies, human, 112. See also names of individual artistes
Flying Dutchman. See Cubanos
Foottit, 214, 217, 218
Foster, Frank, 66
Fövárosi Nagy, 44
Franconis, 30, 32, 38. See also Cirque Franconi
Fratellini, Annie, 229
Fratellinis, 218, 221
Fredericks Family, 39
Frediani, Aristodemo [pseud. Beby], 56, 218, 220
Fredianis, 56, 57, 220, 228
French, 38
French, Harry, 212

Gaona, Tito, 150, 209
Gautier, Dietrich, 29
Gautier, Lulu, 99
Gebel-Williams, Gunther, 138, 141, 228
Gee, Charlene, 185
Georgys, 71
Geraldos. See Rousseau, Madeleine and René

Gérard, Sasha, 50
Gerry Cottle's Circus, 62. *See also* Cottle, Gerry
Ghyka, Countess Fanny, 174
Giants, 68
Ginnetts, 38
Ginnett's Circus, 83
Glenroy, John H., 52–53
Globe-rolling acts, 66–67. *See also* names of individual artistes
Goldkettes, 126
Gondor, M., 206
Gravelet, Jean François [pseud. Chevalier Blondin], 33, 71, 163, 165–66
Grice, Tony, 214, 216
Gridneff troupe, 208
Grimaldi, Joseph, 216
Grix Gregories, 194
Grock and Noni, 220
Gruss, Alexis, 103–4, 181, 228
Gruss, Alexis, Jr., 229
Guérinière, 118
Guerre, Benito, 31
Guyon, 218
Guzman, Richard, 163 n
Gymnasts, 34, 198, 230. *See also* Acrobats
Gypsies, 126, 139

Hachet-Souplet, P., 100, 119
Hagenbeck, Carl, 141, 143
Hagenbeck, William, 140
Hagenbecks, 35, 128–29, 131 n, 146
Haight, Andrew, 36
Hankey, Charlie, 181
Hanlon-Lees, 214, 218
Hanlon-Voltas, 34
Harmston, Willie, 39
Harmstons, 38
Harringay, 40, 66, 67, 71, 102, 104, 110, 121, 159, 160, 161, 181

Hartley Family, 39
Hayden, 214
Hayes, Rich, 189
Henglers, 62, 217
Hera, 188
Hernandez, James. *See* Kelly, Mickey
High divers. *See* Divers, high
Hillier, Joseph, 48
Hilton, Polly, 130
Hoffman, 111
Holtum, 62
Hortobagy Troupe, 206
Houcke, Gilbert, 40, 138
Houcke brothers, 51
Houdini, Harry, 111
Hughes, Charles, 31, 32
Huline, Great Little, 216–17
Human cannonballs. *See* Cannonballs, human
Human flies. *See* Flies, human
Humpsti-Bumpsti acts, 209–10
Hungarian Troupe, Great. *See* Alexanders, Great

Ibarra, Vicente and Ignacio, 40, 150, 208
Ida May's Midship Girls, 161
Ilès and Loyal, 218
Iñas, 212
Ingalese, Rupert, 190

Jackson, Joe, 210
Jacobs, Lou, 218
Jarz, Chetta, 157
Jockey acts, 48–51, 58–59, 228. *See also* names of individual artistes
Johnson, 29
Jolly, 65
Jordan, Nellie, 150
Judge, Billy, 143–44

Judge, Charlie, 143, 146
Juggling, 30, 35, 66, 73, 168–69, 183–91, 195. *See also* names of individual jugglers
Juliette, Mlle., 143

Kaden, 137
Kalmar, Kees, 204
Kara, 185, 189
Karandash, 218
Kasseef, Nelly and Rustam, 139
Kayes, Johnny, 102
Kayes, Tommy, 133, 137
Kayes Brothers' Circus, 102
Kehaiovi Troupe, 205
Keith, Charlie, 39
Kelly, Emmett, 218
Kelly, Mickey [pseud. James Hernandez], 193
Kingston, Chester, 69
Klein Family, 211
Klischnigg, 68
Knie, Frank, 142
Knie, Freddy, 98
Knie, Louis, 138, 142
Knie, Rolf, 59
Knies, 43, 96, 146
Knife-throwing, 73. *See also* names of individual artistes
Knox, Teddy, 185
Konyot, 137
Krall, Karl, 94–95
Kremo, Bela, 187
Kremo, Kris, 187, 190, 228
Kremos, 194
Krones, 42, 131 n

La Roche, Leon, 67
Lane, Ernie, 161
Langeneck, Professor, 144
Laristo, 112
Lauck and Fox, 207

Leers, Luisita, 159
Leitzel, Lillian, 155–56
Lemus, Ron, 157
Lemus, Terry Caravetta, 157
Lena, 150
Lent's New York Circus, 36
Lenz, Johann, 29
Léotard, 33, 151, 153, 158
Lepère, 67 n
Leslie, Harry, 166 n
Levanda, 191
Lipkowska, Gina, 103
Lloyd, Wilkes, 50
Lloyd's Circus, 124
Lockhart, 141
Loisset, Clotilde, 173–74
Loisset, Emilie, 173–74
Loisset, François, 173
Loisset's Circus, 215
Lola, Miss, 115–16
Lorches, 194
Lothar, Great, 161
Loyals, 101–2
Loyo, Caroline, 33, 173
Lucas, 130
Lulu (clown), 224
Lulu (transvestite aerialist), 121
Lupino, George Hook, 222 n
Luppus, 207

M., Tolly, 187
Macarthy [pseud. Massarte], 130
Madison Square Garden, 96, 160, 224
Magyars, 206
Malladoli, Monsieur le Professeur. *See* Raphaël, Albert
Manchester Jack, 128
Manoeuvre, 59
Manzano, Arturo, 181
Marcoud, Ramonde, 159
Marinelli, H. B., 68, 69

Martin, Henri, 128
Martinez, Don, 150
Massarte. *See* Macarthy
May, Ida. *See* Ida May's Midship
  Girls
Mayer, Camillo, 166
Mayorov, 139
Medrano, Jérôme, 58, 116. *See also*
  Cirque Medrano
Medrano Sisters. *See* Swoboda
  Sisters
Melzoras, Flying, 155
Menageries, 35, 123, 124–25,
  128, 131
Mendez, Gene, 164, 166
Menken, Adah Isaacs, 33
Méteors, 158
Midgets, 68
Mijares, Jesus, 181
Mijares, Robledillo, 168
Mills, Bernard, 40, 99. *See also*
  Bertram Mills' Circus
Mills, Bertram, 39, 40, 57, 73, 82,
  93, 121, 181. *See also* Bertram
  Mills' Circus
Mills, Cyril, 40, 65. *See also*
  Bertram Mills' Circus
Mireillys, 159
Molier, Ernest, 118–19
Monbar, Raoul, 106
Monfort, Silvia, 229
Montrose Troupe, 206
Moreno, José, 189
Moung Toon, 188
Moustiers [pseud. Castors], 187
Moxons, 191
Mroczkowski, Czeslaw, 103
Music in the circus, 23, 36–37,
  42, 47, 82, 229
Myer's Circus, 141

Natal, 147
Nazarova, 132

Nicolai, 133
Nicolet's, 163
Nocks, 71
Noiset Troupe, 112
Nomano, Fanny, 86
Norbertys, 161
North, Levi, 52–53
Nouveau Cirque, 57, 217

Oceana, 167
Oghaby, Khalil, 62
Old Wild, 165
Olympia, 39, 40, 57, 67, 71, 76,
  102, 112, 133, 141, 146, 186
Olympians, Five, 56
Omankowskys, 163–64
Ortans, 205
Ortons, 71

Palais de l'Industrie, 166
Palmer, Gaston, 189
Palms, Four, 71
Parade, 27, 36–37, 41, 42, 43, 62
Pas de deux, 58
Pastis, 223
Paulos, 163
Pavlov, I. P., 84, 128–29
Pekouline Troupe, 211
Perch acts, 71–73, 211. *See also*
  names of individual artistes
Perezoffs, 189
Performers. *See* Artistes
Peters, Alois, 110, 112
Pezon, 133
Picchiani Troupe, 205
Pimpo, 220
Pincemin, André, 164 n
Pinders, 31, 38
Pinder's Circus, 42
Pipo and Rhum, 218, 222, 223
Pissiuttis, 58
Polis, 71

Popov, Oleg, 169, 218
Poppescus, 207
Porte, Juan, 31
Porto, 223
Powell, Albert, 69
Powell and Clarke's Circus, 37 n, 62, 121, 217
Powells, 217
Power, 141
Price, Stella, 186
Prices, 186, 214, 217
Publicity, circus, 22–23, 36–37, 93, 106–7, 124–25, 166, 227

Quadrille, 59
Quick and Mead's, 36

Radio Circus, 228
Rainats, 154, 158
Raluys, 106
Ramper, 217 n
Raphaël, Albert [pseud. Monsieur le Professeur Malladoli], 117–18
Rapoli, 185
Raspini, Eduardo, 187
Raspinis, 73
Rasso, Trio, 63
Rastelli, Enrico, 185–87, 228
Rauch, Ludwig, 67
Ravel Troupe, 166
Reco, 168
Regnas, Old, 220
Reinsch Brothers, 51, 58
Renz, Thérèse, 181, 229
Renzes, 42
Renz's Circus, 48, 50, 102, 218
Respinskis, Loyal, 56
Reverhos, 168, 189
Rhum. *See* Pipo and Rhum
Rice, Dan, 37
Richard, Davis, 47

Richard, Jean, 42
Ricketts, John Bill, 31
Ringens, Swan, 110
Ringling Bros. and Barnum & Bailey, 36, 38, 67, 106, 122, 138, 160, 162, 164, 219, 224
Ringling Brothers Circus. *See* Ringling Bros. and Barnum & Bailey
Ringlings, 36, 122. *See also* Ringling Bros. and Barnum & Bailey
Risley, Professor. *See* Carlisle, Richard Risley
Risley acts, 89, 191–95, 207. *See also* names of individual artistes
Rivels, Charlie, 151, 220
Robinson, John, 193 n
Rockleys, 71
Rogana. *See* Rogge, Dora
Rogge, Dora [pseud. Rogana], 66
Rogge, Gerda [pseud. Miss Atlas, the Strong Woman], 66
Rogge, Vera, 66
Roland, 144
Rope acts, 30: bounding, 167; slack, 167, 169; vertical, 162–63. *See also* Tightrope acts; names of individual artistes
Rosaire's Circus, 133
Rossi, 142
Rossi, Alfredo, 50
Rostopchine, Comtesse. *See* Chiarini, Constance
Rouhet, Dr., 94
Rousseau, Madeleine and René [pseud. Geraldos], 23, 40, 121–22, 159–61, 228
Royal Circus, 31, 216

Sadler's Wells, 112
Salamonskys, 126

Salamonsky's Circus, 50, 102
Samel, Erhard and Christiane, 132
Sanchez, Herr, 112
Sandow, 34, 62
Sandwina, Katie, 62
Sandy, 214
Sanger, George, 125
Sanger, Ida, 143
Sanger, John, 220
Sanger, "Lord" George, 33, 37, 38, 124, 217, 220
Sanger, "Lord" John, 38
Sarrasani, 39, 58, 67, 122, 124, 229
Saunders, Abraham, 124
Saunders, Don, 220
Sawade, 133
Scheffer, Severus, 185
Scheffers, 34, 185, 222
Schepp, Dieter, 163 n
Schneider, Captain, 122–23, 137
Schools, circus, 44, 84, 229. *See also* Training
Schreiber, 142
Schreiber, Baptista, 181
Schumann, Albert, 100, 102–3, 104, 181
Schumann, Gotthold, 102
Schumann, Katja, 102, 181
Schumanns, 40, 42, 102, 181, 228
Schwichtenberg, Uwe, 88
Seeth, Julius, 133
Serge, 211
Serges, Alexander, Troupe. *See* Alexander Serges Troupe
Sharpshooting, 73–74. *See also* names of individual artistes
Sherwood, Bob, 53
Shirai, 71
Sholes, Billy, 53
Silaghis, 208

Simoneit, Gerd, 138
Sloans. *See* Yeldings
Smart, Billy, 40, 41
Smarts, 40, 41
Smith, Leon, 146
Sobolewskis, 56
Solohkin Troupe, 207
Soullier, 173
Spalding, "Doctor" Gilbert, 37
Spectacle, definition of, 25
Spelterini, Mlle., 166 n
Spiessert (or Spessardy), Charles, 42
Springboard acts, 204–7. *See also* names of individual artistes
Spurgats [pseud. Crystal Wonders], 65
Stanglemeir, George, 63
Stanecks, Seven, 205
State Circus, 43
Steele, Tony, 150
Stilt-walking, 70–71, 73, 166, 219. *See also* names of individual artistes
Stokes, Spencer Q., 37, 53
Stott, Raymond Toole, 112, 117
Strassburger, Karl, 103
Strassburger, Regina, 181
Strassburgers, 42, 126
Street, L. A., 187
Strong men, 28, 61–64. *See also* names of individual strong men
Sullivan, Rose, 156
Swifts, 189
Swiss National Circus, 43
Swoboda Sisters [pseud. Medrano Sisters], 58
Sword-swallowing, 74. *See also* names of individual sword-swallowers

Tay-Ru, 65
Television and the circus, 40, 227, 230
Terrels, Flying, 157
Theatre, unlike the circus. *See* Circus, unlike the theatre
Thétard, Henry, 58, 62, 128, 132, 134, 138, 228
Tightrope acts, 33, 163–69. *See also* names of individual artistes
Tiller girls, 141
Toch, 62
Tokoyas, 207
Togare, 140
Togni, 96
Tom Arnold's Circus, 66, 67, 102. *See also* Arnold, Tom
Tornados, Two, 73
Tourniaire, 50
Tourniaire, Phillipine, 173
Tower Circus, 40, 229. *See also* Butson, Clem
Training: for acrobats, 198; for animal acts, 75–90, 93–102, 128–31, 134–37, 139–46; for contortionists, 67–68, 70; for trick-riders, 37, 53–55. *See also* Schools, circus
Trampoline acts, 208–9. *See also* names of individual artistes
Trapeze, invention of, 33, 151
Trapeze acts, 149–62. *See also* names of individual artistes
Trick-cycling, 106, 210–12. *See also* names of individual artistes
Trick-riding, 28–29, 31, 47–60. *See also* Training, for trick-riders; names of individual riders
Triskas, 163–64

Trubka, 139
Tumbling, Arab, 212. *See also* Acrobats

Uessems, 66
Unus, 65
Usher, Dickie, 216

Valencia Music Hall, 156
Van Amburgh, 38, 128, 130
Varias, Five, 161
Violat, Mademoiselle, 118
Volta, Ted and Taff, 151
Voltige, 47–48, 50, 228

Wall, Captain, 112
Wallendas, 163–64
Wards, Flying, 161
Weitzmann Brothers, 164
Welch's National Circus, 36
Wells, Adolph, 50
Wentworth, Walter, 69
Westminster Aquarium, 58, 108
Whisky, 223
Wickbold, Arno, 112–13
Williams, Carola Althoff, 138
Williams, Harry, 138
Williams, Jeanette, 138
Willison's Great World Circus, 38
Wirth, Adele, 38
Wirth, May, 59
Wollschläger, 102
Wombwell, George, 124, 128
Woodson, Johnny, 48
Woodward, Captain Joseph, 143
Woolford, Louisa, 60
World War I, effect on the circus, 34
Wulff, Edouard, 101, 104
Wybierala, Leoni and Leinert, 109–10

Yacopis, 206
Yeldings [pseud. Sloans], 219–20
Yokoi, Lily, 211, 228
Young, Selina, 165

Zacchinis, 108, 218
Zaeo, 110

Zavattas, 71
Zay, Freddy, 190
Zazel, 108
Zementov Troupe, 208–9
Zemgannos, 158
Zucker, 93–94